MW00789231

Policing Citizens

What does police violence against minorities, or violent clashes between minorities and the police, tell us about citizenship and its internal hierarchies? Indicative of deep-seated tensions and negative perceptions, incidents such as these suggest how minorities are vulnerable and suffer from or are subject to police abuse and neglect in Israel. Marked by skin color, negatively stigmatized or rendered security threats, their encounters with police provide a daily reminder of their defunct citizenship. Taking as case studies the experiences and perceptions of four minority groups within Israel, including Palestinian/Arab citizens, ultra-Orthodox Jews and Ethiopian and Russian immigrants, Ben-Porat and Yuval are able to explore different paths of citizenship and the stratification of the citizenship regime through relations with and perceptions of the police in Israel.

Touching on issues such as racial profiling, police brutality and neighborhood neglect, their study questions the notions of citizenship and belonging, shedding light on minority relationships with the state and its institutions.

GUY BEN-PORAT is Professor at the Department of Politics and Government at the Ben-Gurion University of the Negev, Israel. He is the author of *Global Liberalism, Local Populism* (Syracuse University Press, 2006), which won the Czempiel Prize, Frankfurt Peace Research Institute, and *Between State and Synagogue* (Cambridge University Press, 2012), which was awarded the Shapiro Best Book Award and the Israeli Political Science Association Best Book Award.

FANY YUVAL is Senior Lecturer at the Department of Public Policy and Administration at the Ben-Gurion University of the Negev, Israel. Her research focuses on municipal systems, management strategies and policy instruments, organizational behavior and public opinion in municipalities, with a particular interest in gender and minorities. Supported by the Ministry of Science in Israel, she recently led a project researching the role played by municipalities in reducing gender inequality.

Policing Citizens

Minority Policy in Israel

GUY BEN-PORAT
Ben-Gurion University of the Negev, Israel
FANY YUVAL
Ben-Gurion University of the Negev, Israel

CAMBRIDGE
UNIVERSITY PRESS

University Printing House, Cambridge CB2 8BS, United Kingdom

One Liberty Plaza, 20th Floor, New York, NY 10006, USA

477 Williamstown Road, Port Melbourne, VIC 3207, Australia

314-321, 3rd Floor, Plot 3, Splendor Forum, Jasola District Centre, New Delhi - 110025, India

79 Anson Road, #06-04/06, Singapore 079906

Cambridge University Press is part of the University of Cambridge.

It furthers the University's mission by disseminating knowledge in the pursuit of education, learning and research at the highest international levels of excellence.

www.cambridge.org
Information on this title: www.cambridge.org/9781108404747
DOI: 10.1017/9781108265164

First published 2019
First paperback edition 2020

A catalogue record for this publication is available from the British Library

Library of Congress Cataloging in Publication data
Names: Ben-Porat, Guy, author. | Yuval, Fani, author.
Title: Policing citizens : minority policy in Israel / Guy Ben-Porat, Fany Yuval.
Description: Cambridge, United Kingdom : Cambridge University Press, 2019. | Includes bibliographical references and index.
Identifiers: LCCN 2018061718 | ISBN 9781108417259 (alk. paper)
Subjects: LCSH: Police – Israel. | Police-community relations – Israel. | Discrimination in law enforcement – Israel. | Minorities – Israel. | Israel – Ethnic relations. | Israel – Race relations.
Classification: LCC HV8242.2.A2 B45 2019 | DDC 363.2/3095694–dc23
LC record available at https://lccn.loc.gov/2018061718

ISBN   978-1-108-41725-9   Hardback
ISBN   978-1-108-40474-7   Paperback

Contents

Tables

Introduction: Policing Citizens

Damas Pikada, an Ethiopian-born Israeli, and Freddie Gray, an African American, shared nothing but their skin color until the spring of 2015. The police beating of Damas Pikada, an Israeli soldier in uniform, caught on tape and aired on national television on June 2015, sparked the rage of young Israelis of Ethiopian descent. The young people who took to the streets and clashed with the police protested against what they described as police racism. A few weeks earlier, African Americans in Baltimore took to the streets after 25-year-old Freddie Gray died during police arrest. International media and the demonstrators them-selves were quick to point to the similarities of young black people protesting against what they described as police racism and brutality. In Tel-Aviv and in Jerusalem young Ethiopian protestors carried signs in English that read "Black Lives Matter," alluding to the events in the United States and the African American protest against ongoing police brutality.

Police violence against minorities, or violent clashes between mino-rities and the police, tell us something about citizenship and its internal hierarchies. These incidents, are often indicative of deep-seated ten-sions, the result of everyday interactions and negative perceptions, that impact police and policing. While policing rests on implied consent, the disenfranchising and de-incorporation of certain citizens from the structures of government and the use of the police to enforce a parti-cular social compliance implies that "in many respects policing is against the resistance of certain communities in order to retain the respect of other communities" (Findlay, 2004: 7). Thus, police legiti-macy and trust in police varies between majority and minority citizens of marginalized groups, sometimes demonstrated in violent incidents that spark public debates.

While it is "shocking" incidents – like those of Pikada and Gray – where the public are exposed to undeniable violence or humiliation that capture attention, everyday encounters matter no less. The relations between

1

minorities and police are embedded in social and political contexts that shape these seemingly mundane encounters, which in turn reshape those contexts. Differently stated, minorities and police officers engage each other not as abstract individuals. Rather, it is an encounter between representatives of state power, carrying also their personal preferences and prejudices, and members of groups with particular perceptions, concerns and expectations derived of personal and collective histories. The fact that particular minorities are vulnerable, suffer from police abuse or neglect and are exposed to violence, is indicative of their status as citizens. For minorities marked by "visible" characteristics like skin color, negatively stigmatized and rendered a security threat, encounters with police (or the fear of them) are a daily reminder of defunct citizenship.

Police not only represent state power and its claim for the monopoly over (legitimate) violence, they exercise them in its everyday interactions. Authorized to provide security and public order, police both serve citizens and hold power to restrict the freedoms of those defined as security threats or disturbing public order. It is hardly surprising, therefore, that police legitimacy is questioned by those citizens subjected to what they perceive as unfair treatment, especially when abuse and neglect are attributed to specific identities. "Minorities" is a generic term that includes different groups with characteristics – language, skin color or religion – that distinguish them from the majority and is often associated with discrimination and marginalization. Minority groups, however, have different goals and prospects for integration, have different experiences with the state and its institutions and, consequently, different perceptions of citizenship and belonging. While the "state" is often an abstract or invisible concept, police and policing are very present in everyday life, especially for minorities. The conclusions that citizens of minority groups draw from significant encounters with police, whether it is their own or of others they relate to, have a direct bearing on perceptions of status and belonging, both shaping and shaped by those encounters.

Setting the study of police and policing within a broader theoretical framework allows us to grasp their institutional role in society, as well as the political and social transformations that police are part of. More important, however, is what the study of police reveals about states and citizenship regimes, namely inclusions, exclusions, privileges and hierarchies. Class, ethnicity or skin color can explain both unequal provision of security, and police violence. Racial profiling, to take one

example, negatively affects racialized minority populations subjected
to police stops and searches with no apparent reason other than their
skin color and their vulnerability. Who is policed and how, therefore, is
a question of status and power established through discourses articulated by government, police and other authorities and by everyday
practices that enforce them. Overall, the study of police and policing
is a study of state and society, their transformations, and the complexity of modern citizenship.

Police violence and public reactions to it are all too familiar in an age
when pictures turn viral and spark emotions and demands for justice.
The year 2015, however, when we began to assemble our data, was an
especially difficult one for Israeli police. In Rahat, a Bedouin town in
the south of Israel, the arrest of a suspected drug dealer ended with the
killing of an innocent bystander. The following day, the funeral turned
into a demonstration and the killing of two more citizens by police,
another milestone in the tense relations between police and the Arab
citizens of Israel. In Jerusalem, a violent attack on a gay parade by a
religious zealot resulted in a young woman being stabbed to death. The
police failed to prevent the assailant – released a couple of weeks before
from prison after serving time for a similar attack – from approaching
the parade. In addition, six officers of the high command had to resign
one after another under different allegations of corruption, misconduct
and sexual harassment. The public image of police was at one of its
lowest points, among minorities and the public at large. The image of
police, however, as we argue throughout this book, is reflective of the
current state of governance and deepening schisms.

Israel and the four minority groups selected for this study –
Palestinian/Arab citizens, ultra-Orthodox Jews and Ethiopian and
Russian immigrants – allow us to explore, theoretically, comparatively
and empirically, different paths of citizenship and the stratification of the
citizenship regime through relations with and perceptions of police. We
study different aspects of policing and society in relation to the context in
which they develop – a conflictual society with deep schisms – but also in
a broader comparative perspective. Israelis of Ethiopian descent are
a visible minority with experiences that resemble those of visible minorities elsewhere. Arab citizens are a national minority demanding equality and recognition, that often clash directly with police, but also suffer
police neglect and insecurity. Ultra-Orthodox Jews are a religious minority determined to protect their way of life and resisting state

intervention enforced by police. Immigrants from the former Soviet Union provide an example of a relatively successful immigration that integrated in society and its views of police and policing, despite past suspicions, resemble those of the majority. Finally, we examine also the perceptions of Israelis who do not belong to any of the minority groups, to learn about the general attitudes and perceptions of police.

Policing amidst Controversies

For the modern state, the institutionalization of police was another articulation of its national identity. Police played instrumental and symbolic parts in the formation and reproduction of modern states and national cultures. The uniformed police force and the police officer on the street provided for the public an "important aspect of the iconography of the nation state" (Loader and Walker, 2001: 20). Beyond the direct provision of essential security for citizens, the police symbolize the promise embedded in the state, its sovereignty, the norms and rules associated with it and the sense of community. The possibility to imagine the nation through the concrete practice of policing and the rules it enforced provided police with authority and the practice of that authority has reenforced the sense of nation-ness and statehood. The police were enforcing a unitary body of law imagined as the consensual expression of the nation, embodied in the rule of the state. In this reciprocal relation, police benefit in terms of legitimacy and effectiveness from the state's capacity to create a community; but at the same time, they symbolize, participate and contribute to this very community.

   The monopoly of the state over violence, always partial, may have further diminished in the era of globalization. "While the nation state still looks imposing in its shiny uniform, and people's bodies and souls are still routinely tortured around the world," writes Manuel Castells, its monopoly of violence is all but a myth. "The state still relies on violence and surveillance, but it does not hold its monopoly any longer, nor can it exercise it from its national enclosure" (1997: 303). The state monopoly over the means of violence may have diminished in the face of global transformations and shifts of authority upwards, downwards and sideways, but functioning states still hold significant powers and violence at their disposal, exemplified by police actions. Indeed, for many citizens, and even more so for noncitizens, the police are the most visible face of government they encounter in everyday life or in critical events. Police and policing, and expectations from them, have accordingly changed in light of new challenges.

Policing has become a fundamentally controversial topic by the late twentieth century in light of two societal changes, diversification and privatization. These changes underscore questions about police authority and new concerns regarding trust and legitimacy. A multicultural reality presents challenges for many contemporary democracies which, in contrast to their image of homogeneity, face new demands from ethnic and cultural groups for equality and recognition. State institutions, among them police, need to accommodate to new needs and demands and to a decline of public trust. The significance of policing to everyday life, mentioned above, is largely about the "heavy symbolic load" it carries (Bradford, 2014: 22). Unfair treatment of citizens communicates to them that they are not valued members of society (Jackson et al., 2012: 1053) and demonstrates the stratified nature of citizenship. Groups who suffer from police discrimination and mistreatment may have low levels of trust towards the state, government and institutions. Indeed, studies from across the world, elaborated upon later, show a marked difference between majority and minority groups in the trust of police. Lower trust is attributed either to direct experiences of police discrimination and/or to minorities' refusal to identify with a single set of legal and political values held by the dominant group, which may lead to alienation from the state, government and its institutions (Michelson, 2003).

The privatization of police forces and the commodification of policing also affect its relation with citizens and raises more questions about trust and loyalty. The so-called privatization revolution of the 1980s included also police services that were partially privatized, either through user-financed police services or by contracting out and allowing for private provision of police services (Fixler and Poole, 1988). These trends accelerated in the wake of the Cold War and globalization and the rising demands for privatized security. The establishment of private security companies across the world has raised questions about their authority and accountability, and concerns over the security gap between those who could afford private services and those forced to rely on public services. Policing provided also by private sources may no longer be a public good, administered by an institution committed to general welfare but rather a service on behalf of those who have the means to pay for it, introducing new forms of discrimination, excluding "undesirable" individuals and groups from public spaces.

Diversity and privatization further erode the nation-state nexus and open new forms of identity, new demands for equality and recognition and new challenges for state institutions. These changes are no less than dramatic for police, previously benefitting from a sense of community that legitimizes their action and at the same time representing and contributing to this very sense of community. Conversely, in divided societies, police are part of a controversial social order, protective for some but oppressive for others. Where marginalized groups seek recognition and equality, and where controversial issues challenge the existing order, police can be a visible and daily proof of their discrimination. Demonstrations broken by police force, frequent stops and searches of visible minorities, crime-ridden neglected minority neighborhoods and occasional police violence are all evidence of marginality. Police discrimination, real or perceived, often more visible than that of other institutions, demonstrates the stratification of citizenship behind the veil of equality. Protests against police, demands for reform and growing distrust are articulations of citizenship demands, demonstrating that police and policing cannot be divorced from politics.

Studying Police

Political scientists have paid scant attention to police and policing, a somewhat surprising neglect considering its presence and impact. Weber's classical definition of the state as the holder of the monopoly of the legitimate use of physical force (or violence) alludes to the importance of two state institutions, the military and the police. Interestingly, while the study of the military has been part of political science literature, police and policing have remained almost alien to the discipline and largely understudied by political scientists (Isaac, 2015). The role police perform in everyday lives of citizens, the power entrusted to police officers, the growing concern of citizens with public safety and the tensions between police and minority groups that exploded in different places, all demonstrate its political significance. The study of police and policing, beyond its immediate relevance, is a study of state and society, their exclusions and hierarchies revealed in the ways citizens perceive police and their treatment by police. Everyday interactions between police officers and citizens, therefore, are political tales of trust and cooperation, or, conversely, of neglect and discrimination.

The debate that surrounds police and policing, both academic and professional, has taken a new course in light of developments and events in different countries that seem to undermine police legitimacy, especially among minority groups. Against traditional conceptions that police can rely on force, deterrence and effective action to gain trust and legitimacy, the decline of public trust became a concern for police officers and policy makers. First, many studies concluded that the ability of police to perform their role requires public cooperation and that without trust and legitimacy cooperation is unlikely. Second, trust in many cases differs between majority and minority groups but also between minority groups with different experiences and needs. Citizens' trust of police, as often measured in surveys, is a "fuzzy" concept that depends on perceptions, expectations and interests. For some groups police will be measured by their "efficacy," namely the ability to provide security or fight crime, while for other groups it is about the "image" of police, the way they treat citizens and their commitment to equality and fairness (Worrall, 1999). Thus, third, police reforms aimed to increase public trust and cooperation must account for a multicultural or multinational reality that presents different challenges to the state and its institutions and requires attention to diversity.

Police is a constitutive element in the production and reproduction of political order and community (Loader and Walker, 2001) but both order and community are often contested markers in contemporary societies. In divided societies, not only the ability of police to secure social order is questioned, the concept itself is politically charged and contested. Contemporary police forces simultaneously embody the quest for general social order and the debates regarding the meaning and consequences of that order, set against inequalities, prejudice and demands for equality and recognition. Almost any examination of police roles and practices suggests that policing is well beyond a bureaucratic task measured by efficiency and is often a "political" question embedded in political and social structures and dynamics. Police, as such, are political in the very essence of their functions as they operate within a political environment (Manning, 2006) that shapes expectations and demands of society, and delineates the authority vested in the hands of police officers.

Police work is somewhat different from other bureaucracies as it is both visible and invisible to the public. Everyday policing involves constant contact with the public, often more intensive than most bureaucrat–citizens interactions, which makes police work visible and under constant scrutiny. At the same time, the behavior of police officers is hidden from the public at large and not systematically monitored by supervisors, allowing police officers great discretion in deciding how to enforce the law (Weitzer and Tuch, 2006). Consequently, policing "is simultaneously both partial and universal, interested and disinterested, divisive and inclusive" (Loader and Walker, 2001: 13). The discrepancy between visibility and invisibility involves questions of power and status, rendering some citizens more vulnerable to abuse and exposed to violence. Consequently, citizens' perceptions of police derive from individual and group exposure to police and policing and from experiences that shape their perceptions of expectations from it. While for some groups, police are a key representative of state, nation and community, and provider of essential service, for others police represent and enforces their marginalization and injustices.

Trust, central to our discussion here, is considered by political scientists essential for effective governance, and declining trust in politics, government and institutions a major concern (Arian et al., 2008; Boggs, 2000), diminishing the capacity of traditional governance (Pierre, 2000) and further undermining trust in governments. This general, and dismal, observation of declining trust alludes to two important questions, first, who (dis)trusts? And, second, how can trust be gained? Theories that explain the level of citizens' trust in the police were mostly developed and tested with "the people" or "the majority" in mind (Van Craen, 2013). But, past or present disenfranchising and de-incorporation of certain citizens and the use of the police to ensure social compliance implies that "in many respects policing is against the resistance of certain communities in order to retain the respect of other communities" (Findlay, 2004: 7). Measured aggregately, trust may provide a partial picture that overlooks ethnic, gender and class differences. Accordingly, political theories of ethnicity, class and identity provide an important supplement for the understanding of trust and legitimacy. These theories can explain why certain groups trust less the state and its institutions, and what particular policies and practices undermine trust of government and specific institutions. Developing a theoretical framework drawn from political science and sociology will enable us to embed the study of police within a wider debate of citizenship, trust and legitimacy and in a wider social context of the changes of states and societies.

Minorities and Police: Context

The encounters between police and ordinary people are a display of citizenship, in its complexities and contradictions. Police discretion on whom to stop and question, separating those determined as normative civilians from those perceived a threat, pertains to existing divisions and stigmas that cut through citizenship. Citizens, who decide to approach police for help, or avoid police at all costs, display their own sense of trust and belonging in state institutions. For minorities, police can be an essential service, to protect their livelihood and property, but at the same time a threat and a proof of their defunct citizenship. Young men in French *banlieue* who flee when they see police officers, Black men in American towns careful not make a suspicious move or young Israelis of Ethiopian descent resentment of being stopped and search, articulate their citizenship in their fears and frustrations. Distrust of police or dissatisfaction with policing may be common to many minority groups, and possibly shared also by minorities, but distrust may reflect particular histories and political agendas. People and groups, to state simply, may have different reasons to distrust police and, consequently, different demands.

The rhetoric used by police to describe neighborhoods as "war zones" and their assignments as "war on crime" or "war on drugs" legitimizes not only their views of the situations facing them, but also the way they work to impose order (Fassin, 2013: 40). The warlike rhetoric, in Fassin's words: "has a cost in terms of democracy, leading to excesses that effect not only the criminals targeted, but also, through collateral damages, citizens who have done nothing wrong" (ibid.). Excesses and collateral excesses include not only overt police force but also daily stops and searches of individuals of stigmatized groups, labeled as security threats and singled out by their skin color or other identifiable features. These practices we describe as "over-policing," the targeting of particular individuals for stops, searches and arrests, and the use of violence against them, are directed against visible, stigmatized and vulnerable groups. Unequal citizenship, however, can take the opposite turn in what we describe as "under-policing," most visible in neglect of minority neighborhoods, more exposed to crime and disorder. Minorities may perceive they are under-policed, over-policed or some combination of the two, and articulate their citizenship status and demands accordingly.

Concerns and frustrations of minority groups, as well as the dilemmas of policy makers and police officers, are part of wider social, economic and political changes. Ethnic and national minorities who protest discrimination and marginality, religious groups demanding autonomy and recognition and immigrants who struggle with integration, all challenge contemporary order. Those groups, and others, have different experiences and develop different expectations and demands, forming different paths for meaningful citizenship. These paths are shaped by overarching identities and ideologies, but also by material concerns of everyday life. Minorities, as argued before and throughout this book, differ in their relation to the state and society. First, they differ in the desire to be included and become part of nation and state. And, second, in the actual opportunities that state and society provide for them to do so. Translated into demands from police, those could stretch between equality and inclusion to recognition and separation, or between ending discriminatory practices of over-policing to providing adequate services to protect them from crime and violence.

Minorities: Experiences and Expectations

Frustrations and declining trust of minorities, part of what we describe as multicultural reality, pose significant challenges for police. We use the term multicultural reality to highlight that with the growing diversity, even in states previously perceived homogeneous, philosophical questions become concrete debates over distribution of resources, equal opportunities, nature of public services, group rights and individual liberties. Policies, planned and executed within a new context of diversity, need to not only ascertain the needs, preferences and demands of the different groups constituting their societies, but also examine whether those policies are likely to meet them adequately. For police, especially in divided societies, those include the provision of services that suit all segments of society, the diversification of the police force so it will mirror society, an improvement in the image of the police among minorities, and serious engagement with hate crimes against minorities (Oakley, 2001).

In the next chapter, we develop three concepts drawn from political science and political sociology, through which we discuss both concerns and expectations of particular minorities: representation, fairness and voice. Using these concepts, we not only identify the reasons behind distrust of minorities in police, but also what reforms can answer their expectations. Representation is a concept often discussed in relation to legitimacy and trust through policies like affirmative action. The symbolic and practical significance of police, and at times problematic historical relations, make representation an especially sensitive topic for minorities. Wearing the uniform, emblematic of the state and nation, may be desirable for minorities who wish to integrate but problematic for those alienated. Individually, enlistment could be a debate between individual aspirations, desire to make a difference and a suspecting community. Collectively, a community debate on whether enlistment of members should be encouraged or tolerated can take place. Finally, individuals and communities may believe that minority officers change the police or rather that they become part of the police and adopt existing prejudices and intolerant culture.

Fairness, referring to the equality of treatment, or the perception of equality, is especially pertinent in the relations of police and minorities. Following our discussion above, to be developed in the next chapter, fairness (or, rather, unfairness) can be assessed in several ways. First, over-policing and policies of racial profiling, whether declared or not, send a strong message of biased treatment. Second, procedural justice relates to the process and the way citizens evaluate police encounters. And third, under-policing can also be perceived as distributive (un)fairness when needs of groups are overlooked. While fairness can be evaluated objectively (who is stopped more; where are police officers present?) it is also subjective and relational. "Relative deprivation" (Gurr, 1970) suggests that people and groups assess their well-being by comparing themselves to relevant others and that intergroup comparisons are particularly powerful in invoking feelings of collective deprivation (Mentovich et al., 2018). Perceptions of over-policing and under-policing, accordingly, develop among minorities in comparison to those perceived more fortunate and often attributed to planned discrimination and subordination. Minorities, therefore, have different reasons to perceive police as unfair and, respectively, different expectations regarding what fairness constitutes.

Minorities might be suspicious of enlistment that would supposedly make police representative, fearing that minority officers would only help perpetuate discrimination. Similarly, "lightweight" reforms related to fairness, like cultural training of police officers, may seem superficial and deliberately avoiding the real issues. Voice, our third concept, is about minority communities' ability to shape policies and oversee police work. The latter is of special significance when police are accused of racial profiling and violence. Public and community involvement in police work that provide voice to citizens includes both cooperation in what is described as "community policing" and forums for engagement that provide for ongoing dialogue between communities and police, but also more controversial possibilities of police accountability and public oversight of disciplinary action against abusive officers involved in violence. Police, drawing the so-called thin blue line, often with some public and political support, is likely to resist any attempts to restrict their autonomy or to challenge their claimed professional authority.

Israel: Citizenship and Policing

Social and political struggles over the boundaries of citizenship and its meaning are central to contemporary Israeli politics. Stratified citizenship and deep schisms make Israel a fascinating case study of police and minorities, unique yet resembling developments elsewhere. Clashes between the police and minorities, in different democratic countries, demonstrate the challenges of diversity and the needs of state institutions to become more inclusive, committed to equality and recognize discriminatory attitudes and practices they hold. Israel has been described as a "non-liberal democracy" because of the monopoly of Orthodoxy over Jewish religious life, entrenched anti-liberal and ethnocentric attitudes in society, and various discriminatory practices towards minorities (Ben-Dor et al., 2003). The flaws of Israeli democracy, discussed by many authors in recent years, largely refer to Israel's difficulty to maintain unity in a divided polity and to accommodate the needs and rights of minorities.

Nationalism, religion and ethnicity are the central fault lines in Israeli society, each division with a life of its own, translated into demands, struggles and identities. Overall, previous arrangements and claims for unity are no longer sufficient as the different divides contain both material and symbolic aspects, relating to struggles over resource allocation demands for recognition and attempts of groups to shape public life or to protect their own way of life. Not only the ethnic state structures alienating and frustrating Arab citizens, but also internal ethnic divisions, religious–secular struggles and other identity questions underscore a tense multicultural reality. The outcomes of these struggles, no longer contained by a dominant center, will depend not only on the demands of ethnic, national or religious groups, but also on the opportunities offered by the state and the ability of Israel's democratic regime to accommodate the challenges. Institutionally, new forms of representation will have to be created and new spaces will need to be devised in order for groups to maintain their identity and for the political system to expand its legitimacy and enhance its capacity to govern. This will include reforms of the institutions related to everyday life, police among them.

Israel is an exemplary case study of national, ethnic and religious struggles, the difficulties of a democratic regime and also of the critical role that police perform in everyday life and in creating and sustaining existing hierarchies and divisions. Because frustrations of citizens in general and minorities in particular have grown stronger and trust in political institutions eroded, the role of the police is ever more critical as they often find themselves in the forefront of civil unrest. Public evaluations of police show a steady decline of trust and a general perception, not necessarily matched by reality (police report a steady decline in crime), that police are unable to effectively fight crime and provide security. While citizens of different groups can be dissatisfied, it could be for different reasons, differing not only majority from minority but also minority groups from each other. Perceptions and frustrations of different groups from the police, whether they are concerned of police violence or neglect, insinuate feelings of belonging and attachment, allude to their place in the hierarchy of citizenship and shape their demands and expectations of a full and meaningful citizenship.

Four Israeli minorities studied in this book (in comparison to the majority of Jewish, nonimmigrant Israelis) provide different viewpoints and the contexts for the study of police and policing. In the chapters of the book we discuss the four minorities in a theoretical and comparative framework. Specifically, we study Palestinian/Arab citizens within the debate of national minorities; ultra-Orthodox Jews, as a religious minority that sets itself apart from the state; Israelis of Ethiopian descent an ethnic/racial minority that suffers discrimination and slow integration; and Russian immigrants, as a relatively strong immigration group that retains its cultural characteristics yet able to integrate.

The Arab minority is qualitatively different from other minorities in Israel: being a national minority within a Jewish state with a history of clashes with police, distrusting police but at the same time in dire need of its protection. Israelis of Ethiopian descent are a "visible minority", vulnerable to discrimination and abuse. Ethiopian neighborhoods are usually poor with relatively high levels of juvenile delinquency and domestic violence that have led to negative interactions with the police. FSU (former Soviet Union) immigrants have integrated better into the Israeli economy and society but have also complained in the past of police discrimination, women suspected of prostitution or men identified with organized crime. Finally, the ultra-Orthodox community has had many clashes with the police throughout the years in their demonstrations against archeological digs, for observance of the Sabbath, etc. Members of these four groups are more likely to have had negative interactions with the police, their perceptions of police a demonstration of status and citizenship.

The dilemmas we explore in Israel, a diverse society with deep schisms and inherent tensions, a stratified and contested citizenship regime, and growing securitization due to external and internal developments, are different but also comparable to dilemmas and paradoxes that appear elsewhere, in different shapes and forms. Consequently, this study of four minority groups in Israel and their relations with and perceptions of police and policing provides insights that stretch beyond the case study and policing. Rather, the relations between police and different minorities – national, ethnic, racial and religious – explored, using original and primary sources, sheds light on political and public policy dilemmas, in Israel and elsewhere.

Methodology and Research Questions

Israel, and the four groups studied, provide for the understanding of the complex relationships between minority groups and the police within the context of citizenship. Our research, based on interviews, documents, media sources and a detailed survey, examines perceptions of policing, needs and demands of minority groups, in relation to wider questions of belonging and citizenship. The research began with focus groups – six of each minority – conducted in different locations. It was followed by a survey conducted among the four minority groups; and a control group, Israeli citizens not belonging to none of the four. The survey included questions about trust, legitimacy, evaluations of police performance, expectations from police and various questions relating to perceptions towards state and society. Finally, we collected secondary data, media and official reports, and conducted several more interviews with community leaders of the different groups.

Focus groups, conducted in the first stage of the research, with the different groups, provided us with an understanding and with important insights about the groups and their perceptions of police, policing and the state. These insights, combined with insights drawn from other studies of minorities, in Israel and elsewhere, instructed us in writing the survey. The survey, conducted by a professional ("Uniseker" Survey Center from the University of Haifa) was carried out between August and November, 2013. A random sample of 2,162 subjects was divided into five different groups of Israelis: Arabs citizens – 507 subjects; *haredim* – 488 subjects; FSU immigrants – 540 subjects; Israelis of Ethiopian descent – 140 subjects; and a control group of 487 subjects. Questionnaires, administered in Hebrew, Arabic and Russian, examined perceptions of police and policing, as well as of citizenship and relations to the state. The questions were divided into several scales identified and included an index for evaluating over-policing and under-policing in diverse areas of police work (Ben-Porat and Yuval, 2012); three additional indices for clarifying the subjects' level of trust in the police in accordance with the three indices known from the literature: procedural justice, police performance and moral alignment (Tyler, 2004). Another cluster of questions examined different questions of cooperation: willingness to enlist, community policing and oversight of police work. Finally, a more general set of questions examined perceptions of state, citizenship and belonging. The indices were composed of a variable number of statements on a Likert-type scale, in which each question had five possible replies.

The transcripts from the focus groups, the analysis of the survey and media reports of significant events of police–minority interactions help answer the following questions in each of the chapters ahead: (a) How do different minorities perceive police and policing, and how do these perceptions relate to perceptions of citizenship? (b) Do individuals of minority groups trust police? What explains trust and distrust? (c) Do minorities perceive police to be fair? Is unfairness related to over-policing or under-policing? How does that affect their trust in police? And how does it affect their assessment of their citizenship? (d) How important is representation in police for minorities? What are the reasons for supporting or objecting to enlistment? And (e) what reforms are likely to make a difference? Do minorities believe they could and should have a voice and oversight of police work? In each of the following chapters, we examine one of the groups, its history, status in Israeli society and relations with the police. We compare their perceptions and experiences to other minority groups and to veteran Jewish Israelis. What can we learn from the different interactions of minorities with the police, their perceptions of policing and their expectations? We draw differences and similarities between the groups, comparing them to "mainstream" Israelis and to resembling groups elsewhere.

Structure of the Book

Our study of police and policing in Israel is set, first, within a theoretical framework we began to delineate above, and will develop in the next chapter. We set the discussion of policing in a multicultural society, and police reform, in the broader context of political responses to diversity, trust, legitimacy and institutional change. The first chapter will demonstrate how these questions pertain to many democracies facing diversity and provide the explanatory model used in the following chapter. In the second chapter, we describe the structure of Israeli society, the salience of security, the history of police and policing, and the state's engagement with diversity and its minorities. The following chapters are devoted to each of our case studies, describing the research findings in relation to our theoretical model developed in the first chapter.

Arab citizens' tense relations with the police came to the fore in October 2000 when demonstrations against Israeli actions in the West Bank, combined with other frustrations, escalated. This violent explosion, thirteen demonstrators killed by police fire, as the investigation committee formed after the events concluded, reflected deep-seated tensions and frustration of an Arab minority in a Jewish state. Our findings, presented in the third chapter, provide another angle of the Arab minority in Israel, its marginal position, the discrimination against it and the perceptions of Arab citizens of their status in Israeli society. The main issue for Arab citizens, as we demonstrate, is not over-policing and racial profiling (although they are certainly present and significant) but rather under-policing and neglect. This is explained by the high levels of violent crime in Arab towns, and expectations from the police to invest resources and efforts to provide security. Distrust of and alienation from the state, on the one hand, and need for state intervention, on the other hand, present difficult dilemmas for Arab citizens explored in this chapter.

The arrival of the Ethiopian community added a new, clear and salient dimension of race to Israel's multicultural reality. Approximately 130,000 Israelis of Ethiopian descent currently live in Israel (about 1.5 percent of the total population). The integration of Ethiopian immigrants was slow and difficult, reflected in socioeconomic marginalization and discrimination. Their descriptions of interactions with the police, Chapter 4 of the book, remind of experiences of "visible minorities" and especially black people elsewhere. Israelis of Ethiopian descent, especially young men, describe racial profiling that singles them out and harsh treatment by police officers. Yet, the majority of immigrants also have strong confidence in the state and its institutions, including police, a paradox explained by their strong desire to integrate. Their experiences and perceptions of police and policing, as the interviews demonstrate, however, suggest a complex picture of alienation and belonging.

Ultra-Orthodox Jews, the subject of Chapter 5, have a long history of clashes with the state and its institutions. Their ambivalent relation to the state stems from their commitment to religious laws and reluctance to accept the laws of the state perceived secular or even anti-religious. Clashes with police have occurred when the ultra-Orthodox demonstrated to protect the autonomy of their neighborhoods from state interventions, against, government policies perceived offensive like the military conscription laws or to prevent gay parades from marching near their neighborhoods. Consequently, the ultra-Orthodox are suspicious of police, reluctant to cooperate and feel they receive harsh treatment from police. This over-policing, unlike among Ethiopians, is not on an individual basis but rather against collective action. Relations with the police, reluctance and suspicious, resonate with the ultra-Orthodox relations with the state, but are also changing in recent years into a more complex relationship.

Immigrants from the former Soviet Union (FSU), Chapter 6 of the book, are a mirror image of Ethiopians. Arriving after the collapse of the Soviet Union, this large immigration of a million people was strong enough and self-confident to set the pace of its integration. FSU immigrants integrated economically, many able to use their human capital or acquire it after immigration and mobilize. Yet, the immigrants retained much of their cultural characteristics, including language, leisure and political culture. Immigrants' relations with police may have been influenced by their experience in the FSU, making them suspicious towards police, but also by early identification of immigrants upon their arrival to Israel with organized crime and stereotypes of Russian prostitutes. Overall, however, immigrants', and even more so their descendants', perceptions and attitudes towards police resemble those of veteran Israelis, dissatisfied with police services but not relating their dissatisfaction to discrimination.

Finally, in the seventh chapter we draw our conclusions from our findings, exploring the differences and similarities between the groups, comparing them to "mainstream" Israelis and to resembling groups elsewhere. The "order" police enforces, in Israel and elsewhere, is a particular order representing the hierarchies of a particular citizenship regime. Thus, when discussing trust, fairness, over-policing and under-policing we measure them against universal concepts of race, migration, national minorities and religion. The perceptions of police and policing we studied here teach us where different groups in Israel position themselves with the hierarchy of citizenship. Combined, the study of police and policing provides a picture of Israeli society, multi-culturalism and the challenges state institutions face.

Acknowledgment

The research was funded by the Israeli Science Foundation (grant 687/11).

1 | *Theoretical Framework*

Policing is not only a basic function of the modern state, providing security for its citizens, but also a display of sovereignty designed to demonstrate the state's claim over the monopoly of legitimate coercion. This well-known definition of the modern state, coined by Max Weber, alludes to the important role of police. The modern state, according to Weber, is to be understood in terms of the "specific means peculiar to it," as "a human community that (successfully) claims monopoly of the legitimate force within a given territory." Thus, sovereignty implies that within state borders the right to use physical force is "ascribed to other institutions or individuals only to the extent which the state permits it. The state is considered the sole source of the 'right' to use violence" (Weber, 1948: 78). For the modern state, the institutionalization of police was another articulation of its national identity and a display of its monopoly over violence. Police played instrumental and symbolic parts in the formation and reproduction of modern states and national cultures. The uniformed police force and the police officer on the street provided for the public an "important aspect of the iconography of the nation state" and a "significant constitutive element in the production and reproduction of political order and community" (Loader and Walker, 2001: 20). The police symbolize the promise embedded in the state, its sovereignty, the norms and rules associated with it and the sense of community it attempts to evoke. The possibility to imagine the nation through the concrete practice of policing and the rules it enforced provided police with authority and the practice of that authority has reenforced the sense of nation-ness and statehood. At the same time, however, police also represent a specific order, nested within a particular power relation and associated interests.

Police, throughout history, are characterized by physical force (exhibited or allusive) used to affect behavior, internal usage and collective authorization (Bayley, 1985: 9). In their symbolic and practical role, police are emblematic of state power and sovereignty, or of their decline.

The monopoly of the state over violence, always partial, may have further diminished in the era of globalization. "While the nation state still looks imposing in its shiny uniform, and people's bodies and souls are still routinely tortured around the world," writes Manuel Castells, its monopoly of violence is all but a myth. "The state still relies on violence and surveillance, but it does not hold its monopoly any longer, nor can it exercise it from its national enclosure" (1997: 303). The state monopoly over the means of violence may have diminished in the face of global transformations and shifts of authority upwards, downwards and sideways, but functioning states still hold significant powers and violence at their disposal, exemplified by police actions. Indeed, for many citizens, and even more so noncitizens, the police are the most visible face of government they encounter in everyday life or in critical events. Police and policing, and expectations from them, have changed in light of new challenges. Major developments in policing include: first, an expanded and more complex role for police; second, a changing image of police and declining legitimacy; third, a gulf between police and some ethnic minorities; and, fourth, an increased reflexivity in public dealing with the police (Newburn, 2003: 102).

The question "what do the police do?" is hardly trivial. While the common answer is that (good) policing reduces crime, several scholars would challenge the claim. David Bayley was explicit: "The police do not prevent crime. This is one of the best-kept secrets of modern life. Experts know it, the police know it, but the public does not know it" (1994: 3). The changing roles and functions of the police, and the expectations from it, allude to the strong connection between policing and politics. "The police are to government as the edge is to the knife," explains David Bayley, "the character of government and police action are virtually indistinguishable" (1985: 189). The power invested in the hands of police by the state, and their ability to exert obedience and cooperation, are both related to their legitimacy, somewhat different than other state institutions. Police work is both visible and invisible to the public. Everyday policing involves constant contact with the public, often more intensive than most bureaucrat–citizens interactions, that makes police work visible and under constant scrutiny. At the same time, the behavior of police officers is hidden from the public at large and not systematically monitored by supervisors, allowing police officers great discretion in deciding how to enforce the law (Weitzer and Tuch, 2006).

Much has changed since Weber's writing: concepts of bounded terri-
toriality are challenged by global transformation, the legitimacy of the
state and its use of violence are questioned and, consequently, police and
policing are debatable institutions and practices. Yet, while the extent to
which current states still hold the monopoly over violence is questionable,
as is their legitimacy to employ violence, policing remains an important
function of the state, a measure for its capacity to rule and a yardstick to
evaluate citizens' rights. Police produce and reproduce order and security
(Loader, 1997), but often preserve specific and present patterns of dom-
ination within the polity, protecting some interests, often at the expense
of others. Because law enforcement is the most visible, immediate and
accessible manifestation of the state, a distrustful relationship with the
police can lead individuals and communities to feel alienated from the
state and civic society altogether (Skogan and Frydl, 2004). At the same
time, police reliance on public support and cooperation encourages,
particularly in democratic societies, to "earn" the trust of citizens
(Kääriäinen, 2007), especially those alienated and marginalized.

Multiculturalism and Diversity

The questions that involve police and policing discussed in this book
cannot be detached from wider transformations of nation-states in
a globalized world and changes of citizenship and governance.
Cultural diversity and ethno-national politics are common to most
contemporary states who, contrary to their image of homogeneity,
must contend with a multicultural and at times multinational reality
(Connor, 1994; Tully, 2001). The growing reality of multinational
and/or multicultural democracies, composed of cultural, linguistic,
religious and ethnic minorities who struggle for and against distinctive
forms of recognition and accommodation, or against inequality and
discrimination, creates new challenges for the democratic regime
(Tully, 2001). Historically, the creation of nation-states not only separated the nation from other imagined communities but also from
domestic groups perceived too alien or politically unreliable to be
incorporated (Wimmer, 2013: 52). States, as Anthony Marx (2002)
explains, have often purposefully excluded some groups to define and
solidify national boundaries. These minorities, in turn, are a constant
reminder of the contested nature of state boundaries and the legitimacy
deficits of its institutions.

The term "minorities" refers to groups that differ from the dominant group in control of the state but may share little beyond that very difference. Skin color, ethnic and national identity, religiosity and class intersect in various ways that, on the one hand, manifest different patterns of discrimination, and, on the other hand, different formations of identity. Some minority groups, for example, are concerned with unequal opportunities that render them second-rate citizens. Others are concerned with questions of recognition and may find it difficult time to align with the state and its institutions that are identified with the dominant majority. And, in many cases it is a combination, or interrelation, of misrecognition and inequality that delineates boundaries and politics. Redistribution, recognition and participation are part of contemporary struggles and debates over social justice (Fraser, 2009). Consequently, as we argue throughout the book, different minorities may have different concerns and needs that reflect and shape their citizenship and, in turn, the demands they make upon the state and its institutions. Minorities, immigrants or indigenous groups, outside or on the margins of national boundaries, may refuse to identify with the state, allegedly justifying their exclusion. Formal citizenship, therefore, does not necessarily overlap with equal status, on the one hand, and feelings of national belonging, on the other hand (Brubaker, 1996). Consequently, trust and legitimacy, essential to any political order, are contested concepts in democracies where the integration of minority groups remains incomplete.

The demands of ethnic minorities, excluded or marginalized, present an acute dilemma not only for "ethnic states" that officially favor a majority (Rouhana and Ghanem, 1998) but also to liberal democracies committed to equality. "Identity politics," claims made by different groups for recognition or equality, are often a response to states' official ideologies, institutions and policies that minorities find unjust, which impact ethnic identity and its political mobilization (Brass, 1985; Enloe, 1981; Rothschild, 1981: 2). Both state and civil society, with their hierarchies and exclusions, are crucial in cementing, creating or attenuating cultural or identity politics (Crawford, 1998), translated into political demands framed in terms of recognition and redistribution. Multiculturalism, accordingly, is not only a philosophy or a description of diversity but also a concrete debate about policy making at different levels. In the face of growing diversity, whether the result of ethnic revival or more recent immigration, states and societies become more occupied with identity questions. This includes, on the one hand, a principled debate on recognition and minority rights within nation-states and, on the other hand, policies and institutions that engage with concrete needs and demands of different groups.

The so-called multicultural turn has changed the political landscape with the rise of different, and often contradictory, perceptions of government, police, the law and appropriate social order, which present major challenges for state institutions in general and for policing in particular (Stenning, 2003). If diversity, and especially its politicization, was perceived in the past as a threat to the state, the remedy being assimilation, in recent years it is also greeted with a more lenient approach, either formally or informally. The belief in national unity, or in the ability of the state to create uniformity, is often replaced by recognition of a need to manage a complex society and the will to face changing and at times contradictory needs of different groups. This approach is reflected in attempts to articulate new definitions of citizenship and to negotiate existing political arrangements, indicating a growing readiness to grant new rights and privileges to minorities (Pieterse, 2004). Some states have shifted towards a more accommodating approach to diversity and formally adopted "multicultural policies" (Banting and Kymlicka, 2003) that go beyond the protection of basic civil and political rights guaranteed to all individuals in a liberal democratic state. Other states still debate how to address the challenges of diversity and the multicultural reality. Multicultural democracies that reform institutions so that they accommodate diversity must take into account not only their contribution to political stability, at times a short-term measure, but also their ability to promote a participatory democracy, fairness, social cohesion and social justice (McGarry and O'Leary, 2006).

Alongside the debate on state-level changes, diversity management has become a common term, shifting from the private sector to the public, to describe various micro-policies at the workplace level. Managers, it is argued, may feel normatively obliged to accommodate people of different backgrounds, are under legal obligation to be inclusive or may try to use diversity as a strategic tool to augment performance (Pitts et al., 2010). Diversity, representation and cultural competence are not only parts of social equity but also "overlapping ways of thinking about a common underlying psychological construct of 'us' versus 'them'" (Pitts, 2005). Social equity has been defined as a pillar of public administration with values and principles to which

public administration should adhere (Fredrickson, 1990). Diversity
management programs were introduced in both the public and private
sector and included different aims: increasing participation of marginalized groups, improving career prospects for their members, incorporating new and wider perspectives into decision-making processes and
helping organizations reach new and formerly untapped markets
(Lorbiecki and Jack, 2000). In the public sector, diversity management
aims extend beyond efficiency and performance. While corporations, in
the face of a diversifying society, run the risk of losing their competitive
advantage, governments run the risk of diminished legitimacy (Soni,
2000). Diversity, as Boston and Callister (2005) argue, must be taken
seriously by policy advisers and policy makers for three reasons. First,
diversity affects the design, delivery and effectiveness of many policies
(Weimer and Vining, 1998). Second, diversity raises questions about
the design of public institutions. And, third, in different countries
diversity is advanced as a policy principle.

The ability, or the will, of states to accommodate diversity, often lags
beyond the needs and demands so that minority groups remain marginalized or excluded. Dominant ethnic groups may successfully resist
changes that would undermine privileged position, while subordinated
groups attempt to change the status quo. State institutions, especially
when dominated by one group, are in a privileged position to make their
preferred ethnic distinctions "politically relevant, publicly acknowledged and culturally legitimate" (Wimmer, 2013: 64). Whether it is
immigrants who do not fully integrate, ethnic minorities who demand
recognition or indigenous groups struggling for rights, the liberal ideals
of equality (rarely fully employed) may not suffice. First, because for
some groups questions of recognition that pertain to needs and sensitivities remain unanswered, and, second, formal declarations of equality
are not necessarily matched by social attitudes and political commitments to fight inequality and abolish discriminatory practices.
Consequently, minority groups may suffer from nonrecognition, discrimination and social-economic marginalization they can relate to the
state and to specific policies. Minority groups, as we argue here, compare
themselves to others and perceptions of relative deprivation (Gurr, 1970)
affect their evaluation of citizenship, identification with the state and the
legitimacy they grant to its institutions. Beyond the philosophical and
theoretical debates, and the looming questions over the future of the
nation-state, the multicultural turn involves mundane, everyday policy

debates and questions regarding institutional practices and articulations of citizenship rights.

Citizenship: Contested

The growing diversification of contemporary states, and the politicization of identity questions, spark debates about traditional conceptions of identity and community, the rights and mutual obligations embedded in citizenship and the gaps between majority and minority populations in the way they relate to the state and its institutions. Citizenship is the most important foundation upon which the modern state guarantees the egalitarian status and rights of all individuals within its territory, equal citizenship considered one of the most basic principles of a democratic state (Axtmann, 1996; Collier and Levitsky, 1997; Kymlicka and Norman, 1994). As the "right to have rights," whose scope and content are negotiated or fought over, citizenship is translated into a "set of practices (juridical, political, economic and cultural) which define a person as a competent member of society, and which as a consequence shape the flow of resources to persons and social groups" (Turner, 1993: 2). In Marshall's classic theory (1950), citizenship evolves and expands in a uniform and linear manner, from civil to political and social rights, as rights accumulate and democracy develops. Yet, Marshall's categories of citizenship – civil, political and social – have largely focused on class divisions and ignored both religion and ethnicity, markers of identity that became central to many societies (Ben-Porat and Turner, 2011). Also, contrary to Marshall's scheme of citizenship, evolving from civil to political and social, the development of citizenship rights has often been cumulative and uneven (Pakulski, 1997), providing different sets of demands and rights to different groups.

Citizenship is a process of social inclusion that provides members of a political community with social status, social rights and the right to take part in collective decision-making (Ben-Porat and Turner, 2011). Ideally, in the context of majority–minority relations, citizenship ensures equality and balance between individuals and collectives, serves as the main component for engendering common bonds to the state and functions as a basic mechanism that underpins the stability of the political system (Kymlicka, 1995; Lijphart, 1984). However, and contrary to its description as linear and uniform, citizenship does not necessarily evolve in a uniform and gradual way inclusive of all individuals and groups but rather provides different and often unequal sets of rights, and a stratified and hierarchical structure (Shafir and Peled, 2002). Cultural, ethnic and racial divisions within society affect the construction of citizenship and reinforce social and political fragmentation. Consequently, citizenship is a contest over rights where individuals and groups articulate their claims sometimes against the state and its institutions, when they believe they are mistreated, and often in competition with other groups perceived as privileged or excluding (Ben-Porat and Turner, 2011). Differently stated, in spite of its universal character, citizenship is the most effective and legitimate institution to discriminate between individuals based on their group belonging, tying universal human rights to membership in a specific national community, granting rights in a differentiated way to citizens of the state, or even completely depriving some groups of rights, often part of the everyday working of the state, even without a legal basis in citizenship laws (Wimmer, 2013: 67).

Citizenship is often a contested ground for individual and group rights, inclusion and exclusion and the very definition of the political community. It is challenged either by demands for rights and entitlements or by changes that undermine notions of common or imagined solidarity (Turner, 2001). These demands can open up citizenship for more rights and inclusions and a change of citizenship regimes. But, opposite developments are also possible, frustrating minorities or immigrants expecting inclusion and equality. Thus, exclusions can be reinscribed when the state is challenged by internal conflicts or external pressures (Marx, 2002), and, similarly, political rights can be limited for the sake of stability and security as witnessed in recent years. As Turner explains, "Who gets citizenship clearly indicates the prevailing formal criteria of inclusion/exclusion within a political community, and how these resources – following citizenship membership – are allocated and administered largely determines the economic fate of individuals and families" (2000: 38).

The very idea of citizenship may be changing, as according to some accounts it is eroding after decades of globalization that undermined the welfare state, transformed national cultures, increased the mobility of people across national boundaries and changed the meaning of national space; overall creating a hierarchy of citizenship, within and between states (Castles, 2005). A crisis, real or perceived, of the nation and the state influences the way citizenship is debated and enacted. In times of crisis, the linear or accumulative nature of citizenship may change in scope and content. Citizenship rights might become constricted, limited or securitized, and, more importantly, forego their universal structure, introducing new hierarchies and exclusions (Ben-Porat and Ghanem, 2017). Globalization brought with it growing insecurity, a securitization of citizenship and its reshaping as "identity management" (Muller, 2004) and security practices that strayed away from liberal ideas of equality and freedom.

Securitizing Citizenship

Unpacking citizenship from its universal and formal egalitarian description reveals not only hierarchies and exclusions, but also security discourses that legitimize them. The securitization of citizenship implies that various issues (as well as groups and individuals) can be "securitized" or made into a "security issue," "if it can be intensified to the point where it is presented and accepted as an existential threat" (Williams, 2003: 516). Acts of security seek to provide protection from danger, freedom from doubt and relief of anxiety. At the same time, however, such acts encourage fear, foster apprehension and feed off nervousness in the population (Nyers, 2004). Thus, "In the ensuing climate of fear, states can flex their muscles with greater impunity, constricting citizenship practices by using national security as a justification" (Dobrowolsky, 2007). Securitization, therefore, can construct specific groups of migrants as "threatening" national identity, state sovereignty and/or social stability (Squire, 2015). Not only migrants, but also minorities within countries or political oppositions to existing orders can all become securitized, questioning democratic citizenship. Minorities in particular are vulnerable unfair treatment when their states feel insecure and fearful of neighboring enemies they are associated with (Kymlicka, 2010). Securitization emphasizes social order and security, severing the connection between social problems and social justice, depoliticizing social questions like poverty and alienation, and exacerbating (real or imagined) public worries and anxieties (Loader and Walker, 2001), justifying suspension of citizenship and human rights.

Securitization allows states to demarcate and exclude minorities residing within them, immigrant or indigenous group, their marginalization justified by social order and stability. Formal citizenship, therefore, does not necessarily overlap with equal status (Brubaker, 1996), citizenship hierarchies preserved by bureaucratic practices. Interactions between citizens and bureaucrats help citizens understand not only how government functions, or its competence, but also of their own status and power as they: "socialize the citizens to expectations of government service and place in the political community ... in a sense street-level bureaucrats implicitly mediate aspects of the constitutional relationship of citizens to the state" (Lipsky, 1980: 4). Interaction teaches citizens about the fundamental properties and commitments of their government but also influences perceptions of political standing, membership and efficacy (Lerman and Weaver, 2014: 12). It allows citizens of different groups to evaluate how people "like them" are treated, with respect or with stigma, in comparison to other citizens.

Police and policing are part of citizenship regimes, separating citizens into those that are entitled to protection, those who remain vulnerable and those depicted as a security threat. The significance of policing for citizens and citizenship extends beyond immediate concerns of security and order to the "heavy symbolic load" the police carry (Bradford, 2014: 22). Fair treatment signals that individuals and the police are "on the same side," motivates individuals to feel like valued members of their social group (Hough et al., 2013) and strengthens the "bonds of citizenship" required for a legitimate state (Bayley, 2002). Conversely, police activity may be detrimental in creating denigrated social categories, communicating stigmatization and labeling individuals as members of marginalized, excluded or denigrated outgroups (ibid.). Police, in Waddington's words, "patrol the boundaries of citizenship: the citizenship of those who are 'respectable' is secured, while those who attack the state exclude themselves from citizenship. Between these extremes are those whose claim to citizenship is insecure and needs repeatedly to be negotiated. Police are the *de facto* arbiters of their citizenship, it is they who are 'police property' and this is a mark of their marginality" (1999: 29). Through their presence and performance police serve as a "vehicle" through which communities are imagined (Loader and Walker, 2001) and citizenship is experienced and evaluated.

Trust and Legitimacy

Trust and legitimacy, essential to any political order, have become contested concepts in democracies where the integration of minority groups remains incomplete and feelings of discrimination are strong. When exercising their powers, governments and their bureaucracies must claim resources and constrain actions in ways that often conflict with the interests and political preferences of their subjects (Scharpf, 2007). Legitimacy is a moral sense of obligation of citizens to obey and cooperate. Accordingly, it is most commonly explained as citizens' acceptance of the state right to rule, or the feeling of obligation to obey, and is a property that is not simply instrumental but reflects a social value orientation towards authority and institutions (Sunshine and Tyler, 2003a, 2003b). Law abidance is often habitual but when discrepancy between required behavior and personal interests and preferences increases, and when low-risk opportunities for evasion exist, legitimacy beliefs may become a crucial factor contributing to the voluntary compliance with undesired rules or decisions of governing authority (Easton, 1965: 278–319). Thus, when authorities are viewed as legitimate, the decisions they make and the rules they create are to a greater extend deferred to voluntarily (Tyler, 2006). Political systems and institutions must, therefore, engender and maintain the belief among subordinates that they are legitimate: entitled to demand obedience and cooperation.

Legitimacy reflects a social value orientation towards authority and institutions (Sunshine and Tyler, 2003a, 2003b) measured in citizens' perceptions and everyday behavior, and alluding to the complexity of contemporary citizenship. Political scientists use legitimacy to evaluate regimes and their stability, as the lack of legitimacy can be a predictor, or more often, an explanation, for regime collapse. While this definition is somewhat circular, regimes make various claims of legitimacy based, in Weber's classical typology, upon tradition, charisma or modern legality, or often a mixture of the three. Those demanded to obey, their acceptance inculcated by shared justifying narratives and discourses (Scharpf, 2007), must accept these claims. Legitimacy, the acceptance of authority, often involves a continuous dialogue between power holders making claims and citizens responding to them, a dialogue taking a different form in different societies (Mazepus et al., 2016; Tankebe, 2013). Beetham (1991) suggests that legitimate authority depends upon lawfulness, the way power was acquired and is exercised, namely by the "rule of law" and principles of due process and equality, the justification of rules in terms of common beliefs, and some evidence of compliance (see also: Tankebe, 2013).

Law, or legality, essential to legitimacy claims, always operates in a social context and must be justified and sustained by shared values and beliefs within society. Conformity to the law bestows legitimacy only to the extent that the law is an expression of recognized and accepted values (Coicaud, 2002). Tyler (2005) suggests that legitimacy (central to people's compliance) is linked to authorities' fair treatment of people. While legitimacy is often claimed from "above," by authorities demanding compliance and referring to legality, it is measured from "below" by citizens' perceptions and evaluations of authorities. Citizens can evaluate legitimacy by "input," authorities' attentiveness to preferences and demands of citizens, reflecting values and norms of society; by "output," their effectiveness in executing policies; and "throughput," their evaluation of the governance process (Mazepus et al., 2016; Scharpf, 2007; Schmidt, 2013). Minority and majority groups may differ not only in their perceptions of institutions' legitimacy, but also by the way they evaluate legitimacy.

Trust, related to but different from legitimacy, "is the belief that a person occupying a specific role will perform that role in a manner consistent with the socially defined normative expectations associated with that role" (Hawdon, 2008). This belief is also relevant to institutions and the expectations citizens hold towards them and citizens' willingness to become involved and cooperate with them. The concept of trust in government and bureaucracy, however, suffers from conceptual vagueness or ambiguity and can relate to past experiences, present observations or future expectations (Bouckaert et al., 2002) often relating to the performance of government and its agencies, or, more likely, to citizens' perceptions of these institutions. Distrust of institutions, however, especially when correlated with class or ethnicity, may be structural and indicative of societal hierarchies and schisms, and of alienation of groups from the state and its institutions.

Political scientists' study of legitimacy tends to focus, almost naturally, on those holding high-level political power and their claims/right to rule. But, the day-to-day use of legitimate force within the state is normally reserved for law enforcement officials and, consequently, the study of the legitimacy of their work is of vital significance to the understanding of politics (Bottoms and Tankebe, 2012). The importance of trust and legitimacy to the performance of governments and their institutions raises two important questions: first, which groups trust and perceive institutions as legitimate? And, second, how can states and their institutions become trusted and legitimate? Theories of ethnicity, class and identity provide an important supplement for the understanding of trust and legitimacy. These theories, on a macro-level, can explain why certain groups trust less the state and its institutions and see them as less legitimate, as marginalized and discriminated groups are likely to be less trusting. On a micro-level, these theories open up different questions on what explains particular trust and distrust, why legitimacy differs between groups, and how different policies affect trust and legitimacy.

Who Trusts? The Policing of Minority Citizens

Police legitimacy and public consent are necessary conditions for the justifiable use of state power: those who are subject to policing must see the police as right and proper (Tyler, 2006). Being the "most visible symbol of state-sponsored coercive control" police are burdened by the need to obtain compliance and, consequently, have the need for legitimacy (Jackson and Gau, 2016). In diverse societies, marked by racial and class divisions and differential citizenship, the "rule of law" and "social order" are inevitably contested concepts. The erosion of the nation-state nexus opens new forms of identity, new demands for equality and recognition and new challenges for state institutions. These changes are no less than dramatic for police, previously benefitting from a sense of community that legitimizes their actions and at the same time representing and contributing to this very sense of community. The tension or asymmetry between state and nation, experienced across the world, suggests that the ability of police to bridge between the authority of the state and the symbolism of national/cultural community is diminishing (Loader and Walker, 2001). The monopoly of violence vested in the hands of the state and, by its order, to the police, is questioned for two interrelated reasons. First, for minorities alienated from the state, police and policing do not necessarily represent a moral order. And, second, practices of police can be perceived as unfair and discriminating against minority groups, further alienating them from society and state.

Diversity, now a common feature in many democracies, even those previously considered homogenous, has a direct bearing on police and policing. Minority groups in different countries demonstrate lower levels of satisfaction with, trust in and legitimacy of the police (Albrecht, 1997; Chakraborti and Garland, 2003; Hasisi and Weitzer, 2007; Tyler, 2001; Wortley and Owusu-Bempah, 2009). Specifically, racial or ethnic identity is often found to be "the best predictor of evaluations of police" (Weitzer and Tuch, 1999). Negative perceptions of police can be attributed to minorities' refusal to identify with a single set of legal and political values held by the dominant group, which may lead to alienation from the state, government and its institutions (Michelson, 2003). Citizens who morally align with the state, having a shared sense of right and wrong, and who perceive the state as legitimate, are more likely to accept the authority of its institutions, police and others, and comply with their demands. Minorities' negative attitudes towards police can be derived from their frustrations from the state policies and citizenship status. With law enforcement being the most visible, immediate and accessible manifestation of the state (Skogan and Frydl, 2004), police are likely to be perceived as executing unjust policies that add to minorities' sense marginality and discrimination.

Alternatively, or often interrelatedly, negative perceptions can be explained by what police do, when they discriminate and stigmatize minorities, or when failing to provide them with security. Under these circumstances minorities compare their status to other citizens, further eroding their confidence in police. Institutions, in other words, might be evaluated, at least partially, independently so that their legitimacy depends also on their own actions and images. Thus, particular institutions are evaluated, first, by their input, how aligned they are with citizens' values and responsive to citizens' needs and concerns. Second, by their output, how effective they are in providing security. And, third, by their throughput, how accountable and transparent they are. Using this typology, therefore, enables both to understand how police forces attempt to secure legitimacy and to evaluate how legitimate they are in the public's eyes. Police treatment of citizens is evaluated not only in absolute terms but also *relatively* to dominant groups. Relative deprivation theory (Gurr, 1970) suggests that the sense of discrimination can be triggered by intergroup downward comparisons (Jost and Mentovich, 2010). Minorities' group position of unfair and exclusionary treatment is directed not only against dominant groups but also against social institutions (Weitzer and Tuch, 2006) and the state. This combination of a lack of moral alignment and perceived discrimination can lead minorities to view themselves as second-rate, or "custodial," citizens:

> Rather than seeing a government that provides for the collective good, their experiences with the criminal justice are defined by domination. As a result, Custodial citizens' "sense of the state" is one of control, hierarchy, and arbitrary power ... Rather than instilling a sense of efficacy, custodial citizens feel that they are not full citizens, that their concerns are not heard by government, that elected officials are unwilling to respond to and help them, and that they cannot trust government to act in their interests, and that taking part or trying to influence the political process is futile (Lerman and Weaver, 2014: 112).

While the combination of racial and class subjugation of African Americans may be more extreme, due to its historical and contemporary dimensions, than that of many other minorities elsewhere, differences between dominant groups and minorities are common. While dominant groups may find it easier to identify with police, minorities may be reluctant to trust and cooperate.

Why Trust? Between Performance and Fairness

Citizens' trust in public institutions combines perceptions of effectiveness, how well institutions perform, and fairness – whether institutions operate with good intentions. These perceptions underscore institutions' attempts to garner trust, and the theories that guide their policies and practices. Performance theory suggests that citizens evaluate government and its bureaucratic agencies by their ability to provide expected services (Bouckaert et al., 2002; Van Craen and Skogan, 2015). Trust in public institutions, therefore, is a function of the extent that these institutions produce outcomes that meet citizens' expectations. In the case of police, citizens' trust and legitimacy depend on the ability of the police to fight crime and provide public safety and, consequently, the police are evaluated by the degree to which citizens are bothered by crime, disorder and

feelings of insecurity (Van Craen and Skogan, 2015). Cooperation
and compliance, accordingly, are a product of self-interest, shaped
by cost-benefit concerns and, consequently, police strategies need to
establish *deterrence* (to reduce crime) and to demonstrate *effectiveness* (to exhibit competence) if they are to secure public cooperation (Piquero et al., 2011). Instrumental legitimacy attributes trust
in police to their effectiveness in performing their traditional tasks
(Tyler, 2005: 326), namely the ability to prevent and control crime
and provide a high sense of security to citizens (Sunshine and Tyler,
2003a: 153). Police, according to this logic, will have legitimacy
and trust if they will perform well, namely provide citizens the
security they expect.

Critics of performance theory suggest that better performance will
not necessarily bring the expected trust. Performance in general is often
difficult to measure and even if improved performance is achieved, it
does not necessarily match public opinion that may reflect different
expectations or limited knowledge (Bouckaert et al., 2002: 64).
Citizens often have difficulty to monitor and control agents' performance, so that their trust is "fiduciary," an asymmetric relation in
which citizens evaluate the moral obligations of agents and place
trust in the agents to act on their capacity (Thomas, 1998). Regarding
police performance, citizens might feel police do not provide enough
security or fail to fight crime. But, rising levels of crime might be the
result of social changes of which police have limited influence over.
Also, while crime statistics may show little change or even some
improvement, public opinion might be influenced by dramatic events
covered by the media that capture attention and create insecurity.
Finally, citizens may differ in their definition of performance based
on their experiences, expectations of and needs from police.
Specifically, minorities may evaluate police performance in relative
terms, comparing themselves to others and consequently, be more
concerned with questions of fairness than effectiveness. For example,
a policy of "quality of life policing," like the "broken windows," was
enthusiastically received by those likely to benefit from it, but the
attention to lower-level offenders has had a negative effect on minorities (Lerman and Weaver, 2014: 45).

Normative models of compliance suggest that citizens pay more attention to the process – input and throughput – than to outcomes.
Accordingly, trust is anchored in considerations of *fairness* (Tyler, 2004,

2006). Procedural justice theory (Tyler, 2001) suggests that citizens' trust in authorities is shaped by judgments of fairness, namely, how decisions are made and how people over whom authority is exercised are treated. This includes perceived politeness and helpfulness of police offices and expectations that police treat all citizens with justice and dignity (Tyler, 2005) that communicate a message that a person is valued and respected. Cooperation and compliance with police, therefore, rely upon the respect, the commitment to their well-being and the fairness police demonstrate in their everyday encounters with citizens. The "heavy symbolic load' (Bradford, 2014: 22) police carry and demonstrate in their interaction with citizens means that citizens can learn about their status in society through how police treat them in specific situations (Jackson et al., 2012: 1053), often in comparison to others.

The way citizens perceive police, both their effectiveness – fighting crime and providing security – and fairness, is often shaped by past experiences, present observations or future expectations (Bouckaert et al., 2002), but experiences, observations and expectations differ among citizens and are mediated through status, class and identities. Police legitimacy, as mentioned before, is often part and parcel of the way they regard the whole political and social order and its institutional framework (Smith, 2007: 34). Consequently, theories that explain the level of citizens' trust in the police, developed and tested with "the people" or "the majority" in mind (Van Craen, 2013; Jackson et al., 2012), may have overlooked important differences between majority and minority groups. Aggressive police tactics, for example, might satisfy some parts of the population, believing it enhances their security, but alienate others who will bear the costs of police aggressiveness. Different histories, contemporary experiences and future expectations of individuals and groups impact their different perception of police and levels of trust and legitimacy.

"Show Me Your Papers": Policing and Citizenship

Policing, following the discussion above, is a test for group and individual citizenship. Democratic policing is identified with procedural regularity and the rule of law, respect for substantive rights and popular participation in policing through civilian oversight or delegation of authority to the community (Sklansky, 2007: 3–4). In the context of a multicultural setting democratic policing can also refer to the capacity of the police, on the one hand, to provide services that fit the needs of different communities and, on the other hand, to uproot existing prejudices and unfair practices towards minorities. Majorities and minorities, however, in practice often experience police, like other state institutions, differently and hold different perceptions of and expectations from police. For the majority, police are an institution associated with the state and with order and they expect police to treat them with respect and provide security. These expectations are not always met: inequalities related to class and gender suggest that majorities are far from homogenous and privatization of police services imply gaps in the provision of security, but in a democratic setting the ideal of police serving the public remains valid. Conversely, for minorities, especially "visible minorities," the police's role is more contested and its intentions questioned. New York mayor, Bill de Blasio, angered his local police force when in an interview he talked about the advice he gave his biracial son. "Look, if a police officer stops you, do everything he tells you to do, don't move suddenly, don't reach for your cell phone, because we knew, sadly, there's a greater chance it might be misinterpreted if it was a young man of color" (Jamieson, 2014).

Fair treatment is a measure of standing in the community and implies that the person is a full and equal member who is deserving of respect. Unsurprisingly, members of stigmatized racial minority groups are especially attentive to fair treatment (Epp et al., 2014: 15). Minorities' perceptions of police unfairness are usually associated with two central problems that can be described as "over-policing," an aggressive approach that singles out minorities, and "under-policing," the neglect of minority neighborhoods (Ben-Porat, 2008b). Over-policing is a clear demonstration of police unfairness, felt mostly by "visible" minorities who are securitized, namely viewed as a "threat" to national identity, state sovereignty and/or social stability (Squire, 2015). This depiction allows and justifies the harsh treatment of minorities by police, and at times the indifference of the dominant groups to discriminatory policies and practices rationalized as necessary.

Police violence against minorities, especially when documented, captures public attention and triggers protest: the beating of Rodney King in 1991 by police officers in Los Angeles, or the more recent series of events that inspired the Black Lives Matter movement, demonstrating police racism against African Americans. Over-policing, however, is experienced also in more mundane practices and everyday events that usually escape the public eye but have detrimental effect on minorities singled out. Police stops, "a frequent and visible exercise of public authority," for example, might have significant repercussions:

Fairly conducted traffic-safety stops tell a driver that they are an equal member of society and are held to the same rule as everybody else. Racially biases investigatory stops tell a driver that they look like a criminal and people like them are subject to arbitrary control befitting their subordinate status; they are not an equal member of society. Police stops that target minorities communicate to those stopped, and those shielded from such stops, that some citizens are not free to move as equal members of society (Epp et al., 2014: 135–136).

Police officers' use of generalizations based on race, ethnicity, religion or national affiliation known as "racial profiling" serve as the basis for suspicion in directing law enforcement actions (Chan, 2011). These practices are usually not part of official policy but are institutionalized and legitimated by rules, training and the law and are expressed in the shared practices of police forces (Epp et al., 2014: 11–12). Racial and ethnic minorities are often more likely to be stopped, questioned, searched and arrested by the police (Walker et al., 2000; Weitzer and Tuch, 1999). The categorization of people through discourses and practices of police and security renders certain groups, often "visible minorities," suspects of criminal or other deviant behavior (Tator and Henry, 2006: 9). Police stops based on racial categories "convey a powerful message about citizenship and equality ... experiences are translated into common stories about who is an equal member of a rule governed society and who is subjected to arbitrary surveillance and inquiry" (Epp et al., 2014: 2). Consequently, "Whites begin their encounters with police assuming that they have full citizen rights and leave these experiences with their status undiminished" (Epp et al., 2014: 48). Visibility (e.g., skin color) exposes minority groups stereotyped "dangerous" to being stopped and arrested more than other citizens. When visibility combines with vulnerability, or marginalization, minorities might also be exposed to police brutality.

Police preferences and the political agendas of policy makers that influence them might leave minority groups, especially in poor neighborhoods, exposed to violence. Decisions to prioritize the safety of some neighborhoods and unequal allocation of police resources can leave other neighborhoods, usually poor and ethnic, "under-policed"

(Brown and Benedict, 2002). Under-policing can also manifest itself in specific policies like police's neglect of complaints about racial harassment and hate crimes, or the overlooking of domestic violence among minority communities, characterized by police as "cultural" or "normative" in these communities, therefore not requiring intervention (Brunson and Miller, 2006). Overall, police may absent themselves from minority neighborhoods regarded as "hopeless" so that poor urban communities suffer from unresponsive policing and high crime rates. Importantly, while members of the dominant group may view rising crime rates a result of general poor police performance, members of a minority group perceive this as a deliberate neglect that renders them vulnerable and insecure. Under-policing, from the minority perspective, is not solely a measure of police performance but also a measure of fairness as minorities attribute under-policing, rightly or wrongly, to discrimination. As such, much like racial profiling, the neglect of minority needs and the lack of commitment to provide them with security is also an indication of their unequal citizenship status.

Under-policing suggests that the debate over police and policing cannot be detached from wider questions of status, class and property, providing more security for those with the political means to demand or the economic capacity to procure. The so-called privatization revolution of the 1980s included also police services that were partially privatized, either through user-financed police services or by contracting out and allowing for private provision of police services (Fixler and Poole, 1988). These trends accelerated in the wake of the Cold War and globalization with rising demands for privatized security and new questions regarding the political restraints and accountability of private companies provided with new powers, as well as concerns over the security gap between the "haves" and the "have nots" and ensuing social fragmentation (Mandel, 2001). Policing provided also by private sources may no longer be a public good, administered by an institution committed to general welfare but rather a service on behalf of those who have the means to pay for it, introducing new forms of discrimination.

Under- and over-policing are not mutually exclusive and can affect different minorities in different ways and may depend also on other factors like class and education. Minorities, especially "visible minorities," can suffer from both under-policing in their neighborhoods where the police are absent and over-policing outside their neighborhoods where they are targeted as suspects (Barlow and Barlow, 2000). Poor, nonwhite and disadvantaged groups are both at risk of violence and exposed to state punitive control (Lerman and Weaver, 2014), suffering a "racial tax," first as victims and second as targets of police intervention (Kennedy, 1997). The fact that under-policing and over-policing can appear separately, in different combinations and different scales of importance, suggests, first, that minorities' perceptions of police are influenced by their perceptions of citizenship and status. And, second, that they are likely to differ in their collective experiences, frustrations and expectations from police.

Reforming Police

Theories that explain the level of citizens' trust in the police were mostly developed and tested with "the people" or "the majority" in mind (Van Craen, 2013). But, tensions and controversies across the world, as well as research data, suggest that minorities have different perceptions of police, different concerns that require attention. Failing to adequately serve and protect minority communities, for different reasons discussed above, further erodes trust in police. To break the vicious cycle police must develop services that suit all segments of society, diversify their force to mirror society and improve their trust among minorities (Oakley, 2001). To engage successfully with minority communities, especially marginalized and alienated, police must overcome their own biases and prejudices in order to serve all groups (Barlow and Barlow, 2000; Casey, 2000; Kelling and Moore, 2006). Post-conflict reconstruction provides an opportunity to rebuild police and a fertile ground for research that examines how a new police force could be part of the solution to the conflict, rather than part of the problem. A police force that can provide security for all political sectors, unlike the politicized and abusive predecessors, must be under civilian control, provide a public service and be ethnically plural and nonpartisan (Nield, 2006). As Nield (2006) argues, "only policing that respects the rights of all citizens and is responsive to their needs can be effective in controlling crime and maintaining order." Differently stated, the new police should rely not on traditional perceptions and patterns of policing that rest on compliance, deterrence and zero-tolerance but on new ideas and methods that stress legitimacy and trust that befit a democratic regime and an inclusive society.

At least part of what is valid for post-conflict states can be relevant also to more stable democracies, where minority citizens remain alienated from the state and distrust police. Changes that took place in police forces, making them more educated, diversified and open than ever before, have not always brought the expected changes in relations between police and minorities (Sklansky, 2007). While in many democratic countries there is broad support for the general principles of good policing (use of minimum force, impartiality, fairness and accountability), surprisingly little is known about the level of popular support for specific kinds of reforms (Weitzer and Tuch, 2006: 37). Police reforms in the early twentieth century sought to professionalize the police, to create uniform standards and make it more effective for crime fighting (Roberg et al., 2002: 49). A change occurred when police in different democratic states shifted from an impersonal, bureaucratic approach to strategies aimed at gaining legitimacy by greater involvement, among other ways through "community policing" discussed below. Later, a multicultural approach was incorporated that included effective engagement with different cultural groups, review of discriminatory policies and provision of services designed to strengthen police legitimacy across society (Chan, 2011; Kelling and Moore, 2006).

Many contemporary police reforms address the idea of "democratic policing," aligning police work with freedoms and equality associated with a democracy.

The goal of democratic policing is to build a web of relationships between the community and the police that helps to control crime by making police aware of the persons and activities in the communities that they are assigned to protect and by inclining citizens to trust and cooperate with police. This also achieves the primary goal of making citizens feel secure in their daily activities, thereby fostering a climate that encourages increased legitimate business activity, investment, and planning for the future (Wiatrowski and Goldstone, 2010).

Democratic police services should operate in accordance with law, be regulated by a professional code of conduct, protect life by minimizing the use of force, be accountable to the public, protect life and property through proactive crime prevention, safeguard human rights and dignity, and act in a nondiscriminatory manner. To the list, especially when diverse societies are concerned, can be added also the effective internal and external accountability and partnership with communities in the achievement of public safety (Bayley, 2005).

Minorities, even in democratic states, often suffer relative powerlessness, marginality, and are alienated from the state and distrust its institutions. Police reforms towards minorities are important both symbolically, acknowledging minority citizens' worth and equality, and practically, everyday interactions with police providing minority citizens with security and treating them with dignity. The different aspects of police reforms, beyond their potential direct impact on trust in police, allude to the deficits in minority citizenship. Consequently, their potential, impact and acceptance by minorities are part of the citizenship debate. Diversifying the police force and making it more representative could potentially affect its legitimacy, if minorities are able to identify with the police serving them. Attention to fair practices, in order to ensure minority citizens are treated equally by police, is another way to enhance trust and legitimacy. Finally, allowing citizens of minority groups to voice their concerns, become involved in policy making and oversee police work may be of central importance. Reforms, therefore, address the gaps between minority citizens and others in representation, effective participation and political voice.

Representation

Clashes between police and minorities and general distrust of minorities in police often raise the question whether the presence of minority officers would make a difference. In divided societies, it is argued, the legitimacy is conditioned by evidence that:

(1) Fellow ethnics are visible among wielders of authority at the political levels of government and state bureaucracy; (2) people of their kind can compete for, attain and hold such positions; and (3) they are able to provide a sympathetic hearing to their fellow ethnics and to protect their interests in the allocation of benefits and the provisions of public services (Esman, 1999: 365).

Representative bureaucracy is a term given to arguments that public organizations should reflect the population that they serve so it can make decisions that benefit the public. Representation of minorities can be "passive" and symbolic, or "active" when representing and defending minorities' needs and interests. (Meier et al., 1999). A representative bureaucracy is argued to be more responsive (Mosher, 1982), held in higher regard among citizens and achieve higher levels of organizational performance. These advantages depend upon organizational strategies and management commitment to diversity (Andrews et al., 2005). Thus, representative bureaucracy provides a means of fostering equity by ensuring that all groups and interests are involved in the shaping of public policy (Coleman and Selden, 2001). A bureaucracy that includes public servants who represent the population as a whole is argued to be more legitimate and accountable. Conversely, an unrepresentative bureaucracy might not only lack legitimacy and accountability in its everyday operation, but also reflects a lack of equal access to government jobs for those not represented (Keiser, 2010). If individual characteristics of bureaucrats influence their values, attitudes and behavior, and because officials could favor members of their own community and discriminate against others (Esman, 1999), the composition of the bureaucracy could be significant.

Scholars distinguish "passive representation," where the bureaucracy mirrors the population and when bureaucrats have limited discretion, from "active representation," when bureaucrats of minority groups are willing and able to take action that advocate the minority's interests. While passive representation may be limited and symbolic, it is possible that it would have a positive effect, both on minority populations who will be able to identify with state institutions and within the bureaucracy itself, the presence of minorities changing attitudes and behaviors. Moreover, it is also possible that passive representation will eventually turn active when bureaucrats of minority groups gain confidence and a critical mass. Yet, the potential for active representation can remain limited, first, because of the restriction on the discretion of bureaucrats and, second, the socialization process of the organization that individual recruits undergo (Keiser, 2010; Meier and Hawes, 2009). Studies of the effect of representative bureaucracy on minorities' perceptions and on performance and legitimacy of bureaucracies in general reveal a complex picture (Pitts, 2005; Pitts and Jarry, 2007), somewhat similar to that of political representation (Mansbridge, 1999).

Representation of police forces was debated in different places. Commissions in the United States that investigated the civil disorders in the 1960s described the mostly white police force in black neighborhoods as an "occupation force" despised by the residents and recommended the recruitment of black officers to diffuse tensions and bolster the image of police (Weitzer, 2000). When police are rebuilt after conflict, diversification is significant, to distinguish the new force from the old, homogeneous, politicized force, associated with the dominant party and illegitimate to the subjugated minority (Nield, 2006). A similar logic can guide more moderate police reforms, hoping that representation of groups hitherto excluded not only has the potential to narrow the distance between the police and these groups but also change police culture from within. Research, from multiethnic settings, however, shows no conclusive support that hiring minority officers will positively affect public perceptions of police (Brown and Benedict, 2002). Moreover, the assimilation of new recruits to existing police culture or their marginalization to insignificant roles further limits the potential impact of diversification (Desroches, 1992; Tinor-Centi and Hussain, 2000).

The presence of women officers in the police force was found to bring higher rates of sexual assault reports, women more comfortable with female officers (Meier and Nicholson-Crotty, 2006). The effects of the presence of ethnic and racial minorities on the force, however, are mixed as it is not clear that minorities prefer to be policed by their own, or have more trust in minority officers. The question of representation in police may be more sensitive than in many other bureaucracies due to its symbolic importance, the type of interaction it carries with citizens and, at times, its problematic history. Minorities may be reluctant to join the police when their histories and practices are considered discriminatory. Minorities are unlikely to enlist if they perceive police as part of a repressive state, an instrument of the dominant group in control of the state, enforcing unjust policies and being part of a wider apparatus of discrimination. Under such circumstances doubts are raised on the actual impact of the recruitment and its ability to change existing discriminatory practices (Desroches, 1992; Tinor-Centi and Hussain, 2000). Also, the motives and allegiances of minority officers can be suspected, being absorbed into police culture or left without discretion, and unwilling or unable to pursue active representation. As a result, minorities can be suspicious of police attempts to recruit them, critical of minority officers serving in the police and expect major changes in the police before considering joining the police.

Overall, diversifying the police force in an attempt to make it representative can be perceived differently by minorities, depending on their perceptions of police and their experiences, relation to the state and their position within it, as well as more mundane interests like the secure employment that police offers. Considering the symbolic importance of police and the role they play in everyday lives of minority citizens, especially in poor and marginalized communities, the debate regarding representation is of major significance. The willingness of minority citizens to serve in the police, or the approval of community members to do so, may be an important indication of citizenship and belonging. The questions whether minority citizens support attempts to diversify the police, their belief that minority officers will make a difference and how they view the impact of community members that currently serve will be examined in the different chapters of the book.

Fairness

Fairness is about how citizens assess the way police operate and interact with people, including both formal and informal policies. Fairness emphasizes the normative or relational dimension of policing (Sunshine and Tyler, 2003b) and rests on the premise that procedures used in citizen–police interactions are essential to public trust (Tyler, 2005). According to this model, and following the discussion of procedural justice above, citizens' trust in the police is primarily dependent on whether they perceive police actions to be fair, respectful and just (Sunshine and Tyler 2003b; Tyler, 2001, 2006). Accordingly, people evaluate fairness by their perceptions whether police officers treat citizens with respect, maintain the rule of the law and allow them to participate in decisions concerning them. When citizens believe they have been treated with respect and dignity by police officers, procedures and decisions appear neutral, and decisions were explained to them and their concerns have been heard, they are more likely to assess the interaction with police as positive, and police as more legitimate and trustworthy.

Assessment of fairness, however, rests not only on interactions with police officers but also on citizens' perceptions that the policies that police carry out are considered just and fair. First, for minorities alienated from the state, perceived as representing the interests and values of the majority, the respectful behavior of officers might not be enough. Second, instrumental outcomes themselves may carry important symbolic value (Bradford, 2014), as the ability and efforts of police to provide security to minorities conveys that they are regarded equal. And, third, when elements of procedural justice adopted by police coexist with practices and procedures that convey an opposite message, their impact might diminish. Racial profiling, for example, is unlikely to be perceived as legitimate, even if officers stopping citizens are polite and respectful. Rather, it is the stops themselves, based on unfair patterns, that make people feel like second-class citizens, as Epp et al. (2014) explain: "People are especially likely to look beyond respectfulness when, as in the case of African-Americans, they are a stigmatized group that is commonly and repeatedly subjected to a process that disproportionately disadvantages members of the stigmatized group."

Measures described as "cultural sensitivity" or "competence" that police can expect a similar fate if they do not address major concerns of minorities. Cultural competence relates to the public administration agencies' ability to deliver culturally appropriate and responsive services (Rice, 2005) and to respond to the challenges diverse societies present through "development of adequate professional skills to provide services to ethnic, racial, and cultural groups" (ibid.). Practice of cultural competency stresses operating effectively in different cultural contexts and providing services that reflect the different cultural influences of constituents or clients. Operationally, it is achieved by integrating and transforming knowledge about individuals and groups into specific practices, standards, policies and attitudes applied in appropriate cultural settings to increase the quality of services; thereby producing better outcomes (Rice, 2005, 2015). The cultural sensitivity training of police officers is designed to uproot police practices considered offensive to minorities, to reduce stereotypes that interfere with police work and to translate commitment to equality into policies that eliminate existing discriminatory practices, such as racial profiling (Chan, 2011).

Cultural training is relatively easy to implement, adding it to the curriculum of officers' courses, but might be of limited value if the problem is deep-rooted racism and animosity towards minorities, and if cultural sensitivity is superficial and glances over the real issues that are of concern to the minority, like police racism. More importantly, training can remain separate from actual behavior and practices as new recruits will receive their "real" training from senior officers, incorporating the traditional and discriminatory organizational culture. Training alone was found to have limited impact unless coupled with practical reforms in management, deployment and supervision (Stone and Ward, 2000). Minorities, therefore, can be suspicious of cultural training either because its effects are limited or because it focuses on their culture as a subject of study rather than the problematic nature of police and the need to uproot discriminatory practices.

Fairness can hold different meaning to different minorities, who develop their own criteria to evaluate police officers and their expectations. Perceptions of police are based not only on individual experiences but also on groups' shared experiences and expectations, common histories and their relation to state and society, shaping interactions with officers predisposing citizens' evaluations. For minorities, who perceive the state illegitimate and policies executed by police unfair, procedural justice and cultural sensitivity might be of limited value. Where deep discrimination is involved, manifested in under-policing and over-policing, micro-changes of fairness may fall short of needs and expectations. Nevertheless, the effect of fairness and unfairness cannot be discounted altogether because, first, it signals to minority groups that their concerns are important and, second, if taken seriously can help uproot discrimination.

Community and Voice

Citizenship, in regard to police and policing, from the point of view of minority groups can be measured in the ability to take part in decision-making, in being recognized as a community with specific needs and concerns, and in having some authority to oversee police work. The symbolic significance of police, as well as their influence on everyday life, means that minorities' perceptions, attitudes and alignment to police are about citizenship. Having a voice, as individuals and communities, and believing that their voice matters, is essential to the idea of democratic policing. Voice, however, often separates weak and marginalized communities from stronger communities and the majority. The interest and ability of minority groups to take part in these processes that involve cooperating with police is a measure of their efficacy and potential alignment. Namely, whether they trust enough to cooperate and believe they can be part of state and society.

Public participation in decision-making is another channel of bureaucratic representation that allows groups to have an impact on the policy process itself. The literature on citizen participation in decision-making (PDM) suggests that citizens' participation is a direct and strong support of the democratic ethos and can improve public sector performance (Adams, 2004; Michels, 2011). Fung and Wright (2001) show that successful participation mechanisms are more likely to be achieved when participation is applied at the local level to relatively simple policy areas. Michels (2011) shows that citizen involvement has a number of positive effects on democracy: it increases issue knowledge, civic skills, and public engagement, and it contributes to the support for decisions among the participants. Overall, the participation of citizens in decision-making processes improves the performance of public agencies and increases the trust in them. Highly involved citizens might become more sympathetic evaluators of tough decisions government administrators are often required to make, allowing government to rule effectively (Irvin and Stansbury, 2004; Putnam, 1993). The positive relationships between PDM, trust in public agencies and performance is significant for police engagement with citizens and even more so for their engagement with citizens of minority groups. Citizens and especially community leaders and activists can be involved with police through different forums. These forums facilitate a dialogue where citizens and police can meet, needs and expectations can be conveyed and different ways of cooperation can be initiated.

Improving relations between the police and minorities can be achieved not only by interpersonal exchanges but also by structural changes through which the community becomes involved in police work and vice versa (Ben-Porat and Yuval, 2012: 240). Community policing, an idea that gained momentum in the 1990s, was part of a broader effort to build trust between police and minority communities, an aspect that includes principles, policies and practices that link the police and community members together in the joint pursuit of local crime prevention (Roberg et al., 2002: 56). While community policing has different meaning and uses, leading some to argue it is more a philosophy than a strategy, it has several common components that include citizen input, broad police functions and personal service. In practice, this often translates to police constant presence (through foot patrol), direct engagement, familiarity with the community served, positive interactions, emphasis on crime prevention, and partnerships between police and community (Cordner, 2014).

Community policing, like other reforms, may face different challenges and have different affects among minority communities. First, disempowered communities that suffer from rates of crime and diminishing social capital might be a greater challenge for community policing than stronger communities that can act collectively and form partnerships with police. Second, "community," in spite of its popularity, is an elusive concept that might also have a "dark side" in regard to minorities, excluded or suspected. Third, suspicion of police and their intentions may complicate the ability to implement community policing that is based on close engagement with citizens. If the idea of community policing is that the public should play a greater role in police work, minorities who do not align morally with police, are alienated from the state and/or distrust police may be reluctant to do so. And, fourth, for minorities who perceive themselves under-policed, namely unprotected, community policing may appear not only as too soft and ineffective, but also a lesser quality policing that supposedly attests to discrimination (Ben-Porat and Yuval, 2012; Skolnick and Bayley, 1988).

Increasing police accountability is an important part of public voice and participation, often resisted by police fearing for their autonomy and clashing with their belief that they are professionals that should not be subjected to lay (and unfair) criticism. The ability for citizens to oversee police work (Lewis, 1999), however, may be of special significance where trust of police is low and suspicion of police misconduct is high. Police boards can be established to allow civilian oversight over the police and include minority members in decision-making (Wortley and Tanner, 2003). Perhaps more important for citizens is to be able to oversee investigation processes of police misconduct and complaints over police violence and abuse. Supporters of civilian oversight argue that misconduct investigations handled by civilians, rather than internally, will be (more) fair, sensitive, trusted and eventually influence positively police behavior.

For minority groups, who believe they are discriminated by police, exposed to violence or racial profiling, oversight might be of special significance. Minorities might be suspicious of police and uncooperative if the oversight proposed is perceived as a facade (Ben-Porat and Yuval, 2012: 240), complaints of police misconduct are perceived as not taken seriously and police officers guilty of misconduct are not reprimanded. The sense of injustice among minority citizens, when police violence is perceived as not taken seriously, not only undermines their trust in police but also signals their marginality within society and state.

History, Trajectories and Questions

In diverse societies, marked by racial and class lines, concepts like "rule of law" and "social order" are disputed and policing is a controversial issue as cultures, religions and competing national identities challenge the existing order that they find unjust and marginalizing. For minorities, the perceptions of police are often embedded within larger questions of citizenship and belonging, discrimination being just another example of their marginality and exclusion. Consequently, the study of perceptions, trust and legitimacy of police enables also a wider understanding of the relation between the state, its bureaucratic apparatuses and citizens. The "war on crime" demand of or declared by police, therefore, means entirely different things for citizens who expect more protection, those doubting that they will receive such protection and those who fear they will be a target of such policies that tighten social control.

While "ordinary" citizens expect police to provide them security, others are more concerned of being targeted and exposed to arbitrary exercise of police power. Ethnicity, race and class are all important factors shaping relations of citizens and police, in different ways. Minorities, other than not being part of the dominant majority, might share very little beyond that. Rather, they may hold different levels of moral alignment with the state and its institutions, and different perceptions regarding their place in society, whether they suffer temporary obstacles or from discrimination deeply ingrained in state and societal structures. Some minorities may be interested and perceive themselves able to successfully integrate, others might feel that integration is impossible and others might not be interested in integration altogether. These perceptions, in turn, affect their legitimacy of and trust in police, the way they define what good policing means and their concerns, needs and expectations from police. Finally, these relations with and to police are part of a citizenship debate we explore in the following chapters.

2 | *Police and Policing in Israel*

After seventy years of statehood Israel is a diverse society, divided by ethnicity, religion and class, engaged with a multicultural reality that calls into question understandings of sovereignty, identity, citizenship, rights and democracy. The description of Israel as an "overburdened polity" by two of its leading sociologists, almost forty years ago, has not lost any of its relevance. The seemingly endless battle over the meaning of a "Jewish and democratic state" is a daily reminder that the meaning of democracy, the meaning of a Jewish state and the ability or need to compromise between them remains contested.

Israel is an immigrant society where 25.6 percent of the majority Jewish population were not born within its borders and a further third of its population are the second generation born to immigrants (Central Bureau of Statistics, 2013, Table 2.6). This diversity is often over-shadowed by the presence of a native Arab-Palestinian minority that challenges the overall definition of a Jewish state and its commitment to democracy, and an "internal" religious schism concerning the state commitment to its Jewish character. These highly intensive and deep divisions (Ben-Rafael, 2013; Smooha, 2009) manifest themselves in different struggles over rights, duties and hierarchies of different social groups.

Like other states, including those that in the past enjoyed hegemonic stability or social homogeneity and are becoming more diverse and less stable, Israel is facing intensifying old and new challenges. These changes have a direct bearing on the state, its institutions and in particular the police (Stenning and Shearing, 2005). The fact that distinct groups are not cut from the same cloth where policing terms are concerned (Murphy and Cherney, 2012) relates both to their relation to the state, alignment or alienation, and the particular characteristics that sets them apart from others. Minority groups differ in their legitimacy of and trust in police, and their willingness to obey and cooperate with them. Israel's diversity, social schisms and intense political environment are the context within which we examine police and policing. Citizenship is the medium through which many struggles are conducted over the rights, duties and hierarchies of different social groups in Israel (Ben-Porat and Turner, 2011), including those that relate to security in general and policing in particular.

A Divided Society

Divisions in Israel intensified in recent decades, underscoring heightened tensions and rapid erosion of trust in the government and its institutions. These divisions occur within, and often in relation to, an external conflict that renders security to be a major concern. These schisms have mostly been present since the inception of the state in 1948, and even before, but intensified with time. The struggles of a growing multicultural reality, like elsewhere, depend not only on what groups desire and their identities but also upon the opportunities that the state and society provide to different groups. For different groups in Israel, unequal distribution of resources and failure to recognize needs, and perceptions of relative deprivation in comparison to other groups, are the cause of frustration, protest and even alienation. As we explore four of those schisms in the following chapters, in depth and with a comparative perspective, we will just outline here the schisms and their impact on state and society.

In early years of statehood, occupied with state and nation building and with a dominant political party (the Labor Party or MAPAI), the schisms were prevented from erupting. A combination of compromises, weakness of immigrant groups and state repression provided the state with sufficient legitimacy and ability to rule. In the 1970s the political center began to implode under pressures from different, dissatisfied groups, leading not only to the defeat of the Labor Party but also of the legitimacy of existing institutions and arrangements. The declining trust of Israeli citizens in the government and its institutions and the growing schism grew in tandem, exposing the divisions within society and the challenges for the state.

The definition of Israel as a "Jewish state" has important implications for its Arab-Palestinian citizens and their ability to achieve equal status. The government treatment of Arab citizens has generally been of neglect and discrimination, resulting in higher rates of poverty and crime, and limited opportunities. This schism is considered the deepest not only because of the economic gaps but also because of the state's difficulty, or unwillingness, to provide an opportunity for this minority to fully integrate as equal citizens. In addition, Israel's control of the occupied territories, where Palestinians live under military rule, further alienates Arab citizens from the state. The demands of Arab citizens for equality and recognition challenge the foundations of the Jewish state and encounter strong resistance from the state and the Jewish majority. Arab citizens are often "securitized," their loyalty to the state doubted and their freedoms restricted. This inherent tension between a national minority and a state, discussed in Chapter 3, has important repercussions for its relations with police.

While the vast majority of Jewish citizens agree that Israel is and should be a Jewish state, they dispute what that definition entails. While for nonreligious Jews a Jewish state is defined in ethnic or cultural terms, for religious Jews this definition should be manifested in the rules of the state and the public sphere. Compromises between religious and secular Jews reached before and established after statehood, known as the status quo, enabled political cooperation although conflicts and frictions often occurred. Changes within the nonreligious and religious camps, as well as wider demographic, political and economic changes, have gradually undermined agreements, heightened tensions and exposed the schism. For the ultra-Orthodox, known as Haredim, whom we explore in Chapter 5, the fact that Israel, being a Jewish state, does not adhere to religious rules, undermines the legitimacy of its institutions and explains their efforts and demands to protect their way of life.

Ethnicity is another divide in Israeli society, often correlated with status and class, and part of the political landscape. The ethnic division in Israel is usually referred to as that between Ashkenazim (Jews of European descent) and Mizrahim or Sefaradim (Jews of Middle Eastern or North African descent). This division began before statehood but became more salient after statehood with the mass immigration of Jews from Muslim countries. The state and its institutions embarked on a project of assimilation that sought to culturally transform the newcomers, often disregarding their cultural identities and preferences. At the same time, many of these immigrants were marginalized, relegated to the periphery and became blue-collar laborers in the developing economy. As a result, an "ethnic gap" was formed between the group reflected in residency patterns, educational attainment and income distribution. Gaps between Mizrahim and Ashkenazim have not disappeared and ethnicity remains salient, influencing, among other things, political identities. In the 1990s two new immigrations arrived. Immigrants from Ethiopia (Chapter 4), somewhat like Mizrahim, suffer from discrimination and were relegated to a peripheral position in Israeli society. Conversely, among immigrants from the former Soviet Union (Chapter 6) while suffering stigmas and hardships, many have made their way into the mainstream.

Israel's main political schism, known as the left-right schism, between those supporting territorial compromises and those who oppose it, has some indirect influence on our discussion here. The territories occupied in the war of 1967, with the Palestinians living there, were placed under military control. Since the 1970s, with growing pace, Israel began to settle Jews in the territories, creating "facts on the ground" and establishing control. Palestinian uprisings and failed Israeli–Palestinian negotiations since the 1990s have heightened tensions both between Israel and the Palestinians and within Israel, including political violence. The ongoing conflict, and periods of escalating violence, increased the salience of security debates, expanded the role of police and had a detrimental effect on Palestinian citizens of Israel. Israel's declared attempt to separate from the Palestinians of the West Bank and Gaza in order to secure the demography of the Jewish state, and various proposed laws in that spirit, have further alienated Arab citizens.

Finally, the economic changes of recent decades introduced new neoliberal policies and growing gaps between rich and poor. Liberal economic policies took a dramatic turn in the 1980s and set in motion the rapid rise of a consumer society resembling, and aspiring to be even more similar to, other Western countries. The growth of the Israeli economy that began in the mid-1980s exploded in the 1990s, influenced by immigration, the peace process and the high-tech industry. The standard of living in Israel, especially for the upper and middle class, measured by ownership of consumer goods, increased almost to the level of the industrialized Western states. State-led economic policies were replaced by neoliberal policies that encouraged privatization and increased socioeconomic gaps between rich and poor. These changes have had different effects on policing and security, with, on

the one hand, the growth of private security services in affluent neighborhoods, and the diminished security of poor neighborhoods, especially in Arab towns (Chapter 3), and, on the other hand, growing
incarceration among young Israelis of Ethiopian descent (Chapter 4).

The schisms and tensions briefly discussed above have also had an
impact on Israel's democratic regime and different institutions.
A recent and comprehensive survey by the Israel Democracy Institute
(Hermann et al., 2018) has found that only a minority of Israeli citizens
feel they have influence on government policies. Israeli citizens distrust
politicians and give a low score to bureaucracies and while overall trust
in public institutions is diminishing, distrust is higher among minorities. Most Israelis believe also that the schisms are deep, especially
between Arabs and Jews, and Arabs show lower trust in the state and
its institutions. Group differences in alignment with the state, perceptions of the democratic regime and trust of public institutions reflect
not only the schisms described above (and discussed later) but also the
hierarchical structure of Israel's citizenship regime.

The Citizenship Debate

The schisms outlined above translate into different struggles that are,
on the one hand, about equality, recognition, redistribution and the
collective boundaries, and, on the other hand, about practical needs of
everyday life. Citizenship in Israel, therefore, is a contested ground and
the medium through which struggles are conducted. The presence of an
Arab minority no longer willing to accept its marginal role, religious–
secular contest over the meaning of a Jewish state and other struggles
"within" Jewish society undermine old arrangements, conventions and
institutions, no longer able to retain their authority. The struggles
demonstrate the contested meaning of citizenship, and the rights and
duties it entails, and expose its hierarchies and inequalities.

The Israeli citizenship law is neutral and contains provisions of
a universal nature, but the Law of Return, granting the right of every
Jew in the world to immigrate to Israel, establishes a formal link
between the state of Israel and the community of world Jewry. This
law, which effectively excludes non-Jews from immigrating and natur-
alizing, is perceived by non-Jewish citizens as unfair and discriminatory. The separation of the nationality category (Jewish) from that of
citizenship (Israeli) is both a source of inequality and exclusion, not

only of Arab citizens. The question "who is a Jew?," critical for entry under the Law of Return, remains in contention between religious and secular Jewish Israelis. Finally, Israeli citizenship has not only an ethno-national classification that excludes non-Jews, but also republican classifications that determine hierarchies with the Jewish majority (Shafir and Peled, 2002). This republican citizenship developed in pre-statehood when the civic virtue of pioneering was recognized as the principal measure of contribution to the common good. Thus, while the ethno-national logic of Israeli citizenship has served to separate Jews from non-Jews, the republican logic has added another level of hierarchy determined by contribution to the state (Ben-Porat and Turner, 2011: 13).

The state has maintained the pioneering ethos of the earlier period, placed high demands on its (Jewish) citizens to serve the collective and evaluated citizenship according to the level of contribution. Ultimately, it was the military service that was deemed the highest service and placed men, initially from the Ashkenazi elite, in the highest rank of citizenship, the heroic male figure or warrior being the ideal citizen. This "republican equation" (Levy, 2008) not only exchanged military sacrifice for social dominance, but also provided the institutions in charge of security with status and authority. This process of militarization and securitization, well entrenched in culture and politics, significantly affects policing and the relations between police and minorities.

Military service became a decisive standard by which rights were awarded to individuals and group hierarchies and exclusions were established and legitimated. The concept of security in Israel, as the late Baruch Kimmerling (1999: 198) argued, "is far more wide sweeping than the term military, at the same time, the ever-expansive boundaries of 'security' are loosely defined, and almost any sphere or subject can be connected expediently to 'security.'" Consequently, militarism serves as an organizing principle of society, based not so much on the formal role of the military and its jurisdiction and more on the way state and society are organized around the management of a protracted external conflict (ibid.). Militarization, therefore, is not simply the dominance of the military but also a "state of mind" and a security discourse that permeates society, defining different social questions in terms of security and providing security experts with authority.

Militarism, "the tendency to view organized violence and wars as legitimate means of solving social problems" (Ben-Eliezer, 1997), has consequences not only for the decision-making process but also to everyday, bureaucratic routines. The protracted conflict yielded a feeling of a constant and imminent security threat, investment of social and material resources for military preparedness and a state of emergency implemented in legislation and administration, able to disrupt or suspend civil and human rights. The heightened importance of security, described in the previous chapter as "securitization," has had important implications for citizenship and policing. First, by providing security organizations with power, responsibility and limited need for accountability. Second, by strengthening and legitimating social hierarchies, depicting groups and individuals as security threats. And, third, blurring the boundaries between military and police, resisting attempts to "civilianize" the latter.

The Historical Foundation of the Israel Police: Structural and Operational

The Israel Police was established on May 15, 1948, immediately after the establishment of the state. The new police were designed as a national force, under the jurisdiction of the Minister of Public Security, that would take upon the responsibilities of the British Mandate police. To enable a continuous and stable transition from the British Mandate to political independence, and in order to take control of the young state and its institutions, the police were modeled after their predecessor, the British Mandate police. A model based on hierarchy and a centralized military-like organization, aimed to serve the government in a society with deep schisms (Shadmi, 2012). The Police Ordinance authorized the police with the sole responsibility to ensure public security and order, prevent violence, safeguard lives and property, and enforce and maintain the law. Yehezkel Sacharov, a former major officer in the British army, was nominated the first police commissioner and about 60 percent of the recruited police officers were former Jewish officers from the British Mandate police (Caspi, 1990). The police in Israel are state-national, under the control of the Ministry of Internal Security. Local or municipal authorities do not have control over police forces (although some cooperation in the form of municipal police has evolved) and police are accountable only to the government and parliament.

Police remained independent from the military, but the boundaries were blurred. To begin with, the vast majority of police officers, male and Jewish, have served in the military. Moreover, a large number of the police commanding officers come from the military, rather than climb police ranks from below. The "border police," established shortly after statehood (and formally in 1953), is a military-trained unit whose initial role was to guard the state borders, but since 1967 has a major role in control of the occupied territories. These units are under the jurisdiction of police, but during wars they were placed under the IDF command. Finally, counter-terrorism, like elsewhere, blurs the boundaries between military and police. The YAMAM, "Unit for Counter-Terror Warfare," was created in 1974, after several terrorist attacks that took the lives of Israeli civilians. Its officers are exclusively from the Israeli army, many of them having served in elite special forces. The unit is involved in counter-terrorism operations, civilian hostage rescue but also with violent crime.

The government decision in 1974 to transfer the authority over internal security to the police was a major turning point. Police authority now extended beyond its traditional roles – crime prevention and law and order maintenance. This change was welcomed by the police expecting it would provide them with more resources and social prestige (Shadmi, 2012: 43). This, however, created a constant tension between the roles police performed, their priorities and image, a fighting force that takes part in security or an organization attuned to citizens' needs and concerns. This underscored a constant tension between a community policing-oriented tendency and an aggressive and combative orientation (ibid.: 44). These contradictory orientations, as discussed in the previous chapter, manifest themselves in different combinations towards different groups. As elsewhere, "securitization" has different implications for individuals and groups, especially those whose behavior or mere presence signifies threat. Social problems are framed as "security problems" and those associated with the latter subjected to profiling and at times violence.

Israel Police: Current State of Affairs

Israel Police splits its deployment in seven geographical districts, under which 71 local or regional police stations are running. The

Israel Police personnel in 2016 was about 30,000. Eighty-eight percent of the force is of Jewish majority, and among the 12 percent of non-Jews, 7 percent are Druze, 1.4 are Arab-Christians and 1.7 Arab-Muslims, indicating that Arab citizens are underrepresented. Women comprise 25 percent of the force. Growing social tensions, especially those that erupted to violence, have raised questions not only regarding the representativeness of police but also their ability to provide adequate services for citizens. This included demands for more tolerance and respect for human rights, but also for effectiveness in tackling crime and providing security. Police, it was suggested, had to adapt themselves to the new reality, by redefining concepts like public order, public safety and personal security, and to be more responsive and sensitive to the needs and demands of different minorities (Shadmi, 2012: 56).

Alongside different reforms, police also began to administer surveys among the public. In the survey conducted in 2016, a little more than 50 percent of the population stated they trust police and are satisfied with their work. Similarly, an almost even split (36 against 35 percent) was found on the question of whether police treat citizens equally. Yet, a majority of Israeli citizens (70 percent) feel secure in their neighborhoods, and an even greater majority declare that they are willing to assist police. Other surveys show somewhat different results: the large survey conducted by the Israeli Democracy Institute, for example, finds that 41 percent of the population trust police, while 59 percent don't trust or have little trust in police (Hermann et al., 2018). Police, also, are less appreciated than other security institutions in Israel, like the military and the secret service (Vigoda-Gadot et al., 2016). More importantly, as described before and demonstrated in the following chapters, different groups hold different perceptions of police and different levels of trust.

Police forces in contemporary democracies seek different strategies to balance the traditional role of effective enforcement and the protection of civil rights and the quality of life of their residents, while applying values of equality, equity and dignity within their procedures and actions towards different citizens and groups (Jones and van Steden, 2013). These debates have also affected Israeli police, like other worldwide shifts of public management paradigms (Pollitt and Bouckaert, 2011; Stoker, 2006). Public management trends generated changes in police core activities and the way they operate. The traditional model of policing, bureaucratic, hierarchical and centered on crime control and prevention with professional universal standards (Ellison, 2007: 248), was gradually affected by the New Public Management (NPM) approach. The latter encouraged more focus on citizens as clients and communities as partners (Hood, 1995) and suggested a more flexible mode of governance.

While traditional policing has led police to draw away from the public (Brown, 1989), under the NPM, the concern for the quality of life of law-abiding citizens offered new possibilities for communication and cooperation with the public. Police forces developed different systems to evaluate citizens' (clients', customers') satisfaction and trust, expecting both to be influenced not merely by police performance but also by procedural fairness and moral alignment (Jackson et. al., 2012), as well as openness and attentiveness to the public (Wünsch and Hohl, 2009: 7). In Israel, police reforms that would collaborate with local communities and develop systems to measure performance were introduced several times. Community police cooperation began in the 1970s with citizens' patrols and shortly after a community relations unit established to communicate with local communities and encourage residents and communities to take an active role in helping maintain public order and personal safety that would enhance the communities' quality of life. Finally, in 1986 the civil guard, composed of volunteers, was placed under police authority (Yanay, 1997).

In 1995, Police Commissioner Asaf Hefetz announced that police will adopt community policing, units intended to closely cooperate with the local community in a manner tailored to the community's tradition and needs (Weisburd et. al., 1988). Community policing models employed elsewhere were modified for the specific circumstances in Israel, involving municipalities, and adopting methods for identifying key problems within communities (Harpaz, 2012). But, when Hefetz was replaced, the community police strategy was neglected (Weisburd et al., 2002). A new strategy adopted, Compstat, first used in the NYPD, focused on performance management and the use of data to measure and set new performance objectives. The *Menahel* (manager) system the police adopted in 2005 and the "Hamifne" (Turning Point), launched in 2012, used measurements and data analysis to improve the effectiveness of police work. This included comparing performance and outputs of various police stations (Gorman and Ruggiero, 2008), transparency and direct access to the system for all members within the organization and strengthening human capital and empowering officers as part of the efforts made to improve the level of service to citizens.

Countries across the world gradually shift from state-national policing to more local-municipal features, and collaborations with local governments (Høigård, 2011: 1–3; Jones and van Steden, 2013). The idea for municipal policing in Israel was first raised in 1995 by the mayor of Raanana, an affluent midsize city, as part of his election campaign (Yanay, 1997). However, it was only in 2011 that the parliament legislated the law that expanded the authority of local government and municipalities, and established partnerships between the local police stations and local authorities (restricted to specific quality of life issues). Policing, however, remained national and cooperation with municipalities remains at the discretion of police officers. Consequently, the relations between the national police and the local authorities is yet to be determined.

Context: Globalization and Securitization

Critical studies of police and policing in Israel point to the growing salience of security debates. Terrorist threats, illegal migration, urban unrest and heightened fear of crime in different countries translated to feeling of "strategic threat" has further blurred the lines between police and military. This threat has also received a global dimension with the rise of terrorism that has affected countries previously immune to it, leading to a militarization of police, often with detrimental effects on minorities. Globalization is also associated with the growing gaps between rich and poor, and the growing reliance on market mechanisms to supply or supplement public goods. Policing, as a result, is exercised not only by states and public institutions but also by private, profit-oriented firms that provide security for those with the means to pay. Minority groups, and poor minority groups in particular, are not only securitized but are often vulnerable and insecure.

In Israel, police reforms and more importantly the demands to implement more far reaching ones were constrained not only by the hierarchies of citizenship described above, but also by growing globalization and securitization. Inequalities between groups, often justified by the "republican equation," impact also the services police provide to different groups. State-led economic policies were replaced by neoliberal policies that encouraged privatization, increased socioeconomic gaps between rich and poor, and underscored what can be described as a "consumer revolution" (Ben-Porat et al., 2016). These changes meant, on the one hand, that social services suffer budget deficits and find it evermore difficult to provide public needs and demands. On the hand, for those able to afford it, private services replace or supplement public ones.

Growing sense of insecurity, alongside new needs and demands, explains the proliferation of private policing in Israel. Private policing includes technologies purchased by citizens to protect their homes and business, private investigators that provide different services to firms and individuals and, most importantly, companies providing security services. The growing number of private security guards, and their expanding authority, impacts public spaces. Guards in shopping malls or universities are allowed to check bags and to prevent suspected individuals from entering (shadmi, 2012). Private policing, supported by the state and even outsourced by state institutions, implicates both class and ethnicity. While the public in general voiced dissatisfaction with police services, and concerns that not enough police officers are present (in spite of the increase), for those with means alternatives could be purchased. In addition, various citizens' initiatives of neighborhood patrols emerged, to provide security police allegedly failed to. It remains to be studied where these initiatives succeed and whether middle-class neighborhoods with higher trust and social capital, or less prone to violent crime, are more successful to provide for themselves what other cannot.

The Second Intifada (uprising) of the Palestinians in 2000 was a turning point in policing, as its effects quickly spilled into Israel. Clashes between police and Arab citizens protesting against Israel's policies escalated, and police killed thirteen citizens (see Chapter 3). Waves of terrorism since have, on the one hand, placed police in the front lines and enhanced their image among Jewish citizens. On the other hand, the events and the new roles of police have strengthened their militarization and societal securitization, with growing concern for safety. Securitization impacted mostly Arab citizens, but also other groups perceived as threatening stability or deemed "radical" (Shadmi, 2012). For Jewish citizens, the wave of terrorism increased support for police, but this rise was only temporary and as terrorist threat declined, so did support for police (Jonathan, 2009). Interestingly, the threat of terrorism has led to greater police performance in Arab neighborhoods (measured by higher clearance rate), but not in Jewish neighborhoods. This does not indicate increased police service in these communities but rather the consequence of heightened surveillance and suspicion of people in those communities (Weisburd et al., 2009).

Growing fears of crime, combined with security concerns, render all problems to be perceived as related to risk and security, ignoring other root causes (poverty, inequality or social alienation) and favoring stronger policing (Shadmi, 2012). Like elsewhere, "tough on crime" policies in Israel are promoted by politicians and readily accepted by the public. This includes not only a demand for more police officers with more authority, but also that the judicial system would administer severe punishment for offenders to deter crime (Rattner et al., 2008). Israel, according to a recent study, is ranked third among OECD countries in incarceration rates with 265 incarcerated for every 100,000 people (www.statista.com/statistics/3009 86/incarceration-rates-in-oecd-countries/). Arab citizens, as well as Israelis of Ethiopian descent, are overrepresented in prisons (Korn, 2003). These differences are the result of structural inequalities that produce crime and delinquency, as well as prejudices in the legal system against Arab citizens (Gazal-Ayal and Sulitzeanu-Kenan, 2010). The consequences of growing feeling of insecurity, on the one hand, and increased securitization, on the other hand, are unequally distributed.

It is not accidental, therefore, that while a small majority of Jewish citizens (50.8 percent) believe that security forces should have a free hand in investigations when terrorism is concerned, a majority of Arab citizens (72.2 percent) disagree (Hermann et al., 2018). This may be indicative of what we explore in the following chapters: the different attitudes towards, and perceptions of, police that reflect wider questions of citizenship.

Citizenship and Policing in Israel

Citizenship in Israel is a complex structure of interrelated hierarchies, institutional transformations and social struggles. Arrangements established in early years of state formation, based on agreements and

coercion, are destabilized by internal–external changes. While the prolonged military conflict and militarism still shape citizenship hierarchies and privileges, new demands posit challenges to Israel's stratified
citizenship. The deepening of schisms – national, ethnic, class and
religious – and the struggles that ensued involve various groups' struggles for recognition and equality. The perceptions of police, namely
evaluations of their fairness and effectiveness, and the expectations
from them, as argued here, are embedded with citizenship.
Specifically, police trust and legitimacy among different groups, the
reasons for legitimacy and trust, and the expectations from police
reflect current citizenship status and future possibilities.

Police are central to the understanding of the dynamics of citizenship
for two main reasons. First, their symbolic importance of representing
state sovereignty provide them with legitimacy (potentially, at least)
from individuals and groups morally aligned with the state.
And, second, the way different groups are policed not only sends
a message about their status as citizens but also has a direct bearing
on everyday life. Thus, police actions and policies towards different
groups, under-policed or over-policed, matter. These policies, often
reflecting structural inequalities and government policies, shape trust
in police and their legitimacy. The relations between minorities and the
police, from the minorities' perspective, reflect the stratification of
Israeli society. Feeling targeted by police or vulnerable and exposed
to violence is a measurement of citizenship, belonging and status.
Similarly, perceptions towards representation, cooperation and oversight, discussed in the previous chapter, provide another layer for
understanding the dynamics of citizenship.

Minorities, when protesting government policies or making
demands for change, will often come in direct contact with police.
Like elsewhere, Israeli police have enforced government policies and,
in doing so, demonstrated that the monopoly over violence is all but
theoretical. Protests of Mizrahim in the Haifa neighborhood of Wadi
Salib (1959) and of the Black Panthers in Jerusalem (1971) met with
strong police response (Chapter 4). Ultra-Orthodox Jews have clashed
with police in many occasions and have also met a strong response. For
Arab citizens, deemed a security threat, police response was more
violent, especially in October 2000 when thirteen demonstrators were
killed. More recently, it was Israelis of Ethiopian descent that were
exposed to police violence. Not only minorities, protestors from the

political left and right have also complained of unnecessary police violence. Direct violence, however, is not the only or the most important measurement of status. Rather, it is the everyday and seemingly mundane encounters that may matter, as the following chapters will explore.

Different Group, Different Experiences?

For the past two decades a continuous decline in public trust of the police has been observed among all groups in Israel, with some fluctuations during the years (Ratner, 2010). Different groups, majorities and minorities are likely to have different perceptions of police, based on collective experiences, ability to identify with police and future expectations from it. Even when groups show similar levels of trust (or distrust) in police they might have different reasons that determine trust. In the following chapters we examine four such minority groups in Israel, studying their perceptions of police and policing in relation to their place within Israeli citizenship. These groups, defined by nationalism, religiosity and ethnicity, we argue, are to some extent representative of their categories and, therefore, can, with obvious limitations, be compared to similar groups elsewhere.

Arab citizens are a national minority that make up about 20 percent of the population and are largely isolated from the Jewish majority. Arab citizens live mostly in defined geographical and municipal clusters, except for a small minority living in quite homogeneous neighborhoods in a number of mixed cities. They maintain a collective Arab-Palestinian cultural-political identity, and a language retained in the educational system, media and literature (Khamaisi, 2013). Arab citizens' relations with the state and the Jewish majority population is sensitive and tense, strongly influenced by the prolonged Arab–Israeli and Palestinian–Israeli conflicts. The relationships with the police in Israel have also seen an unprecedented low point in the tragic events of October 2000 during which thirteen Arab demonstrators were shot dead by the police.

Ethnicity, as discussed above, is an important factor in Israeli society, dividing the Jewish majority and associated with class and social status. The ethnic divide between Mizrahim and Ashkenazim remains relevant when measured in economic and social inequalities, and political affiliations. Also, in early years of statehood Mizrahi protest was met with police violence, demonstrating the hierarchy of citizenship and the

securitization of protest. Israelis of Ethiopian descent, however, provide a more recent and extreme demonstration of ethnicity, both visible
and vulnerable vis-à-vis the state and police, explored in this book.
Israelis of Ethiopian descent, 136,000 citizens (1.6 percent of Israel's
population), many of whom immigrated to Israel in the 1990s, suffered
an absence of available social network to help with their absorption,
limited formal education and skills, and different forms of discrimination that limited integration and led to social segregation (Kacen,
2006). Employment rates among the immigrants of working age
(22–64) is lower (50–55 compared to 70–75 percent among all the
Jews), the percentage of workers in nonprofessional occupations is
higher (37 compared to 7 percent) and the vast majority lives in
relatively homogeneous neighborhoods. Political weakness, social
marginality and being a "visible minority" renders them vulnerable
to over-policing. Consequently, the proportion of teenagers from this
ethnic group among detainees is far greater than their relative percentage in the population (Rattner and Fishman, 2009). Documented
police violence against young Israelis of Ethiopian descent and mass
protests against police violence have brought the relations with police
to public attention.

The integration of immigrants from the former Soviet Union (FSU) is
diametrically opposed to that of Ethiopians. Approximately
one million new immigrants arrived between 1989 and 2001 and
their percentage in the population is about 18 percent. Not only its
size but also human capital and greater acceptance by Israeli society
allowed these immigrants to take control of their integration. A survey
conducted by the Central Bureau of Statistics in 2010–2011 found that
about 42 percent of FSU immigrants defined themselves first and foremost as Jews, 21 percent stressed their country of origin and only
38 percent described their identity as "Israeli." Sixty-eight percent of
FSU immigrants reported that the majority of their friends come from
similar background, and 75 percent still rely on Russian-spoken media
sources. In spite of their largely successful economic integration, more
than half of those interviewed feel they are stigmatized and discriminated. While some of these stigmas included unruly behavior related to
alcoholism or criminal activity, this was proven untrue by crime statistics (Rattner and Fishman, 2009).

Religiosity is a major schism among Jews in Israel, with different
debates over the role of religion in public life and its authority over

nonreligious Jews. Ultra-Orthodox Jews or Haredim constitute approximately 10 percent of society. This group, divided into many sub-groups, is, on the one hand, involved in public life and politics and, on the other hand, maintains segregation and distance from Israeli society and culture (Ben-Rafael and Peres, 2005). Haredi communities live an uncompromising, strict and binding way of life that is independent and introverted so as to retain the defined borders that protect the cultural continuity. These characteristics differentiate between this population and the Israeli public manifestly and demonstrably, some of the communities openly resisting the state and its institutions. Struggles of Haredim to maintain their way of life, often involving imposing it on others, have led to violent clashes with police. Attempts to close roads to traffic on Sabbath, blocking archaeological excavations or preventing pride parades are all examples of struggles and clashes with police. Haredi leaders and the media have complained that police used excessive violence in demonstrators.

The four groups studied in this book represent different minorities, with different citizenship status and moral alignment with the state and its institutions. Arab citizens, a national minority, suffer structural discrimination in a Jewish state and remain alienated and largely separated from the rest of society. Israelis of Ethiopian descent are a "visible minority," an immigrant group that is formally part of the Jewish majority and is strongly identified with the state, yet suffers different forms of discrimination. FSU immigrants provide an example for relatively strong immigration that in spite of stigmas and hardships was able to integrate and gain significant economic, social and political power. Finally, ultra-Orthodox Jews are a religious minority, separated ideologically from the rest of Jewish society and in a constant struggle to protect their way of life but also to establish a role for religion in public life.

The contested nature of Israeli society and polity – widening disagreements and intensified struggles over group rights, collective identity and resources – posits significant challenges to the state and its institutions. For citizens of minority groups police are often the most visible representation of the state in everyday life. Whether it is a young Ethiopian being stopped by a police officer for no obvious reason, or an Arab woman suffering domestic violence, the presence or absence of police tells something about the state's priorities and the securitization of daily life. Minorities' perceptions of policing, due to the symbolic significance and practical importance of police, therefore, provide fertile ground for a discussion of Israel's citizenship regime.

Citizens' encounters with and expectations from police enable us in the following chapters to explore different questions of status and belonging. The four minorities studied here – a national minority, a visible and discriminated immigrant minority, a relatively powerful immigrant minority and a religious minority – enable us to ask different questions about policing and citizenship. The way that minorities differ from the majority by nationality, ethnicity, skin colur, religiosity and class may affect the way they are treated by police (and the state), their perceptions of police (and the state) and expectations from police (and the state). In other words, our discussion of policing and minorities pertains to wider questions of citizenship and to the stratification of citizenship in Israel. Moreover, since these minorities are somewhat "generic" (referring to nation, ethnicity, religiosity and class), and as tense relations between police and minorities are also common elsewhere, the theoretical framework and lessons we draw are hopefully comparative.

3 | *Arab Citizens: National Minority and Police*

In October 2000, in the midst of the Second Palestinian Intifada (uprising), Arab citizens in Israel staged mass demonstrations to protest Israel's policies in the West Bank and Gaza. Footage from the violence in the territories enraged Arab citizens, especially the death of a 12-year-old child in Gaza, caught in the cross-fire between Israeli soldiers and Palestinian militias. The demonstrations in the northern part of Israel escalated and the police responded with live ammunition. The riots lasted for several days during which twelve Arab citizens (and one Palestinian from Gaza) were shot dead by the police. The Orr Investigation Commission, nominated by the government and headed by a Supreme Court Justice, stated that the "events of October 2000 shook the earth." While the committee criticized the police for their excessive use of force, and also Arab leaders for inciting violence, the events, it concluded, were the consequence of deep-seated factors:

Government handling of the Arab sector has been primarily neglectful and discriminatory. The establishment did not show sufficient sensitivity to the needs of the Arab population and did not take enough action in order to allocate state resources in an equal manner. The state did not do enough or try hard enough to create equality for its Arab citizens or to uproot discriminatory or unjust phenomenon. Meanwhile, not enough was done to enforce the law in the Arab sector, and the illegal and undesirable phenomena that took root there (Orr Commission, 2000).

The tense relationship between Arab citizens and the police has neither began nor ended with the events of October 2000, although these have negatively affected perceptions of police and the state (Hermann et al., 2017). Rather, they are embedded in the history of the Arab minority in a Jewish state and ongoing debates of identity, rights and citizenship. Three events that took place during the final stages of writing this book demonstrate the severity of the relations between the police and the Arab citizens. In January 2017 police shot

68

and killed Yacoub Abu Al-Qia'an in the Bedouin unrecognized village of Um-Al-Hiran. Police entered at night, heavily armed, to demolish houses and evacuate the residents of the village, where a new Jewish community will be built. Abu Al-Qia'an was shot driving away from the scene and his car hit and killed a police officer. Police and the Minister of Internal Security were quick to state that Abu Al-Qia'an was affiliated with terrorist groups and was shot while attempting to kill police officers. It was only weeks later, when evidence contradicted the claims, that the minister admitted that "mistakes were made" (*Times of Israel*, 2017).

Several months later, on June 6, a security guard at the entrance of Kafr Qasem police station shot and killed a local resident, 28-year-old Mohammed Taha, during clashes of residents with police. Clashes erupted after police arrested a member of a local committee that took upon itself to fight against local crime, which police, they claim, fail to prevent. Arab leaders, following the incident, accused the police for both using excessive force and failing to deal with organized crime in the Arab communities (Efrati, 2017). A month later, on July 29, Arab residents of Jaffa took to the streets and clashed with police, after police officers shot to death 22-year-old Mahdi Sa'adi. Suspected of being involved in a shooting, Sa'adi and a friend were chased by police who in an attempt to apprehend them opened fire. The angry residents who clashed with police accused them of "cold blooded murder" (ibid.).

Excessive use of force and the securitization of Arab citizens, how-ever, are not the only cause for distrust of police. Rather, growing concerns over violent crime in Arab neighborhoods and perceptions of police neglect imply that Arab citizens are simultaneously under- and over-policed. In such circumstances, minorities develop a complex relationship with police, mixing disdain and dependency, embedded in wider questions of citizenship and belonging.

The Jewish–Arab cleavage is considered the deepest schism in Israeli society. Arab citizens are a nondominant, nonassimilating, working-class minority considered by the Jewish majority as dissident and enemy affiliated (Smooha, 1990). Um-Al-Hiran, Kafr Qasem and Jaffa are not isolated events, police violence combined with the high rate of violent crime, demonstrates both the tense relationship between Arab citizens and police and Israel's stratified citizenship. Securitized and subjected to the use of excessive force, on the one hand, and vulnerable to crime and violence, on the other hand, Arab citizens' perceptions of police and policing are embedded in wider questions of citizenship and inequality, demonstrating the complex relations of a national minority with the state and its institutions.

National Minorities and Police

A police officer will not dare treating a Jewish person the way he treats Arabs because the Jewish person will not let him. He will talk back to him and even sue him. But we, Arabs, we are unaware of our rights, and because we are a minority, and because of the wider Jewish-Arab conflict we are always afraid of police officers and they take advantage of our fear and treat us differently (focus group, Nazareth).

The presence of national minorities in many contemporary democracies presents everyday challenges to the legitimacy of state institutions and policies. National minorities often find it difficult to fully integrate into states that refuse to recognize their identity. The state, and its institutions on its behalf, might, formally or informally, discriminate against national minorities, further eroding their trust and exposing the stratified nature of citizenship. National identities, held by national minorities, may be less flexible and hybrid than some theorists would suggest, as if integration is simply a matter of choice. Rather, minorities are often constrained in the choices they make as state and national boundaries are imposed upon them. States in their attempt to achieve legitimacy and mobilization select whom to include, reward and encourage loyalty from, and simultaneously play off antagonism against groups excluded (Marx, 2005: 22). In some instances, loyalty to an in-group is solidified by discrimination against an out-group, distinguishing friends from enemies and an us/them mentality. Thus, contrary to the assumption that modern states sought to unify "all within," nationalism has been institutionalized in particular and exclusionary forms (Marx, 2005: 25).

   In theory, citizenship ensures equality and balance between individuals and collectives, serves as the main component for engendering common bonds to the state and functions as a basic mechanism that underpins the stability of the political system (Lijphart, 1984; Kymlicka, 1995). Formal citizenship, however, does not necessarily overlap with equal status, on the one hand, and feelings of national belonging, on the other hand (Brubaker, 1996). Citizenship often involves hierarchies and divisions and, as a result, is challenged either by demands for rights and entitlements or by changes that undermine notions of common or imagined solidarity (Turner, 2001). This is especially acute in instances where the state is an "ethnic state," identified with one dominant group, minorities might find themselves excluded and discriminated and, consequently, find it difficult to identify with the state and its institutions. Minorities' claims of unfair and discriminatory treatment by police can be countered by security arguments made to justify policies and protect the "thin blue line" of police.

In the national security discourse many minorities constitute a threat to the state's territorial integrity (Brubaker, 1996) as well as to national identity (Olesker, 2014). Minority demands can be rejected when framed as security threats, questioning the loyalty of the minority to the state and, consequently, justifying its treatment as a question of national security. Securitization as a concept refers to framing political demands and debates as a "security issue," that "can be intensified to the point where it is presented and accepted as an existential threat" (Williams, 2003: 516). This translates into "acts of security" that promise (the majority) to provide protection from danger, freedom from doubt and relief of anxiety, but at the same time encourage fear, foster apprehension and feed off nervousness in the population (Nyers, 2004) especially towards groups depicted as a threat to national identity, state sovereignty and/or social stability (Squire, 2015). When their states feel insecure and fearful of neighboring enemies, minorities' rights can be sacrificed for promised security and, at the same time, the space for moral argument and democratic debate shrinks (Kymlicka, 2004: 158).

National minorities, at the same time and in spite of securitization, can also be vulnerable to crime and violence that make the presence of police necessary. Discrimination in the labor market and unequal allocation of resources can leave minority neighborhoods in dire poverty, exposed to crime and violence and (among other things) also lacking adequate police services. This, as mentioned in Chapter 1, means that they can be simultaneously over-policed (or securitized), but also under-policed and neglected. This precarious position is likely to negatively affect police legitimacy. The difficulty for moral alignment, being distanced from the national values police represent and their symbolic role, suggests that the potential for legitimacy may be limited. However, the dire need for security, as described below, might underscore acceptance of police's role and expectations for equal service, both fair and efficient. It is not only the symbolic importance of police, emblematic of state sovereignty, but also their practical significance in providing security and order, with fairness and justice, that sets apart minorities from other citizens.

By its very nature police's exercise of authority threatens to curtail the liberties expected by citizens of a democratic state. But, underneath formal equality citizenship is often coupled with various exclusions and hierarchies, demarcating those protected and those protected from. Under these conditions of constricting citizenship (Ghanem and Khatib, 2017), national minorities' relation to police reflects and amplifies their position in an ethnic state. The way minorities are policed, in comparison to other citizens, with both excessive use of power and neglect, allows them to draw lessons about their status (Bradford, 2014) and, possibly, to challenge it. Policing in Israel, therefore, is a contested site of citizenship where, first, Arab citizens find it difficult to identify with the state and its representative institutions. Second, where concrete concerns of discriminatory practices of policing render them both a security threat and vulnerable to crime and violence. And, third, discrimination and its reform, regarding both securitization and neglect, is embedded in issues and questions beyond police and policing.

Palestinian/Arab Citizens of Israel

Primordial Jewish solidarity and ethno-national exclusion explain the status of Arab citizens in Israel as Judaism performs a central role in political integration and exclusion (Kopelowitz, 2001). The Arab or Palestinian citizens of Israel, 80 percent Muslims and 20 percent Christians, constitute a national minority of 18 percent in a predominantly national Jewish state. Unlike other (Jewish) ethnic minorities in Israel Arabs are an unassimilable national minority, not only because they are linguistically, culturally and religiously different from the majority Jewish population, but also because Jewishness is the primary factor informing state identity that by definition excludes non-Jewish citizens from full participation (Ben-Porat, 2013). Although officially citizens, Arabs are not full members of the imagined community for which the Jewish nation-state was established (Smooha, 1990). In addition, the Arab–Israeli and Israeli–Palestinian conflicts pose difficult identity questions for Arab citizens of the Jewish state, on the one hand, and render them suspect for the state and the Jewish majority, on the other hand.

Scholars describe Israel as an "ethnic democracy" (Smooha, 1990) where the state privileges the ethnic majority and discriminates against the minority (Kook, 2017). Arab citizens' formal citizenship is contrasted with the ethnic Jewish-Zionist character of the state, and a republican discourse that negatively implicates Arabs' belonging and citizenship and their ability to attend to the common good (Peled, 1992). The definition of Israel as a Jewish state is protected by a Jewish political consensus and by legislation that prevent parties from standing for election if they negate the status of Israel as the state of the Jewish people or the Jewish character of the state. While Arab citizens have the right to vote, Arab members of parliament have negligible influence as Arab parties never took part in governing coalitions and a strong majority of 80 percent of Jewish citizens believes that decisions central to the state security and peace must have a Jewish majority (Hermann et al., 2017). Accordingly, the symbols of the state (flag, emblem and national anthem) derive from Jewish heritage and religion and are representative of the Jewish people rather than the citizens of Israel.

The distinction between the state, of which Arab citizens are full members, and the nation they are excluded from has practical Implications. Israeli law includes many provisions that guarantee privileges for the Jewish majority and neglect and discriminate against Arab citizens (Rabinowitz and Abu-Baker, 2005), demonstrating "degrees of citizenship" (Shachar, 1998). Arab citizens suffer residential, educational and occupational segregation; higher unemployment and poverty; overcrowded and underdeveloped cities; and discriminatory land allocation policies (Lewin et al., 2006; Lewin-Epstein and Semyonov, 1993). While legal and political struggles succeeded through the years in challenging some discriminatory practices, new plans for developments were introduced, and an academic and professional elite grew (Manna, 2008), gaps remained significant, and even if the socioeconomic situation has improved, the gap between Arab and Jewish citizens has widened (Lavie, 2010). The vast majority of Arab citizens, about 90 percent, live in Arab towns and villages, and even those who live in so-called mixed cities usually live in segregated neighborhoods.

Arab citizens struggled for political equality and recognition and the expansion of citizenship through demands that challenge the Israeli system of control (Lustick, 1980). These struggles took a new turn in the 1990s with the rise of an assertive voice, described as the "Stand-Tall Generation" that unlike their forebears perceive citizenship as a collective entitlement rather than a personal affair (Rabinowitz and Abu-Baker, 2005: 3). They locate themselves within a Palestinian national identity, described as a distinct indigenous group with national, cultural, religious and linguistic characteristics. Politically, they reject the Jewish definition of the state and demand not only individual achievements but also collective indigenous rights (Jabareen, 2015; Jamal, 2011; Ghanem and Mustafa, 2011). A vanguard of academics and professionals searched for new and different ways to promote rights and demand recognition and inclusion, challenging the foundations of the Jewish state in several position papers ("future vision documents") published in 2006. The new consciousness is not shared by all Arab citizens, as others hold more compromising positions towards the Jewish state, believe that inclusion would occur gradually and take comfort in improvements that have been made. Surveys indicate that the Arab community holds more moderate positions than its leaders and seeks integration (Lavie, 2010). But, the number of Arabs voting for Zionist parties has significantly declined in favor of Arab parties representing the new identities and demands.

Identity conflicts (that preceded this new generation) were depicted as "Palestinization," growing identification with the Palestinian nationalism and the struggle in the territories, matched by "Israelization," imperfect integration to state and society, enabling individual achievements, measured by education and status (Smooha, 1999). Exclusion of Arabs seemingly allows them no choice but Palestinian identity but everyday life might allow de facto absorption and accommodation. In a recent survey, 39 percent of Arab citizens chose "Arab" as their primary identity, 34 percent chose religion, and only 14 and 10 percent, respectively, chose Palestinian and Israeli (Hermann et al., 2017). By the late 1990s it appeared that Israelization, measured in social and economic integration and political acceptance of the state, has taken some place (Smooha, 1999). This was reflected in educational achievements and the growing presence of Arab citizens in civil service and industry. Moreover, struggles for equality waged by politicians and NGOs have successfully challenged some discriminatory practices and policies. But, demands for full inclusion and equality could not be fully met without structural changes involving the Jewish definition of the state. When these demands were made explicit by activists and politicians they encountered not only resistance from the Jewish majority but also a securitization and delegitimization of Arab citizenship.

Arab citizens' difficulties are exacerbated by their identification with their Palestinian brethren in the West Bank and Gaza. For many within the Jewish majority Arab citizens not only identify with state enemies, opposing the occupation, but also make demands that threaten their own identity, when calling for full equal rights and challenging the idea of the Jewish state. Under these circumstances relations between Jewish and Arab citizens, in spite of some advancements, remain problematic. In a survey conducted in 2015 a small majority of Arab citizens (57.5 percent) saw Zionist Israel as "racist" and 66.5 percent of Jewish citizens regarded an Arab citizen as potentially disloyal if he identified himself as Palestinian (Smooha, 2015). This distrust explains Arab citizens' pessimism that full equality could be achieved within a Jewish state, and Jewish citizens' concern that Arab citizens seek to undermine the Jewish state. Jewish right-wing politicians, including Avigdor Lieberman, a former defense minister, have publicly announced that Arab politicians should be prevented from being elected and that citizenship rights must be conditioned by loyalty to the state. This disagreement is central, as 67 percent of Arab citizens do not believe Israel has the right to be a nation-state of the Jewish nation and 58 percent of Jewish citizens believe that voting should be denied from those not recognizing the Jewish state. It is hardly surprising that 54 percent of Arab citizens do not believe Israel is a democracy where their rights are concerned (Hermann et al., 2017).

Security and Securitization

"National security," often invoked when police power is exercised and civil rights are violated, is a contested term when state and nation do not overlap and when security is largely serving one group, at the expense of other groups' freedoms and equality. The securitization of Arab citizens is hardly new. After the war of 1948 the new state awarded citizenship to Arabs who remained under its jurisdiction, but at the same time placed them under military control, justified by security concerns that they will take part in the Arab–Israeli conflict.

Military rule, which among other things restricted Arab citizens' right to travel, was dismissed in 1966. But, Arab citizens remained suspect for the state and its institutions. Consequently, Political activists, parties and NGOs, and school teachers and directors remained under surveillance of the state.

Securitization responded not only to the concrete terrorism threat, in which Arab citizens did not usually take part, but also to identity threat that the presence and demands of Arab citizens conjured, perceived an existential threat to society and the (Jewish) state (Ghanem and Khatib, 2017; Olesker, 2014). Demands for recognition and equality, under these circumstances, or any breach of the law regardless of context, can be depicted in terms of security. Recently, a government minister has described unrecognized settlement of Bedouins in the southern Negev area not as a legal problem, as questions of land ownership remain contested with Bedouin claims for lands confiscated by the state, or a social problem, Bedouins being one of the poorest sectors in Israel, but as a security threat:

The south is under attack, and not only from Gaza, but also from illegal takeover of land that undermines Zionism in the Negev. We are under the threat of a hostile takeover (Nardy, 2018).

Securitization has a popular appeal among Jewish Israelis, answering real and imagined threats, both manipulated by politicians. A large majority of Jewish Israelis (68 percent) do not believe that an Arab citizen who feels part of the Palestinian nation can be loyal to the state of Israel, and hold that security decisions require a Jewish rather than a simple democratic majority (Hermann et al., 2017). Waves of Palestinian terrorism in past decades have also taken their toll on security, used by Israeli right-wing politicians to further undermine the status of Arab citizens (Peffley et al., 2015). In the wake of the Second Intifada, a political climate fueled by fear and violence and legislation targeting Arab citizens accelerated the securitization process (Olesker, 2014). The decline of terrorism was not matched by that of securitization and further attempts to marginalize Arab citizens' political power through legislation and other restrictions.

Policing in recent years in Israel, like elsewhere, and probably to a larger degree, is associated not only with law and order, but also with combatting terrorism. Police in Israel have traditionally been involved in military roles, and the military in policing (see Chapter 2). During the Second Intifada (2001–2002), facing a wave of suicide bombings, the police were given the authority to handle threats for homeland security (Hasisi and Weisburd, 2014). Fighting terrorism by police was accepted by the Jewish majority as necessary, attributing some social prestige to the police for their role. Arab citizens, conversely, were concerned with the negative ramifications, namely higher securitization (Hasisi and Weisburd, 2014). Somewhat ironically, heightened securitization has improved some aspects of police performance in Arab communities (measured in clearance rates) but this does not necessarily have a positive effect on Arab citizens' perceptions of police as it is perceived to be the result of heightened surveillance and profiling (Weisburd et al., 2009).

The embedded securitization discourse affects even inadvertently the perceptions of police intentions. When in the fall of 2009 the police announced it intends to form an undercover unit that would fight crime and illegal activities in Arab towns, it referred to it as *mista'rivim*. The term, familiar to all Israelis, describes Arabic-speaking undercover military units operating in the occupied territories. For Arab citizens, the use of the term not only invoked that police equate operating in their towns with military operations, but also the fear that the unit would be used for security purposes and control rather than for serving and protecting. This seemingly minor event demonstrates the dilemmas not only of Arab citizens, but also of policy makers and police officers concerned with rising violence in Arab neighborhoods.

Minorities, however, in spite of marginalization and discrimination, may demonstrate surprising levels of trust towards the state, government and its institutions (Maxwell, 2010). Our data, as well as other sources, show a complex picture of perceptions towards police: limited trust but also a demand for police to be more involved in face of growing crime and violence within Arab towns and neighborhoods. In the last decade, Arab citizens, 20 percent of the state's population, account for more than 50 percent of murders related to crime and killing of women. Arab politicians and intellectuals describe the high levels of violence in terms of a social disaster, threatening to break apart Arab society. While only 14 percent of Jewish citizens believe there is a serious threat of violence in their neighborhoods, 54 percent of Arabs believe so (http://go.ynet.co.il/pic/news/pre1.pdf). "We are on a slippery slope to internal collapse of Arab society," stated Taleb el-Sana, a former member of parliament (Khoury, 2016). Whether the

blame is placed on state discrimination, Arab society's internal problems or police apathy, the seemingly unending violence underscores
an ambivalent perception of and expectations from police.

The perceptions of police, discussed below, are part and parcel of
Arab citizens' identity dilemmas. First, the memory of the 2000 events
that casts a shadow on the relationship between Arab citizens and the
police. Second, the growing securitization, exacerbated by growing
presence of Islamic politicized identities and minor involvement of
Arab citizens in terrorism. And, third, an internal crisis of Arab society
with growing violence and insecurity, leaving citizens vulnerable and in
dire need of policing and, no less important, improved services and
opportunities to relieve poverty.

My State? My Police?

Fairness of authorities communicates to citizens their inclusion and status
(Bradford, 2014) and often demarcates differences between majorities and
minorities. Just a few hours after Yacoub Abu Al-Qia'an's vehicle hit and
killed officer Erez Levi, a police spokesperson issued a message stating that
"the terrorist is an active member of the Islamic movement, his connection
to ISIS is examined" (Dolev, 2018). Neither of the allegations were true.
A month later, the Minister of Internal Security referred to the event as
"sorrowful and tragic" and explained that

the event should not overshadow the relationship. No one should take
a single event in which, unfortunately, an officer and a civilian were killed
and project this on the relations between the Bedouins, the police and the
state. It is wrong and not representative (ibid.).

Seventeen years earlier, the Orr Commission, after its investigation
of the 2000 events and the killing of thirteen citizens by police, saw the
problem as structural and not just a tragic event. The commission
expressed great concern that the discrimination of Arab citizens by
state institutions in general, and their troubled relationship with police
in particular, negatively effects their trust in police. In its conclusions
the committee referred directly to the need that police will take upon
themselves to treat Arab citizens in an equal manner:

It is important to assimilate, at every level of the police force, the importance
of level-headed and moderate behavior in relations with the Arab sector. At

the same time, it is important to uproot the phenomena of negative prejudice toward the Arab sector that have shown themselves among veteran and esteemed officers in the police force. The police force must impress upon its policemen the comprehension that the Arab public in its entirety is not their enemy and that it should not be treated as such (Orr Commission, 2000).

The legitimacy of police for Arab citizens is impacted by their troubled relations with the state, and difficulty for moral alignment due to structural discrimination. However, as discussed before, legitimacy is also affected by trust and the ability, as well as the commitment, of police to be effective and fair. "Police treat us like garbage," stated a resident of Rahat, a Bedouin town, commenting on the visit of a newly appointed Arab police officer, "in their eyes, every citizen here is either a criminal or a terrorist. That is why they allow themselves to use violence against citizens for no reason" (Har-Zahav, 2017). Almost twenty years after the events, and in spite of declarations and attempted reforms, Arab citizens still treat police with suspicion. Police, like other state institutions, too often symbolize their exclusion and the gap between formal citizenship and its hierarchies. A majority of Arab citizens (77 percent) believe they are treated unfairly by the state and its institutions (Hermann et al., 2017). While a majority of Arab citizens (64 percent) do not think that fair treatment will change their perceptions towards the idea of a Jewish state (ibid.) it remains to be examined whether this could affect the legitimacy of specific institutions.

Our survey (see Tables 3.1, 3.2 and 3.3) also demonstrates the differences between Arab and Jewish citizens. Only 29 percent of Arab citizens declare they trust state institution (between 6 and 10 on a 0–10 scale) compared to 45 percent of the majority group. Still 45 percent of Arab citizens feel part of Israel and 55 percent are proud to be Israelis, demonstrating the complex relationship with the state, as numbers are much lower than the majority group, respectively 88 and 90 percent. In a series of studies based on extensive surveys of Arab citizens, Smooha (1999, 2015) argues that Arab citizens while deprived and marginalized, economically, socially and politically, are also gradually embedded into Israeli society, desiring to mobilize and, importantly, have no real and immediate alternative.

Legitimacy is not only a product of adherence to objective and formal standards of good conduct, but also of people's perceptions that the institutions represent particular value systems people can

Table 3.1 *Trust and Legitimacy*

Question/statement (%)	Group	Strongly disagree 1	2	Strongly agree 3	4	5	Mean (S.D.)
I trust the police	Arab	18	12	30	20	22	3.17 (1.4)
	Control Group	11	14	34	25	16	3.21 (1.2)
I have respect for the police and police officers	Arab	13	8	18	27	34	3.61 (1.4)
	Control Group	7	8	23	28	35	3.74 (1.2)

Table 3.2 *Identifying with the State*

Question/statement (%)	Group	Strongly disagree 1	2	3	Strongly agree 4	5	Mean (S.D.)
I feel I belong to this country	Arab	15	13	27	21	24	3.26 (1.4)
	Control Group	3	1	8	18	70	4.52 (0.9)
I am proud to be an Israeli citizen	Arab	14	8	23	20	35	3.53 (1.4)
	Control Group	1	2	7	10	80	4.64 (0.8)

Table 3.3 *Trust in State Institutions*

Can state institutions be trusted? (%)	No 0	1	2	3	4	5	6	7	8	9	Yes 10	Mean (SD)
Arab	10	2	4	10	10	34	9	11	4	1	4	4.68 (2.4)
Control Group	8	3	7	8	8	22	11	16	11	3	4	5.06 (2.6)

identify with based on shared ethical frameworks or on "moral align-ment" (Jackson et al., 2012: 1054). For Arab citizens obedience to police is not related to legitimacy in the form of decision and policies made in accordance with citizens' values and morals (Jackson and Bradford, 2010), but rather to police deterrence. "We all obey police because we are afraid of them, because we don't feel police provides us security and we don't feel it is there to protect us and our rights. On the contrary, we feel it is against us and against our interests" (focus group, Daburiyya). The moral alignment, which provides for deeper and more stable legitimacy, is missing, "I accept police values if police officers stand up to these values, but if police officers abuse their power, I do not respect them" (focus group, Nazareth). This lack of trust and legitimacy, demonstrated later, has also negative effects on cooperation necessary to fight crime and provide security.

Our survey data, however, show that there is no significant difference in the trust in police between Jewish and Arab citizens, a result of the overall low trust for police, different perceptions and expectations within Arab society and the dire need for police to protect from the threat of violence. In a more recent survey, however, the trust of police was much lower among Arab citizens (42 compared to 27 percent among Jewish citizens), more in line with what we heard in the focus groups (Hermann et al., 2018).

Fairness

The words "unfair" and "discrimination" were mentioned many times in the focus groups with Arab citizens, referring to both the state and police. "It is not a Jewish and democratic state, only a Jewish state" (focus group, Daburiyya); "it is the police of the majority" (ibid.); "discrimination is everywhere" (ibid.). Being stopped by police, usually for traffic violations, was attributed not to the drivers' wrong-doing but for being targeted by police. Similarly, as discussed later, the inability of police to curb crime in Arab towns and neighborhoods was related not to objective difficulties but to police priorities or to purpo-seful neglect. Several participants have explicitly made the connection between the treatment by police and wider citizenship concerns. "There is discrimination we feel everywhere, because this is a Jewish state whose very existence is based on discrimination of Arabs." Consequently, some were rather pessimistic that things could change:

"police treatment of minorities is based on how the state treats us and there is discrimination we feel everywhere. Because this is a state that is only a Jewish state that since its inception was based on discrimination between Arabs and Jews. This makes any improvement difficult" (focus group, Daburiyya).

Arab citizens, on the one hand, hold negative views of police and believe they are victims of police violence, therefore wanting to keep police at bay. But, on the other hand, escalating violence raises demands for police to take responsibility and increase their presence. This ambivalence can be observed in debates over presence of police officers in Arab towns and villages. Following the Orr Commission recommendation, new police stations were to be built in Arab towns, providing services and bringing police closer to Arab citizens. While the plans were at most partially implemented, with resources not allocated, Arab citizens themselves were split on the issue, as several politicians raised concerns that these would be used for control rather than for service. "Police treat Arab towns as enemy zone, and then they come to open a station. The minister instigates against Arab citizens and then wants to impose a police station upon us. You need to achieve some trust first" (Nardy, 2017). Contrary to Arab politicians that raised objections, town mayors, in Tireh, Illut and Jisr a Zarkah, concerned with rampant crime and violence, demanded police stations in their cities (Daghash, 2011: 33).

General questions of fairness in the survey find some differences between Arab and Jewish citizens (Table 3.4), though they are not very large due, again, to the low standing of police also among Jewish citizens and differences between Arab citizens regarding evaluation and expectations from police. However, in line with relative deprivation theories, Arab citizens tend to believe they are likely to be treated worse than others (Table 3.4).

In the focus groups, frustrations with police were more explicit, pointing to specific concerns and experiences we described before as "over-policing" and "under-policing." In Table 3.5 we see that Arab citizens do not differ much from Jewish citizens in their perception regarding the lack of police, or their excess. However, what is no less important are, first, the "objective" facts of Arab insecurity. Second, their particular dilemmas resulting from being both securitized and neglected. And, third, the explanations they provide vis-à-vis their citizenship discourse alluding to the hierarchical nature of Israel's citizen regime. This complex picture of perceptions towards police is

Table 3.4 *Fairness*

Question/statement (%)	Group	Strongly disagree 1	2	3	4	Strongly agree 5	Mean (S.D.)
Police treat people fairly	Arab	19	16	40	16	9	2.81 (1.2)
	Control Group	10	18	43	23	6	2.98 (1.02)
If you would file a complaint of a crime, how would you be treated by the police, compared to others?		Far worse				Far better	
	Arab	13	10	67	5	5	2.79 (0.9)
	Control Group	5	6	64	16	9	3.17 (0.9)

Table 3.5 *Over-Policing and Under-Policing*

Question/statement (%)		Far below requirements 1	2	3	4	Far above requirements 5
To what the extent are the police in your community involved in each one of the following domains:						
Traffic violations	Arabs	21	14	21	20	24
	Control Group	16	19	25	22	18
Handling crime	Arabs	18	19	24	21	18
	Control Group	11	21	33	23	12
Dealing with domestic violence	Arabs	17	13	29	20	21
	Control Group	12	18	33	24	13
Disputes among residents or between neighbors	Arabs	25	19	32	15	10
	Control Group	19	23	30	19	9

reflective of citizenship concerns of a national minority struggling for equality and recognition. In Israel, the securitization debate adds to the complexity, Arab citizens' identity dilemmas and the state's suspicion of them. Demands for equality, seemingly trivial for democratic citizenship, are not easily answered in an ethnic democracy where they are perceived as a security threat, symbolic or demographic, to the state. Hence, a simple request that "police should treat us equally, not as second-rate or third-rate citizens" (focus group, Daburiyya) requires understanding what inequality means and what measures of equality are necessary. What exactly are Arab citizens' expectations from police? As Table 3.5 demonstrates, more Arab citizens than Jews tend to think that police services, in different realms, are both far below and far more than required, attesting again to dilemmas and differences among Arab citizens.

Securitization and Over-Policing

The lingering memory of the shooting of thirteen demonstrators in October 2000 by police officers still haunts the relations between police and Arab citizens. For police, as for many Jewish Israelis, this was an unfortunate outcome of demonstrations that went out of control, instigation of Arab leaders and a justified police response. For Arab citizens, however, the shooting (and the reaction of Jewish citizens) was another proof of their precarious citizenship status. Arab citizens could draw on their collective memory to argue this was not an isolated event. In 1956 border police killed forty-nine villagers for allegedly violating a curfew; all police officers found guilty served less than a year in prison. In 1976, six Arab citizens were gunned down by the army and police during demonstrations against land confiscation. Yet, the 2000 events were significant because they happened in a period when Arab integration seemed to have made significant progress. The peace process with the Palestinians that began in 1992, the important political role Arab parties had in support of the government headed by Yitzhak Rabin, and the investment in Arab towns and villages were all optimistic indicators.

The investigation committee formed shortly after criticized both police conduct and state policies that left Arab citizens behind, and Arab leaders for instigating the violence. But, to the dismay of Arab citizens, no charges were pressed against police officers. Theodor Orr, the High Court Justice who headed the investigation committee, criticized the Police Investigation Unit (PIU) in charge of investigation for not making an effort to find those responsible for the shooting (Weitz, 2010). Upon retirement, Herzl Shviro, the director of PIU, explained there was not sufficient evidence to press charges. In the same interview, he also alluded to police culture and the ability to investigate police:

There is no chance, no chance. I can count on one hand the number of times that an officer reported a criminal violation of a friend on an illegal use of force. You know what, not even one hand. It is a code of silence. It is not that police officers conspire before the event, but truth to the matter is that they don't talk and don't tell the truth about the use of force against a citizen (ibid.).

For Arab citizens, the decision not to indict officers was telling. "Nobody seriously investigated their death, because they are Arab." One activist compared the decision to the events of Kfar Kasem (1956), where a symbolic fine was placed on officers and concluded that "Arab citizens are step-sons of this state." Another asserted that "This simply means that Arab citizens are treated differently ... this report means one thing, after 57 years you Arabs are still regarded as a problem" (*Yedioth Aharonot*, 2006).

More than thirty Arab citizens were killed by police in different incidents since the violent events of 2000, while only three Jewish citizens were killed by police in the same period. Police investigations either found the shooting necessary and justified or, in some incidents, described it as a "mistake." In one case, when a police officer was sentenced to prison, charged with unnecessary shooting and killing a car burglar, fellow officers and senior commanders escorted him to jail displaying comradery (Rabad, 2010). Arab leaders, relatives of those killed and others exposed to police violence perceive the acquittal of officers as a deliberate policy that has little regard for Arab lives and differentiates Jewish from Arab citizens. Mahmud Taha, whose son was killed by police in Kfar Qasem during a demonstration, blamed the police for excessive use of force: "there was not excuse for this shooting. He shot straight to his upper body and head. If these were clashes with Jewish citizens, like those with Ethiopians or Ultra-Orthodox, none of this would have happened ... it is obvious that the hand is very easy with the trigger" (Efrati, 2017).

Riots erupted in a northern town after a young man who attacked a police car with a knife was shot while trying to escape and when no present danger to officers was present. Arab citizens took to the streets described the killing as an "execution" (Shaalan, 2014). In the Bedouin town of Rahat, Sami el-Jaer, an innocent bystander, was killed in January 2015 by police fire during a drug raid. Sami's father, Khaled el-Jaer, was arrested after he confronted the officers who shot his son, and claimed he was beaten severely by officers in the station. During el-Jaer's funeral, violence erupted again as a police car entered the procession, was stoned and ran into the crowd, with more wounded, one citizen who died from heart arrest, and more arrested by police, including a sixteen-year-old who was hit by the police car but blamed for instigating violence (Har-Zahav, 2017). El-Jaer family's demands for an open investigation were not answered and the officer charged with the shooting was not indicted. His sister, Manar, expressed her dismay: "We feel this is a police state, not a state for all its citizens. Just a police state, not a democratic state. the rule of law applies only for Jews" (Abu Suiss, 2016).

Arab citizens since statehood have fought land expropriation by the state and discriminatory policies of land allocation. Mapping, allocating and zoning is a display of sovereign power, but also the hierarchies of citizenship. In the Israeli case, ethnicity rather than citizenship is the main criteria for land distribution, favoring Jews over non-Jews and limiting Arab citizens' rights to land. Denied of building permits and new development plans, and contesting state confiscation of lands, Arab citizens often build without permits. State orders to expel unrecognized villages and demolish houses built without permits have put police in direct and often violent encounters with Arab citizens, further diminishing trust in police, on the one hand, and the securitization of Arab citizens, on the other hand.

In the Bedouin unrecognized village of Um-Al-Hiran, to be demolished by a court order and replaced by a Jewish settlement, police entered during the night, heavily armed. Interestingly, in the same week, in an operation to demolish houses in a Jewish illegal settlement in the West Bank, police entered unarmed and in spite of resistance and several officers hurt, no serious injuries were inflicted. In Um-Al-Hiran, described in the beginning of this chapter, police shot and killed Yacoub Abu Al-Qia'an and a police officer, Erez Levi, was killed after being hit by Abu Al-Qia'an's car. Khaled el-Jaer, who lost his son to police shooting a few months earlier, described his perception of the events in Um-Al-Hiran:

police violence, of an organization that does not examine itself, does not question its own mistakes ... not mistakes, this is murder after murder, our children are murdered ... my problem is not only with the police, but with the war the state declared on the Bedouins. The talk of [Jewish] territorial continuum, the birth rate, the demographic threat. Police officers hear what leaders are saying and develop hate . . . we are part of this country for god's sake (Knesset Committee for Internal Affairs, 2017).

Atia El-Asam, Chair of the Unrecognized Villages Committee, summarized the feeling:

I have no doubt that for police we are enemies, not citizens. This is shown by the violence treatment . . . we know we can't change this when police officers are instigating against the Bedouin population, when the Prime Minister and Ministers are instigating, this is the result. I want to tell you that as a citizen, I am afraid of police. The police is supposed to provide me with security, but when I see a cop, I am afraid (ibid.).

Securitization is not only about violent clashes but also of everyday practices that limit minorities' freedom of movement. While Arab citizens suffer less from racial profiling, being often indistinguishable in appearance from other citizens, they are profiled where they are identified. The Association for Civil Rights in Israel (ACRI) appealed to the Supreme Court (4797/07) to order the Israel Airports Authority (IAA) and the Ministry of Defence to stop using national criteria for security checkups. The ACRI described how Arab citizens were subjected to thorough, humiliating and often long examinations that caused them to miss flights. The IAA declared that new procedures and new technologies would be implemented soon, eliminating the need for profiling. This example does not relate to everyday policing, but is exemplary of securitization that sets apart Arab citizens and demarcates them as potential security threats. What many Jewish citizens perceive as an unavoidable necessity is a humiliating and discriminatory practice for Arab citizens.

Police, Use of Force and Perceptions of Over-Policing

Securitization for Arab citizens implies that national security is first and foremost the security of the Jewish people, that security concerns often trump citizenship rights and, consequently, that Arab citizens are over-policed. Some make the connection between Israel's policies in the West Bank, employed by soldiers now turned police officers against Israeli citizens (Har-Zahav, 2017). More importantly, when over-policing means police violence, Arab citizens are certain that police officers can get away and that justice is not on their side, separating them from Jewish citizens. In the focus groups, police violence and excessive use of force was mentioned several times; being stopped for no reason, other than speaking Arabic or wearing traditional clothes, and experiencing harsh and rude treatment by police officers.

There is discrimination everywhere. In airports where Arabs are treated differently, in shopping malls where you are asked to provide an ID only because you are Arab, in football stadiums where Arabs are harassed (focus group, Daburiya).
   In shopping malls, hospitals, bus stations ... if you are not in the right mood things can really turn bad ... you say something and it can add with violence or imprisonment (focus group, Dir-El-Asad).
   Police don't treat us with respect and dignity ... they abuse their power. When an officer stops me he yells at me, he is disrespectful ... he would not dare act the same way with Jewish citizens ... there are many instances when people are in public places and because they are Arab officers are rude to them and even use violence against them for no reason (focus group, Nazareth).

In one of the focus groups, the over-policing and the differential treatment of police was related to social and economic marginalization of Arab citizens:

There is racism in police and the way it treats Arabs is worst than the way the US police treats minorities ... but it is the same everywhere. We have poverty, unemployment and lack of resources [that cause more crime] and, consequently are treated differently (focus group, Jerusalem).

Over-policing, in these accounts, is underscored by a securitization ethos that renders Arab citizens vulnerable to police abuse and violence. The vulnerability of Arab citizens, depicted as a security threat, also, they believe, provides police with impunity to charges of unfairness.

Securitization of Political Dissent

Over-policing takes place also against Arab citizens involved in politics, especially during times of heightened security tension. In demonstrations against the war in Gaza in February 2009, for example, police arrested demonstrators, the majority of them Arab citizens. The high number of Arab citizens arrested for illegal demonstration, or for waving Palestinian flags, was interpreted as an attempted silencing directed by the government. More recently, in May 2018, in demonstrations against Israel's military operation in Gaza, police were blamed by demonstrators for using especially excessive violence. Jafar Farah, the chairman of the Mosawa Human Rights Organization, was arrested in a demonstration in Haifa, together with his 18-year-old son. The arrested, Arab citizens, complained they were beaten and verbally attacked by police officers. Footage of his arrest show Farah, handcuffed, walking on his own feet to the police car. Later that night, he was brought to the hospital with a broken knee after being hit by a police officer. The next day, pictures of Farah in the hospital chained to the bed raised more outrage.

MK Ayman Odeh, chairperson of the United (Arab) List, criticized police brutality: "The wild attack on us by police in Jerusalem and the attack and arrest of the demonstrators in Haifa, over claims that raising the Palestinian flag constitutes incitement, is untrue and also illegal" (*Times of Israel*, 2018). Farah refused to put the blame on one officer: "This cop," Farah added, "and other cops at the Haifa station along with him, did what they did under their commanders' supervision. The commander of the Haifa police station is responsible for what happens in his house. I trust no one" (Rabad, 2018). In another interview, Farah stressed the political aspect of his beating:

The purpose of beating me was humiliation in front of the other detainees. That is how I feel. To hit me, humiliate me and send a message to the others – if we could not arrest one of your parliament representatives, we will take a leader and humiliate him in front of his children. This came from the commander, it was not a cop that lost it (Fishbein, 2018).

The number of Jewish citizens that agree with the statement that "human rights organizations cause damage to the state" has risen in 2016 to 71 percent (from 56 in the previous year), compared to only 23 percent among Arab citizens. Also, while a slight Jewish majority (50.8 percent) agrees that the police and other security forces should have a free hand when involvement in terrorism is suspected, the majority of Arab citizens (72 percent) object (Hermann et al., 2017). This confluence of political dissent, against what Arab citizens perceive as structural inequality, and terrorism, explain their resentment of

securitization. In the survey and most of the focus groups the suppression of political dissent and the place of human rights organizations did
not receive much attention. This could be the result of political activity
involving only certain groups, or other concerns that overshadowed. In
some of the focus groups, however, political suppression was raised as
another example of the difference between Arab and Jewish citizens
and the flaws of Israel's democracy:

They will not let us demonstrate, but protect the right of Jewish citizens to do
so (focus group, Daburiyya).
    They always arrest more people when the demonstration is of Arabs.
When Jewish people demonstrate, because they want to make things better,
they are hardly arrested. But when Arabs want the same thing and demonstrate, police treat them as a security threat, arrests and humiliates them"
(focus group, Jerusalem).

Insecurity and Under-Policing

Sheikh Kamal Ryan, who founded an NGO to fight violence in Arab
towns and villages in Israel, describes the grim reality that begets
violence:

Apathy of the state and its institutions to the causes that breed violence that
stems from poverty, economic instability, lack of law enforcement, police
neglect, the deterioration of the education system, lack of informal education
for young people when out of school and a bleak future. Combined with this
are the rapid changes in the family structure, and the erosion of values and
morality of a society that lost its compass in an absence of a strong leadership
(in Ali, 2014: 17).

National minorities, under such circumstances, can suffer from harsh,
and at times violent, treatment of police, but at the same time feel
insecure. Securitization and insecurity, therefore, are not mutually exclusive. Not only in Israel, a Muslim citizen in Britain captures well the
feelings of being both targeted, stopped and searched, and excluded:
"The police see me as a terrorist, and then I'm invisible" (Parmar, 2011:
377). Arab citizens' complaints of over-policing in general, and police
violence in particular, are matched by a severe crisis of security and
feelings of vulnerability. While 50 Arab citizens were killed by police
since 2000, more than 1,200 were killed during the same period in

crime-related events. More than 40 percent of murder victims in Israel are Arab citizens, who constitute only 20 percent of the total population (Ali, 2004). Victims include those involved in crime and gang warfare, but also disputes between families, murder of women by their families and innocent bystanders, caught in gang crossfire, all creating the feeling of vulnerability as well as of intended neglect by the state, demonstrating marginality and defunct citizenship.

Security feeling is often subjective, and also based on comparison to other groups perceived to be better off, described above as "relative deprivation." While police took pride that crime-related violence was successfully curbed among the Jewish citizens, among Arab citizens the picture was very different. Crime rates soared, the murder rate being three times higher than among Jewish citizens, insecurity rose and trust in police declined. By October, the number of homicides in 2017 reached fifty-eight, the last one a young pharmacist shot in the entrance to Tira (Shaalan, 2017a). The novelist Saed Kashua, a native of Tira, described how fear rules in the city he left:

Violence is part of everyday life. With lawlessness, and being unable to rely upon state institutions, violence mediated by criminals became a way to resolve conflicts. Namely, enforcing solutions of the powerful on the weak. A hundred armed men can make the life of 50 thousand into hell, to make fear part of their everyday life and life without security unworthy of living (Kashua, 2016).

It is not surprising, therefore, that Arab citizens were four times more likely (54 percent) than Jewish citizens to report that there is a problem of violence in their neighborhood (Ben-Porat and Yuval, 2012). The rising violence in Arab communities is attributed to both internal and external causes. The collapse of traditional sources of authority and family structure, common to societies in transition, created a vacuum of authority in Arab society. This vacuum is coupled with economic and social marginality, breeding frustration. And finally, the availability of illegal weapons and the rise of organized crime combine to make Arab neighborhoods unsafe (Ali, 2014). Samah Salaime, a social worker and activist, said:

All the mothers are scared to death. What if a brawl starts and someone has a pistol? If your child goes with friends to some narghile hangout in Tira or Taibeh, in the length of a second, someone who's armed can get uptight over something and chaos will erupt. Some weeks ago, a boy of 9 was murdered in Lod when he went to buy falafel. The youth really have a serious problem (Shani, 2016).

Muhamad Barake, a former member of parliament, referred to the growing violence as a "social disaster." Others use the term "disease" or "existential danger" (Ali, 2014). Among the victims are women subjected to violence by their spouses and their families. In the city of Lydia (Lod), to take one example, fifteen women were murdered between 2010 and 2016. Arab leaders and activists have fought to remove the term "family honor killing," used in the past to describe these murders. In a parliamentary committee hearing, shortly after the fifteenth victim, 32-year-old Dawa Abu Serach, was shot in front of her children, it was reported that eighty women in Lod were considered under threat, sixty of them Arab (Knesset Committee for Women and Gender Equality, 2016). In the hearing, the family of the victim and other women under threat described the difficulty to get help from police. Police officers, conversely, described efforts made to protect women threatened by their families and the reluctant cooperation they receive. Similarly, while Arab citizens, women and men, complain that police fail to prosecute violent men even when sufficient evidence exists, police argue that families, neighbors and sometimes the victims themselves don't provide information or refuse to file complaints. In a parliamentary hearing, a police officer described the difficulty: "We arrive at the crime scene minutes later, it is washed, evidence has disappeared and no one saw anything" (Knesset Committee for Women and Gender Equality, 2003).

With staggering numbers of murders and violence, Arab leaders acknowledged their responsibility to fight violence, but claimed that only police have the capacity to fight organized crime and confiscate illegal weapons. Local attempts to fight violence, either by traditional forms of appeasement ("sulcha") or by organized neighborhood watches, offer at most limited hope in face of gun violence. In the focus groups, people referred to internal problems and the culture of violence that evolved, but have also pointed the finger at police, blamed for having the ability, but not the will, to put an end to violence:

Our problem is not with their qualifications and skills. We know Israeli army and police are well-trained. Our problem is with their attitudes towards us and their commitment to solve problems in the Arab sector. They need to be told that they should treat Arabs as human beings, not look at them as lesser (focus group, Jerusalem).

Everybody knows who killed and everybody knows who has guns. Why don't they do something and arrest them? (ibid.).

For Arab citizens it is evident that their insecurity is very different than that of their Jewish neighbors and they are certain that police make greater efforts, and succeed, when Jewish citizens are involved. Not only the failure of police to prevent the escalation of violent crime, but also the fact that many murder cases remain unresolved, is a proof of discrimination:

In the Jewish towns police is more invested, therefore faster and can provide security. Not in Arab towns (focus group, Dir-El-Asad).
  If in the Jewish towns there is a murder, police will do everything possible. In Arab towns the police make no effort, just a superficial work to get away with it (focus group, Nazareth).
  Murder in Jewish towns is solved in days . . . we are willing to cooperate, police is not willing to help (focus group, Daburiyya).

Some of the participants relate the failure of the police to provide order to years of neglect and unfair allocation of resources, which has left them incapable to provide order. Others believe this is a deliberate policy not to interfere and at most to contain the crime within the Arab neighborhoods.

Sometimes I feel that the police wants to let us fight and kill each other (focus group, Nazareth), or, police wants to destroy us (focus group, Dir-El-Asad).

These feelings and perceptions match the findings of the survey (Table 3.6): while Arab citizens do not necessarily differ from Jewish citizens in their personal feeling of security, and even slightly agree more than Jews that police provide them with security, relative deprivation is high. Arab citizens believe that police services they receive in their neighborhoods are of a lower quality than what Jewish citizens receive and that police would be slower to respond to a call in an Arab town or neighborhood.

The abundance of illegal weapons, used by criminals or in domestic disputes, underscores the feeling of insecurity, due to the perceived absence of police, and of an arms race where young people, for status or out of fear, purchase weapons and at times, use them. Here again, 49 percent of Arab citizens think that illegal weapons are a major

Table 3.6 *Insecurity and Under-Policing*

Question/statement (%)	Group	Strongly disagree 1	2	3	4	Strongly agree 5	Mean (S.D.)
How would you rate the quality of services police provide for you?		Very low quality				Very high quality	
	Arab	20	13	35	18	14	2.92 (1.3)
	Control Group	12	22	36	23	8	2.94 (1.1)
Police provide security for me	Arab	20	16	25	19	20	3.02 (1.4)
	Control Group	15	22	32	21	10	2.88 (1.2)
How quickly would respond to a call from your neighborhood?		Very slow				Very fast	
	Arab	7	20	29	19	15	2.94 (1.3)
	Control Group	10	13	35	28	15	3.25 (1.15)
Police service in your neighborhood compared to others is better/worse		Worse				Better	
	Arab	24	19	33	12	12	2.69 (1.3)
	Control Group	8	10	45	22	15	3.26 (1.1)

problem where they live, while only 7 percent of Jewish people think so (Abraham Fund, 2018). It is estimated that there are about 400,000 illegal weapons in Israel, most of them in the hands of Arab citizens. Moreover, according to police sources, 68 percent of the illegal use of firearms is in Arab neighborhoods (Zoabi, 2018). In a demonstration in front of the Taibe police station, following another killing, MK Ahmed Tibi explained: "we are raising our voice in front of the police station to put a stop for this crime wave, collect illegal weapons and fight the crime gangs and the murderers" (Shaalan, 2017b). A high school principal in Umm el Fahem told a reporter: "I cannot be sure that some of my students don't have a weapon in their house. I haven't seen, but I live here and am aware of the reality. There are many young people that hold weapons for self-defense and also as a status symbol" (Kubowich, 2016).

Illegal weapons got more attention when a terrorist attack in Tel-Aviv involved an Arab citizen. "When the weapons of Wadi Ara were directed to the people of Wadi Ara, nobody cared," scolded MK Ahmed Tibi his colleagues, "now, when it is pointed to Tel-Aviv, against Jews, everybody cares, and rightly so. But, this outrage should have come earlier, after hundreds of victims" (Knesset Committee for Internal Affairs, 2016). A police initiative to allow Arab citizens to turn in illegal weapons without facing charges achieved less than minimal results – a mere fourteen weapons collected. Not entirely surprising considering the low levels of trust in police and the feeling of insecurity among Arab citizens, making guns evermore popular.

Police Officers Like Us

The presence of national minorities in the police, representing state sovereignty and authority, can be a test case of citizenship and police legitimacy. The fact that police can be perceived by minorities as the oppressive arm of the state, and personal and collective experiences of police violence, may deter minorities from the police. Similarly, the securitization of minorities and the doubt of their loyalty to the state could, formally or informally, prevent their hiring. Recruitment of minorities, however, can be considered beneficial for both minorities and the state because, first, it can potentially enhance police legitimacy among minorities. Second, allow minority officers to influence police work changing both under- and over-policing. And, third, provide individuals an opportunity for mobilization and integration they might want to take advantage of. For national minorities, however, recruitment might be an especially sensitive topic due, on the one hand, to their securitization and the role police performs, and, on the other hand, the lack or limit of moral alignment with the state and its representative institutions.

In recent years Israeli police have made efforts to recruit Arab citizens: in 2016–2017, for example, 325 Arab officers joined the police. Still, Arab citizens, and especially Muslims, are underrepresented in police. Until the 1980s police recruited only Arabs who served in the military, namely Druze and Bedouins. The policy was relaxed in the 1980s but the policy change had little effect on the numbers of the recruited (Weitzer and Hasisi, 2008). In 2010, there were less than 400 Muslim police officers, out of 22,000 – 1.8 percent (Ronen, 2010). Unsurprisingly, enlistment remains controversial among Arab citizens, unconvinced of police intentions. Arab politicians have often voiced opposition to the plans announced for the recruitment of Arab citizens to the police, arguing that this will only serve to strengthen the state hold on Arab citizens and not change police attitudes and commitments. In a radio interview MK Aiman Awda explained that the relationship with police is problematic and that recent events of police violence make Arab citizens reluctant to join (KAN, 2017). Jafar Farah, director of the Mossawa Center for Arab Rights, was more explicit:

Police should change its policies, stop violence against demonstrators and detained, really fight crime in Arab society, that is what really should be done. But they do everything except this. Recruitment of Arabs to police will not solve anything (Yanovsky and Shaalan, 2016).

Public opinion, however, does not match the strong objection of politicians and political activists. In a recent survey, 72 percent of Arab citizens supported the incorporations of Arab police officers and 77 percent were interested in a police station in their neighborhood (Abraham Fund, 2018). Similarly, Arab mayors, weary of the growing and unending violence in their town, were supportive of more police presence. "Whoever has an alternative to the police – bring it," explained Shuaa Mansour, the mayor of Taibeh, "we have no alternative" (Hadid, 2016). In focus groups and in the survey the perceptions towards recruitment were ambivalent, on the one hand, with skepticism and criticism of Arab citizens serving in police and political objections to the idea of joining the police. But, on the other hand, voices supporting the recruitment of Arabs in hope for change were also heard.

Like elsewhere, recruitment of minorities raises question of loyalty, minority citizens concerned that recruited officers will "switch sides," aligning with the police rather than serving their communities and adopting the institutional culture rather than helping transform it. Indeed, Arab officers, some claimed, were harsher than the Jewish towards Arab citizens, or were at best insignificant:

They want to show they are in control and will treat us worst (focus group, Dir-El-Asad).
I was stopped once by a police car with a Jewish and an Arab officer. The Arab officer simply followed the orders of the Jewish (focus group, Nazareth).
They train them in a certain way and we cannot even distinguish an Arab from a Jewish officer. They don't even speak Arabic with us (focus group, Daburiyya).
They are more Jewish than Jewish. We are stopped by an Arab officer and he talks to me in Hebrew. I respond in Arabic, and he asks again in Hebrew … that shows how shallow and stupid they are (focus group, Jerusalem).

Participants also doubted the motivations of those who chose to join the police, claiming they were mostly instruments and removed from the community's needs and concerns:

Arab officers join the police and want to have a career. Therefore, he will do everything he is told (focus group, Daburiyya).

Those who consider joining the police are not concerned with our concerns. They are usually people lacking values and that can't find a job and that why they join the police (focus group, Jerusalem).

Others, however, were more positive and believed that Arab police officers could and should make a difference. The attitudes against the recruitment of officers like the ones above, they argued, damage Arab citizens' interests and the potential for change.

I think we need more Arab people in the police. I considered it and will be happy if more talented people will join the police (focus group, Daburiyya).

We have created discrimination against ourselves. Why? Because there are not enough Arab officers ... I think police is a good job and Arabs should join in big numbers until at least in Arab towns there will be Arab officers (focus group, Dir-El-Asad).

The reluctance regarding Arab police officers was about their will and ability to take it upon themselves to represent the community or to change police and policing from within. Supporters argued that even if not assuming the role of "active representation" the very presence of Arab police officers could make a difference. Passive representation, and the familiarity with Arab society and needs, could influence the way they work and eventually help improve police service for Arab citizens.

I think an Arab officer will make a difference. He will take into account our values when he works, he is familiar with the Arab mentality ... it will also improve police, they will internalize our values and cultures and take them into account (focus group, Jerusalem).

[The language they speak] is not the most important thing. That is not what we expect from police. There are more important things we need to protect our lives, to protect us from crime (focus group, Daburiyya).

Despite concerns and skepticism, research has shown in recent years support for recruitment of Arab officers, although no preference for Arab officers in their own communities was found among Arab citizens (Weitzer and Hasisi, 2008). Indeed, police reported a sharp rise in the number of Arab citizens applying to enlist. In 2015, only 425 Arab citizens applied to join the police, but before the end of 2016 already 1,420 applied (Yanovsky, 2016). Interviewed for the *New York Times*, the new recruits described their motivations as both personal challenges and a secure job, and their desire to contribute to their society. "If we had a Palestinian state, we would serve that one," explained one of the new policewomen, "but we are here" (Hadid, 2016). Arab police officers appeared in campaigns designed to encourage enlistment among Arab youth and an Arab police officer was promoted to the rank of a deputy commissioner.

Findings from the survey (Table 3.7) also demonstrate the ambivalence towards representation. Overall, both Arab and Jewish citizens strongly agree that police should be representative of society (72 and 80 percent, respectively). Yet, only 40 percent of Arab citizens believe that the recruitment of Arab police officers will have a significant positive impact on police and Arab society relations. Furthermore, there is no expectation that Arab officers will serve in Arab communities, with a strong preference for the professionality of the officers over their ethnicity and tepid support for cultural training. The rejection of ethnicity and training and the demand for professionality (and fairness) seems also to defy attempts of policy makers to frame violence and crime in Arab neighborhoods as "cultural." Arab citizens' demands from recruited police officers, in other words, is to provide them with adequate services, similar to Jewish citizens. Finally, Arab citizens remain personally reluctant to join the police, as only 25 percent would consider it (compared to 41 percent among Jews), but only 43 percent would object to a friend's or relative's decision to do so.

Cooperation with Police

National minorities' cooperation with police displays similar dilemmas of recruitment, with limited legitimacy and trust, on the one hand, and the need for effective policing, on the other hand. The alleged reluctance of Arab citizens to cooperate with police is often used by the latter to explain their difficulty to provide security and solve crimes in Arab neighborhoods. David Cohen, a former police commissioner, in response to a double homicide in Kufr Kara', explained that Arab citizens do not cooperate and, as a result, crimes are not resolved:

Table 3.7 *Representation*

Question/statement (%)	1	2	3	4	5	Mean (S.D.)
How would recruitment of police officers from your community affect the relations between the community and police?	Negatively				Positively	
Arab only	13	9	38	22	18	3.22 (1.2)
Would you prefer police in your neighborhood to be:	Arab only	mixed	Not from my group	Not important, professional	NR	NR
Arab only	4	11	7	78		
[For a salary meeting your expectations] Would you consider becoming a police officer?	No		maybe		Yes	Mean (S.D.)
Arab	58	7	11	10	14	2.16 (1.5)
Control Group	38	6	15	18	23	2.81 (1.6)
If a friend or a family member decides to join the police, would you support him/her?	Strongly object	2	3	4	Strongly support	Mean (S.D.)
Arab	35	8	15	17	26	2.90 (1.6)
Control Group	8	8	18	22	44	3.86 (1.3)
Police officers lack proper training to understand real problems in my neighborhood	Strongly disagree	2	3	4	Strongly agree	Mean (S.D.)
Arab	15	13	37	17	18	3.09 (1.3)
Control Group	22	16	24	8	20	2.97 (1.4)

It is not reasonable that a crime is committed in the presence of some of the citizens and no information is provided to the police. Without the cooperation of the residents with the police it is not possible to rein the phenomenon of violence and crime.

The mayor, in response, explained that

people want the crime to be solved and are willing to work with the police. What stops them is not the label of collaborator, it is the fear of retaliation (Daghash, 2011).

Arab citizens reluctance to cooperate is not necessarily about "political" considerations and the lack of moral alignment, but rather because they do not trust police to act in their interests or to protect them if they cooperate.

It simply does not make sense that police, with all its power and authority can not put an end to shooting and murders . . . Police make all kinds of excuses that we do not cooperate, but police itself works against the interests of Arab citizens (focus group, Daburiyya).

In a report submitted to the Minister of Internal Security, Arab MKs provide specific examples where police failed to protect those who cooperated with them from retaliation of crime organizations (Zoabi, 2018). The vast majority of Arab citizens (70 percent) state that they are willing to take part in the fight against crime (Abraham Fund, 2018), a sentiment found also in the focus groups accepting a duty to cooperate with police to "eradicate crime" (focus group, Jerusalem). But, the reluctance to cooperate with police was attributed to the fear that police will not be able to protect them.

Arabs are afraid to cooperate with police and testify because they know police cannot protect them (focus group, Dir-El-Asad).
    I will not be a witness. Because I am afraid. I have a family, a clinic and patients, and police can not provide me security (focus group, Nazareth).
    How can we cooperate when police does not care? we cannot cooperate without security (focus group, Daburiyya).

It is not surprising that the idea of community policing, often popular among minorities for being sensitive and avoiding use of force, is less popular among Arab citizens (Table 3.8). In a previous study we conducted (Ben-Porat and Yuval, 2012), Arab citizens saw community policing as weak, unable to resolve insecurity and, generally, as a force of low quality.

Table 3.8 *Community Policing*

Community policing provides an answer to the needs of my community (%)	Strongly disagree 1		2	3	4	Strongly agree 5	Mean (S.D.)
Arab	21		14	28	19	18	2.99 (1.4)
Control Group	10		10	28	25	28	3.51 (1.3)

The survey (Table 3.9) shows that Arab citizens are ready to obey officers even if they disagree with the order, differing little from Jewish citizens, but the reasons for obedience may differ. Arab citizens declare they would report to police incidence of violence in their neighborhoods (80 percent), but less so reckless driving (48 percent) or to identify offenders (46 percent). More surprising, more Arab citizens than Jewish citizens (62 and 42 percent, respectively) agree with the statement that the problem is not policing but rather citizens who do not respect the law and more punitive measures are required. Yet, this statement can be explained by the dire situation of growing insecurity and resentment towards criminals responsible for the violence. James Forman (2017) describes a similar pattern among African Americans in the US, supporting punitive measures against criminals, in spite of the fact it hurts mostly black men. As the head of NAACP Washington office explained:

If we're not safe within our homes, if we're not safe within our persons, then every other civil right just doesn't matter (ibid.: 202).

The desire of national minorities to be safe and free from the threat of violence, and perceptions of under-policing, therefore, explain the demand for more police and even more force, ostensibly aligning with police. At the same time, however, as long as trust of police remains low, it is likely that they would also demand that police be supervised and transparent, a demand police would usually resist.

Oversight

For many, and especially for political activists, the fact that police officers allegedly responsible for the killing of Arab citizens, or for using violence

Table 3.9 *Cooperation with Police*

Question/statement (%)	Group	Yes	No
I would call police to report violence in my neighborhood	Arab	80	20
	Control Group	85	15
I would call police to report reckless driving in my neighborhood	Arab	48	52
	Control Group	66	34

		Strongly disagree				Strongly agree	Mean (S.D.)
		1	2	3	4	5	
Would you identify to police a person you saw commit a crime?	Arab	24	10	20	18	28	3.16 (1.5)
	Control Group	16	8	17	18	41	3.60 (1.5)
I would obey a police officer even if I disagree	Arab	19	7	16	18	41	3.52 (1.5)
	Control Group	9	8	21	24	39	3.76 (1.3)
The police are not the problem, it is citizens who don't obey the laws and must be disciplined	Arab	8	6	24	20	42	3.83 (1.3)
	Control Group	17	16	26	18	24	3.08 (1.4)

against them, are not punished is a reason not to trust the police and policy makers in charge. Human rights NGOs like Adalah (www.adalah.org) published several reports that raised questions over the decisions not to press charges against police officers responsible for the shooting and killing of civilians in October 2011. More recently, the family of Sami el-Jaer, killed by police in Rahat in 2015, demand that his death be investigated.

We feel that this is a police state, not a democratic state ... the law only applies to Jews, not to Arabs ... the accused must be brought to a trial, if Israel claims the rule of law exists, they must be brought to trial (Abu Suiss, 2016).

The family of Yacoub Abu Al-Qia'an, shot and killed by police, after the allegations he was attempting to run over officers were proven false, has also demanded justice when the state attorney decided to close the case (Ben Zikri and Breiner, 2018).

Arab citizens, and others, distrust the office in charge of investigating police officers (MAHASH), under the Ministry of Justice. The vast majority of complaints filed to MAHASH (93 percent) are rejected or not handled (Kubowich, 2014). For Arab citizens, with cases that involve severe police violence, the decisions not to press charges against officers are of special significance. The residents of Um-Al-Hiran, where Al-Qia'an was killed, published a letter after MAHASH decided to close the case and stated that:

The closing of the case without prosecution should concern every Israeli citizen, it is the moment where police officers receive a license to kill without any legal consequences (Channel 10 News, 2017).

In the following chapters we will see that other groups also complain that police violence is not checked and that violent officers are rarely punished. However, for Arab citizens, the fact that human lives are involved is a clear demonstration of vulnerability and the high price of their securitization. In 2010, then years after the October riots, a report published by the Israeli Democracy Institute reviewed the investigations of the killing of thirteen citizens, and criticized the decision to close the cases without charges:

against these findings it is difficult to avoid the question if the same conclusions would be reached if these were 13 Jewish citizens? Or, is there no connection between the possibility that there was unjustified or excessive use of lethal force towards Arab citizens and the avoidance of investigation shortly after the events, the decision not to investigate later and the decision to close all cases for a lack of evidence? Can we see in the way the security forces operated during the event against Arab rioters a policy of "lets teach them a lesson" and with the failed investigation of the events the adoption or compliance with this policy? (Saba-Habesch and Kremnitzer, 2010)

The lingering memory of the events and the fear of police violence, however, are matched by the reality of insecurity that requires police intervention. Consequently, Arab citizens want to see police authority both exercised (to provide security) and restrained (against violence). Both Arab and Jewish citizens strongly agree that officers who use unnecessary violence should be punished, and Jewish citizens also reject (though not as strongly) the statement that police should prioritize fighting crime even if it involves hurting innocent people. While both groups agree that police must be fair and courteous when engaging with citizens, even at the expense of deterrence, Arab citizens are more insistent. The dilemmas of Arab citizens are evident in the final two questions (Table 3.10). First, Arab citizens support more than Jewish citizens providing the police with more authority, but at the same time also stronger oversight of police work. This seeming paradox can be explained by a conflicting reality in which a national minority is simultaneously over-policed and under-policed, both attesting to discrimination and marginality.

Table 3.10 *Police Oversight*

Question/statement (%)	Group	Strongly disagree 1	2	3	Strongly agree 4	5	Mean (S.D.)
Police must treat citizens with fairness and dignity,	Arab	4	2	9	14	71	4.46 (1.0)
even at the expense of deterrence	Control Group	5	7	15	20	53	4.08 (1.2)
Officers who use unjustified force should be punished	Arab	4	1	2	7	86	4.72 (0.9)
	Control Group	2	2	5	10	82	4.67 (0.8)
Police should prioritize public order and fighting	Arab	27	14	28	14	17	2.82 (1.4)
crime even if innocent people are hurt sometimes	Control Group	26	18	26	16	15	2.76 (1.4)
Police should have more authority and autonomy	Arab	12	11	28	23	27	3.42 (1.3)
to be able to protect the public	Control Group	19	12	22	21	26	3.23 (1.4)
Strong oversight of police is necessary	Arab	3	2	11	23	60	4.34 (1.0)
	Control Group	3	5	17	27	48	4.12 (1.1)

Conclusions

The presence of minorities, unable to assimilate yet demanding equality and recognition, challenges democratic commitments of states and the legitimacy of their institutions. Police and policing teach citizens about the fundamental properties and commitments of their government (Lerman and Weaver, 2014: 12), allow them to evaluate how people "like them" are treated in comparison to others, and are often indicative of the contested and precarious citizenship of national minorities. The ethno-national classification of Israeli citizenship marks the gap between the formal citizenship of Arab citizens and their unequal status. Arab citizens are perceived by the Jewish majority as non-loyal and at times a security threat, and remain politically and economically marginalized. The Jewish state's limitations on their equality and the prolonged Israeli–Palestinian conflict further distances them and securitizes their demands and struggles. Accordingly, their relations with and perception of police are characterized by suspicion, securitization and neglect.

The legitimacy of police is negatively affected by Arab citizens' alienation from the state and its institutions as well as it execution of state policies perceived by Arab citizens as discriminatory. Moral alignment with police, therefore, remains difficult, if not impossible, for a national minority alienated and securitized.

Legitimacy of police, however, can rely also on more particular measurements of trust, where citizens believe that police are fair and effective, able to provide security. Minorities, like Arab citizens who are securitized and alienated, suffer simultaneously over-policing and under-policing, relating both to unfairness. For Arab citizens, the perceptions of being targeted by police, more exposed to police violence and politically suppressed, strengthen their assessment of the limits of their citizenship. At the same time, the rising crime and violence in their neighborhoods are perceived as a result of intended neglect by police and the state, another example of their marginality. Rampant crime and disorder, underscoring violence and crime, themselves the result of poverty, poor public services and lack of opportunities.

Arab citizens feel insecure due to rising crime, illegal weapons and sporadic violence harbor resentment towards police, for their alleged lack of commitment. At the same time, however, under these circumstances there is hardly an alternative for police, so that minorities, despite resentment, might demand not only stronger police actions but more punitive measures towards criminals and more incarceration (Forman, 2017). But if it appears that interests of police and government, on the one hand, and minorities suffering from crime, on the other hand, converge in the demand for authority, significant differences between them remain. While government and police tend to see authority or the firm exercise of law and order as the solution to all problems, minorities might be more concerned with the root causes of violence and also demand eradicating discrimination and poverty. Referring again to the Orr Commission's recommendation, structural causes of inequality need to be addressed, and not only by police. Moreover, it is unlikely that minorities would exchange criminal violence with police's unchecked power, and trust police without proper voice and oversight, an indication of equal citizenship.

It is hardly surprising that police reforms, recruitment of Arab officers and new stations in Arab neighborhoods have not changed the perceptions, improved trust or ameliorated concerns. While Arab citizens and police might agree on the need to fight crime, making police more effective, the question of fairness, requiring oversight of police and tackling police violence, seems to set them apart. Under these circumstances, with limited trust, Arab citizens' perceptions of neglect and police claims of lacking cooperation, the impact of changes remain limited. For a securitized national minority, under constant suspicion, in an ethnic state, where majority's needs and interests take precedence, police and policing may be another (significant) example of inequality, marginality and segmented citizenship.

4 | The Skin Color Effect: Police and the Jews of Ethiopian Descent

It was the documented beating of Damas Pikada, a young Israeli soldier of Ethiopian origin, by a police officer that sparked a series of riots in the spring of 2015, demanding that police officers involved be brought to trial. The beating, that sparked the events, was not an isolated event, despite what many Israelis wanted to believe. The demonstrators, mostly young Israelis of Ethiopian descent (hereafter, Ethiopians), expressed their frustration not only with police and with being targets of police violence, but also with wider ongoing discrimination and marginalization, and many times, the racism they face in Israel. As one demonstrator explained:

We came to Israel because we were Zionists, not like others who came for a better job. When you are a Zionist, you believe with all your heart that this is your country, that our forefathers lived her and that we deserve to be here. But what is happening here is a catastrophe, racism everywhere ... we will not by silent any more. We are not the generation of our parents that accepted everything. This age is over and in the new age there is a young generation demanding his rights (Kubowich, 2016b).

The demonstrations, in Tel-Aviv and Jerusalem, escalated, with police and Ethiopians blaming each other for use of violence. The demonstrators, some carrying Israeli flags, defied any attempt to depict them as subversive or disloyal, insisting it was the state that betrayed them and breached the republican equation: "We serve, Ethiopians are first in line for top combat units, sacrificing their lives in all wars. And, in return, the state, how does it treat them?" (ibid.). Demonstrators not only stressed their military service, but repeatedly chanted two more names, Avera Mengistu and Yosef Salamsa, whose stories are emblematic of the state's betrayal of its Ethiopian citizens. Avera Mengistu, a troubled young man, crossed the border to Gaza in September 2014 and since disappeared, presumably held by Hamas. During the demonstrations in 2016, most Israelis were unfamiliar with the name as the affair was silenced in hope that it would help his release. For the demonstrators, however, and activists supporting the family, it was clear that had Mengistu not been Ethiopian greater efforts for his release would have been employed. Yosef Salamsa, another young Ethiopian man, was arrested by police officers who used a taser gun, handcuffed him and left him for hours outside the police station. After the event, Salamsa withdrew to himself, fell into depression and four months later was found dead in what was declared a suicide.

For the young Ethiopians, the stories of Mengistu and Salamsa were a clear demonstration of systemic racism and the significance of skin color. The words of demonstrators often echoed those of the Black Lives Matter movement in the US:

I don't think that what is happening in Baltimore affects us, but there is some commonality and understating, there are some similarities. They suffer from racism and we suffer from racism, only there it is more extreme – people were killed by police officers. Here, for the time being, we are only beaten.

I don't know if things here are related to what is happening in Baltimore, but we can identify with them, as black people (ibid.).

The relations of Israelis of Ethiopian descent with police reveal a different story than the Arab citizens and a different part of the hierarchical and segmented structure of the Israeli citizenship regime. Being Jewish, Ethiopians are formally part of the national collective, morally aligned and entitled to equal rights. In practice, set apart by ethnicity and skin color, they are often discriminated by different policies, marginalized within Jewish society and vulnerable to police abuse. Again, perception of and relations with police attest to broader questions of citizenship and to the gap between its formal inclusivity and manifestations of hierarchy.

Citizenship and Skin Color

The status of minorities, especially so-called visible minorities, often demonstrates the hierarchies and exclusions of citizenship. Ethnic groups, unlike national minorities, can, at least potentially, be part of the imagined nation and within its formalized boundaries, but at the same time marginalized, racially categorized and subjected to different abuses or differential treatment. While many states and societies have seemingly moved beyond and away from racial classifications, "race," in spite of lack of scientific grounding, and racism, in more subtle forms, has not disappeared. Race, ethnicity and nation share common traits, all referring to descent and common origin (Fenton, 2003: 51), that can change with time and place. Jews, for example, are a national group in Israel, an ethnic group in the US and were considered a race in earlier times (Spinner, 1994: x). Like nationalism and ethnicity, race is made up of classificatory systems, representations and symbolic elements (Fenton and May, 2002). While ethnicity at times is defined in terms of race, it is often perceived as socially made and subjective, unlike race which, in previous times, was perceived naturally created and objective (Nobles, 2000: 14).

The concept of race has been abandoned, with its attempts of scientific hierarchies (Fenton, 2003), and grim past of racist ideologies and practices. But, while race may no longer be valid as a scientific category, states have dropped the category "race" from censuses (Loveman, 2014: 5), and racist ideologies are discarded, "race" remains politically and socially significant. No longer considered an essential trait, race is depicted as a socially constructed and contingent outcome of practices and processes of exclusion (Fox et al., 2012), which can exist even in the absence of (formal or scientific) racism and of (self-declared) racists. Thus, even when states refrain from legal racial discrimination or the use of racial categories, political and social construction of racial divides exist (Loveman, 2014: 5) and shape the hierarchies of citizenship. As "an ascribed set of character traits with which individual groups are labeled by others" (Treitler, 2013), race is often associated with skin color, or other attributes that are "visual" and detectable.

Racial paradigms organize the way in which "race" operates in different times and places and the categories and hierarchies it contains. The sociologist Eduardo Bonilla-Silva describes a new racism that includes "practices that are subtle, institutional and apparently nonracial" (Bonilla-Silva, 2006: 15), which continue operating even while racist attitudes are in decline. This new racism no longer relies on biological tropes but rather on cultural ones more difficult to discern but serve similar purposes of exclusion and hierarchies. "Racialization" is defined as the "extension of racial meaning to a previously racially unclassified social relationship, social practice, or group" (Omi and Winant, 2014: 111) and a process of "permanent othering" (Gans, 2017). It impacts residential segregation, educational achievements, job and advancement prospects and is often intersectional, as class, gender, age and other identities are part of the process (Gans, 2017). Thus, even where states and institutions are seemingly racially neutral, skin color can remain associated with economic and educational gaps, de-facto segregation and ill treatment by institutions, "resulting over time in replication of old lines of racial inequality or the construction of new ones, even as still others seem to dissolve" (Harris and Lieberman, 2013: 17).

Much of the discussion of race and racism comes from the American history of slavery, Jim Crow laws and the evolvement of African American identity, or from colonial experiences. But, race and racialization can be found elsewhere, within different institutional settings and practices, constructed in daily interactions or "everyday race-making" (Lewis, 2003). In the absence of overt racism and self-identified racists it is more subtle and less explicit than older forms, used in inverted commas, without explicit "ethnic projects" that formally define hierarchies (Treitler, 2013). Yet, race continues to exist in everyday encounters between state authorities and citizens and within societies.

Policing and Race/Racialization

The use of racial categories in policing is an example of what Bonilla-Silva (2006: 14) describes as racial "micro-aggressions" used to maintain boundaries by signaling who belongs and who does not through discourses, categorization, policies and practices. The targeting of "people of color" or "visible minorities" as suspects and their vulnerability to police violence sets them apart from other citizens and has wider and negative social repercussions. Like other institutions, police would deny the existence of racism or practices of racialization, yet, their practices often reveal the opposite. The U.S. Department of Justice, to take one recent example, in its investigation of the Baltimore Police Department following the death of an arrested citizen and other complaints of police discrimination and violence, stated the following:

BPD's targeted policing of certain Baltimore neighborhoods with minimal oversight or accountability disproportionately harms African-American residents. Racially disparate impact is present at every stage of BPD's enforcement actions, from the initial decision to stop individuals on Baltimore streets to searches, arrests, and uses of force. These racial disparities, along with evidence suggesting intentional discrimination, erode the community trust that is critical to effective policing (U.S. Department of Justice, 2016: 7).

It is hardly surprising, therefore, that race is one of the most consistent predictors of citizens' attitudes towards the police (Weitzer and Tuch, 2006). Excessive use of force against racial minorities was in several cases a trigger for riots and, in their wake, investigating commissions that identified police malpractice and demanded or recommended reforms. In the US, it was the documented beating of Rodney King in 1991 by the Los Angeles police, and the acquittal of the officers involved, that led to violent riots. More recently, the shooting of unarmed Michael Brown by police in Ferguson, Missouri (August 2014), the choking to death of Eric Garner by New York police officers (July 2014) and the death of Freddie Gray while in custody of Baltimore police (April 2015) were some of the incidents that led to the creation of the Black Lives Matter movement.

In Britain, it was not direct police violence, but police racism associated with the death of Steven Lawrence in 1993 that evoked rage. Lawrence, a young black man, was stabbed to death in a racially motivated attack. A parliamentary inquiry report (MacPherson, 1999) described in length the police's (and other authorities') mistreatment of the investigation and of the victim's family:

We assert that the conclusion that racism played its part in this case is fully justified. Mere incompetence cannot of itself account for the whole catalogue of failures, mistakes, misjudgements, and lack of direction and control which bedevilled the Stephen Lawrence investigation (MacPherson, 1999: 6.44).

In France, riots erupted in 2005 after a police chase ended with the death of two young boys. The boys, who returned from a football game, ran away from police because they did not have their documents with them into an electric substation. The police who pursued the boys saw them enter the substation and did nothing to prevent their death (Schneider, 2008).

Police violence, especially when documented and followed by riots, captures attention, but the distrust of police is often the result of everyday practices, seemingly neutral policies that do not mention race and interactions that appear ordinary or banal to outside observers. Not only the use of excessive force against racial minorities, also their targeting as suspects for no other reason than their skin color, conveys a message about citizenship (Epp et al., 2014). The investigation of the Baltimore police revealed how African Americans are more likely to be stopped and searched, simply for being black and residing in neighborhoods where police are engaged in particular practices:

BPD's pedestrian stops are concentrated on a small portion of Baltimore residents. BPD made roughly 44 percent of its stops in two small, predominantly African-American districts that contain only 11 percent of the City's population. Consequently, hundreds of individuals—nearly all of them African American—were stopped on at least 10 separate occasions from 2010–2015. Indeed, seven African-American men were stopped more than 30 times during this period (U. S. Department of Justice, 2016).

The significance of the Baltimore police report, and others, is the opportunity provided to go beyond the events that triggered the investigation (the Steven Lawrence case, the death of Freddie Gray or the October events in Israel discussed in the previous chapter) to the causes underlying them. The reports, and academic studies, shift our attention from individual acts of racism and overt violence to "institutional racism" embedded in police conduct. In the Macpherson Report of the Steven Lawrence investigation institutional racism was defined as

the collective failure of an organisation to provide an appropriate and professional service to people because of their colour, culture, or ethnic origin. It can be seen or detected in processes, attitudes and behaviour which amount to discrimination through unwitting prejudice, ignorance, thoughtlessness and racist stereotyping which disadvantage minority ethnic people (Holdaway and O'Neill, 2006).

While this definition is wide and open to interpretation it also allows to capture the significance of policies and interactions devoid of overt racial connotations.

Institutional racism translates into what was described previously as "over-policing," a mistreatment of minorities by the police, either by excessive use of force or by discriminatory practices against them (Findlay, 2004: 101), at times harder to detect. "Racial profiling," the most common practice, refers to the use of generalizations based on race, ethnicity, religion or national origin as the basis for suspicion in directing law enforcement actions (Closs and McKenna, 2006; Wortley and Tanner, 2003). In this process of racialization, skin color becomes a category that triggers police actions, from stop and search, to arrests and, at times, more use of force than otherwise (Walker et al., 2000). Consequently, racial and ethnic minorities are often more likely to be stopped, questioned, searched and arrested by the police (Epp et al., 2014; Walker et al., 2000; Weitzer and Tuch, 1999). In the United States, this has further consequences in higher rates of incarceration of African Americans, and deleterious consequences that arise after being incarcerated in job prospects and poverty (Kahn and Martin, 2016).

In policing, like elsewhere, racial discrimination does not require explicit prejudice (Kahn and Martin, 2016) and racial negative stereotypes can exist even when profiling is not a policy. Ingrained negative stereotypes, which link racial minorities with violence and criminality, on the one hand, and wide discretion, on the other hand, can lead officers to treat racial minorities as suspects, and the latter to view police stops as an infringement of their citizenship rights. The judgments based on skin color that officers make require people to justify presence in a certain neighborhood or to be exposed to a body search only for being in the "wrong" neighborhood. The search, a racially framed, institutionalized practice of police (Epp et al., 2014: 12) signals to minorities their unequal status and suspended citizenship rights. It is hardly surprising, therefore, that a consistent racial trust gap of police exists, and that racial minorities trust police less and are more likely to believe that police officers engage in racial profiling (Kahn and Martin, 2016).

Thus, while documented police violence against racial minorities captures attention and raises awareness of racism, racialization is also part of everyday, seemingly mundane practices and actions, which demarcate hierarchies of citizenship. These practices, often more subtle and harder to detect than police violence, render minorities vulnerable, and, when persisted, strengthen negative stereotypes of minorities, minorities' resentment of police and a segmented citizenship regime.

Israelis and the Jews of Ethiopia

Despite the obvious similarities in racially based discrimination of Ethiopian Jews in Israel and African Americans in the US or immigrants in Europe, differences are important (Kaplan, 1999). Ethiopian Jews, known also as Beta-Israel, did not arrive as slaves or guest-workers. Rather they came to take their place as citizens of the country they belong to as Jews and, consequently, their arrival was celebrated as a successful Zionist enterprise. However, regardless of statements, declared policies and intentions, Ethiopian Jews' experience in Israel, especially of young people, is entrenched in racist and anti-racists discourses (Ben-Eliezer, 2004). Notwithstanding the danger of imported models, and avoiding the trap of simplistic comparisons, it is vital to explain the process of Ethiopians *becoming black* (Kaplan, 1999) through the particularities of their experience. Adam, an Ethiopian attorney, has explained, in response to fellow Ethiopians celebrating Obama's victory, why the comparison of Ethiopian Jews in Israel to blacks in America is both wrong and dangerous:

Your attempt to link us to the blacks in the United States has always been dangerous and has caused our young people to degenerate to the lowest levels, because, like you, our youth admires black singers, just because they are black. I am not naïve. Unfortunately, there are racists in Israel. Their racism derives from the fact that they think like you ... they look at the color of the skin and they compare (quoted in Mizrachi and Zawdu, 2012).

Ethiopian Jews for many years had no contact with Jewish communities elsewhere and developed their own customs and religious forms. Like other Jews, they were considered strangers in their land, suffered discrimination and developed the idea or return to Zion (Ben-Eliezer, 2008). From the nineteenth century, European Jews, and later Jewish and Zionist institutions, who "discovered" the Jews of Ethiopia, attempted to solidify their Jewish identity along the westernized model of clear boundaries. Until 1974, Ethiopian Jews were prevented from immigrating to Israel because their religious status was considered ambiguous by the religious authorities. After their status as Jews was recognized, Ethiopian Jews could take advantage of the Law of Return and immigrate to Israel (Offer, 2004). Immigrants, after significant hardships, during which many lost their lives, arrived in two major operations, "Operation Moses" in 1984 and "Operation Solomon" in 1991. Approximately 136,000 Israelis of Ethiopian descent currently live in Israel, constituting 1.6 percent of its population.

Ethiopian Jews entered Israel and were granted citizenship by the principles of the Law of Return. Like elsewhere, formal citizenship did not translate automatically to full and meaningful membership. Initially, Ethiopian Jews were received with enthusiasm, their arrival depicted by the popular press as part of Israel's mission of bringing all

Jews to Israel with the dramatic details of their hardships and rescue, adding to the sympathy. But, more than twenty years after their arrival, the Ethiopian community constitutes one of the most disadvantaged segments of Israeli society. Since their arrival, Ethiopian immigrants have occupied the lower strata of the socioeconomic ladder in Israeli society (Offer, 2004). Many Ethiopian Israeli families live below the poverty line, use public assistance as their main source of income, and reside in poor and segregated neighborhoods (Kaplan and Salamon, 2004). In addition, their Jewishness, previously recognized by the former Chief Rabbi of Israel Ovadia Yosef, was once again doubted, with different demands for conversions they found humiliating and degrading. Ethiopians often refuse to apply the language of race to explain discrimination (Mizrachi and Zawdu, 2012; see also Abu et al., 2017), but gradually racial discourse became hard to avoid.

Police violence was the trigger, but hardly the only cause, for the resentment formed among young Ethiopians that exploded in the demonstrations in the summer of 2016. The demonstrations, and the anger expressed by young people who took to the streets and clashed with police, brought to the surface what was previously denied or ignored, but could no longer go unnoticed. The Israeli government, in response to the events, formed a committee, headed by the Ministry of Justice to "eradicate racism against Israelis of Ethiopian descent." The use of the word "racism" was of special significance, indicating that the topic could not be avoided. The report (one of the authors was a member of the committee) acknowledged:

the reality in which Ethiopian young men and boys report feelings of insecurity when they walk in the streets and are exposed, regularly and continuously to harassment for being stereotyped as "different." A reality where Ethiopian women are not treated with equality and respect. A reality where black-skin citizens stand out and are identifiable in the public, and at the same time so transparent (Ministry of Justice, 2016: 7).

Ethnic inequalities and discrimination are not new to Israeli society, which is highly divided and stratified along ethnic lines. Not only Arab citizens, but also Jews originating from Muslim countries (Mizrahim or Sefaradim) suffered discrimination, justified or explained by Israel's "westernization project" led by the Ashkenazi (European descended) elites (Khazzoom, 2003). Discrimination, often based on negative stereotypes, translated to unequal allocation of resources and relegation to the periphery where education and employment opportunities were limited and underfunded. Inequalities between center and periphery still persist, as well as the ethnic boundaries they demarcate (Sasson-Levy, 2013). While the term "black" was used at times as derogatory against Mizrahim (compared to European "whiteness"), skin color in practice was an elusive marker (often difficult to differentiate between groups) and was an ethnic label marking differences and hierarchies (Sasson-Levy, 2013).

Ethnicity is part of the political and social landscape dividing the Jewish collective, demarcating hierarchies and shaping political identities. The efforts of the state to erase ethnicity and delegitimize it involved also the police when ethnic protest was perceived as a threat to social order. Mizrahi protest in the 1950s (and in the 1970s) was securitized and, accordingly, met violent response. In July 1959 police officers in the Wadi Salib neighborhood of Haifa shot and wounded Yaakov Akiva, a Jewish immigrant from Morocco who was under the influence of alcohol. The shooting sparked a protest of residents in the neighborhood, mostly Mizrahim, frustrated with the poverty and housing conditions and with their discrimination, compared to Jewish immigrants from Europe who often received better housing (Weiss, 2007). Newspapers described the events as an "ethnic uprising" and government and politicians blamed the opposition for instigating the riots and demanded action be taken against what they described as vandalism and reckless behavior. In the following weeks riots took place in other ethnic neighborhoods across the country. In Beer Sheva, a southern city, the riots led to many arrests and the rioters were described by the press and police as delinquents who do not represent the community. Yet, while only a minority took part in the riots, the rioters' claims of discrimination of Jews from North Africa in housing and employment were far from unfounded (Bar-On Maman, 2018).

Riots in different cities, expressing pent-up ethnic frustrations and demands for equal citizenship, were on the one hand marginalized by government officials as nonrepresentative, but on the other hand securitized and met harsh police response. Protestors in Haifa described to journalists the poverty and discrimination they suffer and asked if police officers would use live ammunition in the wealthy neighborhoods of the city like they did in Wadi Salib (Strassman-Shapira, 2012). Uri Avnery, the editor and owner of the antiestablishment newspaper *HaOlam HaZe* (this world), argued shortly after the events that police violence was directed at marginalized groups, first Arab citizens and then Mizrahim:

He who shoots Muhamad (an Arab name) will shoot Rachamim (a typical Mizrahi name), he who arrests and deports without trial Suliman, will arrest and deport Nissim ... what happened yesterday in Wadi Nisnass (an Arab neighborhood of Haifa) must happen today in Wadi Salib (quoted in Weiss, 2007: 14).

In the early 1970s it was an ethno-class struggle of the "Black Panthers" for equality and against poverty and discrimination that raised similar concerns and reactions from the government. The group was described by the government as "anti-Zionist" and manipulated by radical left organizations and the protest was quickly securitized – members of the group were criminalized and described as a "violent mob." The "moral panic" ensued by the government and the police depicted the group as a public threat, to be closely followed by the police and concerned citizens. Informers were recruited, activists were followed by police, arrested and demonstrations were forcefully dispersed (Lev and Shenhav, 2010).

The intersection of policing and ethnicity in Israel is reflective of social hierarchies and the stratification of citizenship. Ethnic inequalities – economic, political and social – render groups more vulnerable to unfair and discriminatory practices. While securitization is largely reserved for non-Jewish citizens, other groups can become its targets, especially vulnerable and visible ones. The discourse surrounding Ethiopians, and ensuing institutional practices, presented a new, clear and salient dimension of race (Mizrachi and Zawdu, 2012). Again, as mentioned before, race is a constructed category, but once constructed it received "real" dimensions through institutional policies and seemingly mundane bureaucratic decisions, formal and informal. The segregation of Ethiopians, and their consequent racialization, was not the result of official government plans, as ministries devised different plans to integrate them into Israeli society (Ben-Eliezer, 2008). The segregated outcomes of Ethiopian (and poor) neighborhoods can be attributed to "objective" conditions (immigrants' low scale of material and human capital) that marginalized them, but also to discrimination, racialization and "cultural racism" (Ben-Eliezer, 2008) that affected the prospects also of those born or raised in Israel. This "societal" and "everyday" cultural racism developed in a multicultural and neoliberal society, where discriminations are hidden under cultural and economic logics and individual preferences (ibid.).

Segregation was the result, among other things, of mayors' demands to curb government plans to settle Ethiopians in their towns. Mayors, and residents, complained that the plans would hurt real estate value, and that their welfare services could not take any more "weak" populations. As a result, many Ethiopians found themselves in separate neighborhoods and schools, on the margins of society. The cultural racism, which posited "insurmountable cultural differences" (Balibar, 1991: 31), not only kept Ethiopians apart from the rest of society but also established a paternalistic system of racial categorization and bureaucratization turning the group into an object of management, further enforcing negative stereotypes. Ethiopians were considered a weak population requiring special care (Offer, 2004) so that while Russian immigrants received cash grants that allowed them to rent or purchase apartments wherever they chose, Ethiopians were sent to absorption centers. This system created dependency on government support, strengthened the stigmas of Ethiopians' weakness and their marginal status.

Racial consciousness, in response to segregation, intensified among Ethiopians and a racial rhetoric and claims of racial discrimination became more common (Offer, 2004). But, at the same time, Ethiopians stress their Israeli and Jewish identity and highlight their patriotism, often downplaying racism. Government policies, institutional practices and societal attitudes present Ethiopians with a constant dilemma between the desire to be included and the reality where racism prevented integration. Racialization has made an impact on various aspects of Ethiopian life in Israel, including lifestyle, identity (Shabtay, 1999, 2001) and acculturation (Kaplan, 1999; Kaplan and Rosen, 1993). While racialization was significant for the group's interactions with Israeli society and institutions (Ben-Eliezer, 2008; Salamon, 2003), distance and marginalization were matched by their desire for inclusion and the use of their Jewishness as a cultural resource (Mizrachi and Zawdu, 2012). Thus, when tear gas was used against Ethiopian demonstrators, one retorted with anger, "what are we, Arabs?" (Kaplan, 1999). In different instances military service was raised to demonstrate sacrifice and the breach of the republican equation by state and society. Being part of the Jewish collective, even if not fulfilled, Ethiopians demarcate themselves from other stigmatized and marginalized groups, stressing a strong feeling of national belonging and demands for a fully inclusive citizenship.

The survey results demonstrate that Israelis of Ethiopian descent perceive themselves as part of the collective, and by so doing they claim their place within and defy the attempts to marginalize them.

While feelings of belonging are weaker than those of veteran Jewish Israelis and Russian immigrants, they are far greater than those of Arab citizens (Table 4.1). Similarly, Ethiopians are proud to be citizens like other Israelis (Table 4.2) but their trust of the state and its institutions is lower (Table 4.3), indicating the dilemma of desiring to belong while suffering discrimination.

Table 4.1 *Belonging*

I feel I belong to this country (%)	Not at all 1	2	3	4	Very much 5	Mean (S.D.)
Ethiopians	4	10	14	17	56	4.12 (1.2)
Arabs	15	13	27	21	24	3.26 (1.4)
Ultra-Orthodox	10	11	21	18	40	3.67 (1.4)
Russians	2	2	11	27	58	4.37 (0,9)
Control Group	3	1	8	18	70	4.52 (0.9)

Table 4.2 *Pride*

I am proud to be an Israeli citizen (%)	Not at all	2	3	4	Very much
Ethiopians	3	2	9	8	78
Control Group	1	2	7	10	80

Table 4.3 *Trust*

Can state institutions be trusted? (%)	No 0	1	2	3	4	5	6	7	8	9	Yes 10	Mean (S.D.)
Ethiopians	22	3	3	12	10	19	7	7	7	2	7	4.26 (3.1)
Control Group	8	3	7	8	8	22	11	16	11	3	4	5.06 (2.6)

Racialization of Ethiopians in Israel

The initial enthusiasm that surrounded the arrival of Ethiopians was gradually replaced with more mundane questions and with racialized practices and a growing racial divide that came to the fore, among other things, in police violence. Police violence, however, is embedded in wider institutional racism and public sentiments. In the day after the demonstrations erupted in May 2015, Dany Adeno Abebe, a journalist, who immigrated from Ethiopia with his family to Israel as a child, wrote:

Violence and Racism towards us are not only the problem of police, it is your problem [Israeli Society]. You, the regular Israelis, meet us everywhere: in the army, work, school and the supermarket. Therefore, you must understand that the protest that erupted expresses our frustrations of what happened to us in the past thirty years. You may have felt sorry for us, but you never looked at us as equals ... what do we want? What everyone wants, to be treated as human beings ... we are not transparent blacks, but citizens of the state, just like you (Abebe, 2015).

The protest of 2015 was intense, as discussed below, but not the first time that Ethiopian frustrations erupted. A landmark event in the relationship between Ethiopians and Israeli society and state happened twenty years before. In 1996 a newspaper report revealed that blood donated by Ethiopians is thrown away in fear that it might be contaminated with the HIV virus. The Ministry of Health explained that this was a procedure used for many groups considered of higher risk, to protect the public and the blood was thrown out in secret in order not to stigmatize the donors. The symbolic meaning of discarding the blood, drawing a wedge between Ethiopians and the rest of the nation and implying they are sick and contaminated, regardless of reasons and intentions behind the decision, evoked an emotional response. It was also pent-up anger and frustration over the ongoing discrimination, and the continuous doubt over their Jewishness, that for the first time mobilized Ethiopians in large numbers.

More than 10,000 gathered for a demonstration in front of the Prime Minister's office in Jerusalem, the long demonstration escalated to violence, tear gas was used by the police, and dozens of demonstrators and police officers wounded. The placards carried by the demonstrators were explicit, stating "we are Jews: stop the racist apartheid" (Ben-Eliezer,

2008), but also "our blood is red like yours and we are just as Israelis as you are." It was not only the blood: demonstrators have also mentioned that twenty young Ethiopian army recruits committed suicide in the past two years, incidents of racial discrimination and a broader sense of not feeling accepted. The rejection of blood seems to encapsulate all feelings, as a demonstrator explained:

I did two years in the army to become a citizen of Israel like everybody else. When they tell me that since 1984 they've been spilling the blood, it feels like the army means nothing, that I'll never be part of Israel, because my color is black and my blood is contaminated (Schmemann, 1996).

The police, surprised by the violent reaction, claimed that they were not prepared because they "knew the Ethiopians to be a quiet and retiring community" (Seeman, 1999). Ethiopians, however, did not place the blame on police, regretted the fact that police officers were wounded during the demonstrations and explained this was a result of anger with government policy. At the same time, however, Ethiopians resented the violence police used against them, comparing it to measures used against Palestinians (ibid.), stressing again their rights as citizens. The events of 1996 quickly subsided for most Israelis but were indicative of future developments and dilemmas of Israelis of Ethiopian descent, the demand to belong and the desire to integrate against racialization and marginalization.

Policing: Story of Belonging and Difference

Contrary to the events in 1996, in 2015 police were a major target of the frustrations of Israelis of Ethiopian descent and remained at the center of the debate. In a controversial comment, the Police Commissioner, Roni Alsheikh, stated that "when a police officer encounters an [Ethiopian] suspect it is only natural that he suspects him more than if this one someone else" (Pulwer and Kubowich, 2016). Later, the commissioner tried to explain that in his comment he was addressing a problematic situation, rather than justifying a policy. Regardless of what the commissioner meant, data published by the Ministry of Justice has shown that Ethiopians constitute 3.5 percent of the arrested whom charges were pressed against, twice their share of the population, and 8.5 percent of juveniles in prison, more than four times their share (ibid.).

Demonstrators in the 2015 events chanted "we are all Yosef Salamsa," identifying with a victim of police violence and suggesting they are all potential victims. Police officers, responding to a report of an attempted break-in to a school, arrested 22-year-old Salamsa, a man with no criminal record, who was sitting on a bench nearby with a friend, drinking beer. The officers who shot Salamsa with a taser gun during his arrest claimed he was violent, a claim disproven later by investigative reporters. Salamsa was taken to the police station, left outside, handcuffed, until found by his family who took him to the hospital. Afterwards, he was released and no charges were pressed against him. According to the family, after a complaint was filed against the officers, police began to harass them, by phone and house visits, looking for Yosef. Police claimed that Salamsa did not cooperate, therefore the complaints filed by the family had to be dismissed, and that police came for him because he was needed for investigation. Several days after the police visit to his home, on July 4, 2014, Salamsa's body was found in a nearby quarry and his death was ruled a suicide – a ruling the family rejected.

After Salamsa's death, the case was reexamined by the Unit for Investigating Police Internal Affairs (MAHASH). The investigation revealed that police officers lied when they stated that Salamsa was warned before fired at, that leaving him handcuffed outside the station was a violation of procedures, as were the threats to the family made by officers. Yet, no charges were pressed against any of the officers involved. For his friends and family, the reasons were clear:

Salmsa was black, Ethiopian and therefore a target for police abuse – and they are certain that if a "white" Israeli would suffer a similar fate, his death would not be ignored (Burstein-Hadad, 2014).

Ethiopians' moral alignment with police is high, similar to other Jewish Israelis, but at the same time the incidents exposed racism and racialization that could not be ignored. In the demonstrations, alongside the placards denouncing police and state racism, some of the demonstrators were holding Israeli flags, others, in interviews to the media, stressed their military service and the betrayal of the state they served. Tal Yalo, a reserve army officer who took part in the demonstrations, said:

I served this country for 9 years . . . 3 in active duty and 6 in reserves . . . .in the last war I served for 30 days . . . but I feel this country is no longer for me . . . that this country is neglecting me, is hostile towards me. I receive a different treatment, not in a good way and nothing is done to change it . . . We see this happening also in the US, and I really hope that things here will not be the same . . . someone should do something about violent police officers (Yalo, 2015).

The contradiction between the demand to belong, often by evoking the "republican equation" of sacrifice (Levy, 2008) and denial of the race category ("we are all Jews"), on the one hand, and the constant reminder of racialization in everyday policies and practices, on the other hand, was very clear in our data. In the focus groups, the words "black" and "white" were often used. The power that "white kids" have, different treatment that "white people" receive and the attitudes of "white police officers" were a central part of the conversation. But, against the feeling of being singled out because of their skin color, and vulnerability compared to "whites" of "Israelis," was also high trust in police, what we explain as attempts to fight stigmas and feel that inclusion is also possible. As Table 4.4 demonstrates, differences between Ethiopians and veteran Jewish Israelis are minimal in their trust of police, respect of police officers and moral alignment with police. We try to explain this paradox later, but important differences

Table 4.4 *Trust, Respect and Moral Alignment*

Question/statement (%)	Group	Strongly disagree 1	2	3	Strongly agree 4	5	Mean (S.D.)
I trust police	Ethiopians	19	12	24	15	29	3.23 (1.5)
	Control Group	11	14	34	25	16	3.21 (1.2)
I have respect for the police and police officers	Ethiopians	9	7	14	20	50	3.97 (1.3)
	Control Group	7	8	23	28	35	3.74 (1.2)
Police protects values important to me	Ethiopians	18	16	27	17	22	3.08 (1.4)
	Control Group	13	16	36	20	15	3.09 (1.2)

do come up when particular practices and policies are asked, and in open discussions in focus groups.

Singled Out and Over-Policed

Interactions with government representatives in general, and criminal justice institutions in particular, expose citizens to the political world they live in, and shape individuals' perceptions of their political standing, membership and efficacy (Lerman and Weaver, 2014: 10–12). Encounters with police officers signal to people whether they are regarded as citizens of worth, equal to others and deserving respect. When citizens' concerns are ignored and their security feels compromised, or, when they feel they are targeted by police and regarded as suspects, their citizenship is perceived hollow. In a meeting between young Ethiopians and police officers in a neighborhood where many Ethiopians reside, one of the young people described the encounters with police they experience and their consequences:

Almost everyday police come into this neighborhood. There are kids here that don't need to know what police is and criminals are, for police to stop by and talk to the in patronizing way. It makes you feel that you are worth less than others, that something is wrong with you ... for every little thing they will be pulled into the police car, then marked as criminals, and then believe they are criminals (Blecherman, 2015).

In the focus groups, over-policing was a central theme, especially among young men, the targets of these alleged policies. Participants talked about racial profiling and described feeling insecure, and reluctant to call police.

I feel unsafe to call police because there is a chance they will think I am guilty. When I am near a police officer I feel I am under examination. So instead of feeling safe I feel insecure near a police officer (focus group, Kiryat Gat).

When I was stopped the first time it was like in American movies where every black person is stopped and questioned (ibid.).

They work by profiles they build, based on stereotypes and stigmas. And to justify the profiles they frame that population ... if in regular cases of domestic dispute will end with a warning, when you work with stereotypes it will end in arrest. [You become] another statistical item (ibid.).

The latter comment is of special significance, for many of the participants it was not only that young Ethiopians were stopped and searched, but that the searches end in arrests and criminal records, setting them apart from others. "They charged me with obstructing a police officer ... charges against Ethiopians, 3 out of 5 are about assaulting an officer. This is nonsense" (focus group, Rehovot). Comparisons were often made with non-Ethiopian ("white") Israelis who, they strongly believe, are treated differently. "They will not approach Israelis the same way. They will speak nice to them ... for us, it is 'get out'" (focus group, Lod).

"Over-policing" refers to different practices of profiling and harsh treatment of different groups; these practices include not only stops and searches, but also violence. Some of the violence, when extreme and documented, received public attention, but in the focus groups participants described more obscure events of being abused and humiliated:

They really hit hard ... they abused me ... took me to the car, through me on the floor on top of a friend and they sat with their feet on us, all the way. In the station, they kept hitting me, real hard.
– and then?
I got charged with obstructing police work (focus group, Lod).

Participants were certain that skin color is the determining factor for police harsh treatment and violence, black skin associated by officers with criminality ("there worst nightmare," one stated), that allows them "to take all their aggressions against us" (focus group, Kiryat Gat). Hence, participants in the focus groups, mostly young people, more exposed to profiling and encounters with police, relate their negative experiences to their identity and skin color. Their visibility, combined with discrimination and negative stereotypes, renders them vulnerable to mistreatment and violence.

Vulnerability

Inequality, racial profiling and especially police violence is explained by Ethiopians as a result of their weakness, as a group and as individuals, compared to "white" Israelis. "If a white guy gets a report (or, arrested)," it was heard in the different focus groups, in different versions, "his mother will come to the station and raise hell" (focus group, Lod). The words "weak" and "vulnerable," or in Israeli slang "with no back" were repeated, explaining that officers, when they come to us, they look down on us. They know we have "no back" and they can cover up everything they do. There is no justice (focus group, Kiryat Gat).

The vulnerability is often referred to the parents, immigrants unfamiliar with the language, marginalized and unable to help their children when they are profiled and abused by police officers, or when they face charges and a criminal record likely to negatively impact their future.

Our parents have not been here long enough to understand the rules of the game so they use our weaknesses. They use their power against us … they know who to come at and whom to avoid. That is how the mind of a police officer works (focus group, Lod).

It is very easy for the police to say things about Ethiopian youth, to treat them in a certain way. But I think that if parents will have more courage and be more involved things can change (focus group, Rehovot).

Vulnerability, to the participants, means that they do not raise their voice when mistreated, are not familiar with the legal system and their rights as citizens and defer to police, not pressing charges against abusive officers. This vulnerability, in turn, they believe, brings on more abuse by police, who are able to take advantage of them:

They are used to the fact there are Ethiopians, the scapegoat that can fill the quota of arrests. We don't have the means to fight it. We also lost our trust in the system (focus group, Rehovot).

Stigmas, they explain, combine with vulnerability, so that young Ethiopians are once and again being stopped and arrested in larger numbers than others, simply for being visible and vulnerable. Even when it is about violations like drunk driving, they believe, Ethiopians are treated differently than others.

When there are parties of Ethiopians you see long lines of police cars who patrol the area and stop drivers to check if they are drunk … there is extra law enforcement … we feel the police is out there to get us (focus group, Kiryat Gat).

Domestic violence, some argued, is also treated differently when Ethiopians are involved. In the past, police and welfare services were blamed for not taking measures to prevent severe domestic abuses among Ethiopians. Now, they argue, stigmatization implicates everyone: "the feeling is that all Ethiopian men for them are potential killers" (focus group, Kiryat Gat).

Participants have made the connection between their racialized identity, poverty and vulnerability, again drawing the difference between themselves and "white" Israelis, and a strong sense of relative deprivation:

Sometime they will come here, to a place where young people sit and treat them as if they were criminals. In Tel-Mond, where rich people live, if a police officer will mistreat their sons they will hire a big shot lawyer and put the officer in Jail ... You understand? His father will raise hell. Here? we will accept the beating and shut up ... go back home ... that is how it works ... they [the rich] will hire a lawyer ... In our community the parents will blame their child, he will have a public defendant and in 99.9 percent will be found guilty" (focus group, Netanya).

Being secure is about class. The rich, the educated, who live in their own neighborhoods will get better protection. Every call will be answered, every complaint handled. In weak populations, "problematic" for police, things are different ... I don't feel I can receive service or that even that I should be in contact with police. It is a problem (focus group: Kiryat Gat).

Some of the participants in the focus groups expressed not only distrust of police, but also resignation. Complaints, they felt, would be useless, as would attempts to fight police abuse. The hierarchical nature of Israeli citizenship, and their powerlessness within it, was overwhelming:

In my neighborhood there are police patrols. It makes me anxious, I feel like I am in Harlem, really. Like, what are they looking for? I also hear that they stop and question young children ... they took a 13-year-old to the station because they suspected his mobile phone was stolen ... (focus group, Haifa).

So if I come and complain to internal investigation? These are police officers, officers investigating other officers, how does that sound to you? They are friends and they will protect each other. You will never hear of a complaint that led to a punishment of an officer. It doesn't happen, that's the way things are (focus group, Netanya).

I gave up ... let them do what they want. If they stop me, I don't even talk to them, give them my papers ... nothing ... go ahead, do your job ... what's the point arguing ... enough (focus group, Netanya).

Somewhat surprisingly, however, the majority of Ethiopians in our survey demonstrated confidence in police (Table 4.7), alongside the strong feelings of being over-policed and mistreated. Most Ethiopians, like other Israelis, have not personally suffered police abuse (Table 4.5) or been arrested and stopped by police, the latter more common for young men being victims of profiling. But, among those who were, more Ethiopians report unfair treatment (Table 4.6). Ethiopians believe more than the control group that police arrest and stops citizens for no reason (Table 4.8) but do not fear officers more than others (Table 4.9). Similar contradictions surfaced in the focus groups where some of the participants downplayed racialization or its ramifications. We have attempted to explain this elsewhere, in a joint work with Ofir Abu (Abu et al., 2017) as an attempt to fight stigmatization.

Table 4.5 *Police Abuse*

Have you personally experienced biased treatment by police officers? (%)	No	Yes
Ethiopians	78	22
Control Group	80	20

Table 4.6 *Arrest and Treatment*

In the past three years, were you stopped or detained by police? (%)		No	Yes			
	Ethiopians	79	20			
	Control Group	78	22			
If, yes, did police treat you fairly? (%)		Very unfairly	2	3	4	Very fair
	Ethiopians	38	10	14	14	24
	Control Group	21	13	12	9	45

Table 4.7 *Expected Treatment by Police*

If you would file a complaint of a crime, how would you be treated by the police, compared to others? (%)	Worse 1	2	Same 3	4	Better 5
Ethiopians	27	8	47	13	5
Control Group	5	6	64	16	9

Table 4.8 *Over-Policing*

Police stop or arrest people in your neighborhood for no reason (%)	Strongly disagree 1		2	3	4	strongly agree 5	Mean (S.D.)
Ethiopians	22		13	24	21	20	3.04 (1.4)
Control Group	38		26	19	9	8	2.23 (1.3)

Table 4.9 *Fear of Police Officers*

I fear police officers (%)	Strongly Agree 1		2	3	4	Strongly Disagree 5	Mean (S.D.)
Ethiopians	67		11	9	8	11	1.96 (1.4)
Control Group	56		18	12	9	6	1.90 (1.2)

De-Stigmatization and Citizenship

For many Ethiopians the strong desire for inclusion in Israeli society, namely participation and recognition as equal members of nation and state (Mizrachi and Zawdu, 2012), creates a moral alignment with the state, and even with police, despite discrimination. To be able to do so, they employ different de-stigmatization strategies (Lamont, 2009), which include efforts to assimilate to the dominant group, individual efforts to distance oneself from the negative characteristics associated with their group, attempt to demonstrate that negative views of their group are baseless, emphasize shared religious and/or national affiliation and adherence to state or national ideologies as a way to express identification and belonging (Lamont, 2009: 159; Lamont and Mizrachi, 2012: 369). As our survey data demonstrates, Ethiopians' trust in police does not differ from other Jewish Israelis (Table 4.4). Expressing trust in and positive attitudes towards government and state institutions is another way to demonstrate inclusion (Maxwell, 2010). Those who downplay or minimize racialization respond to their stigmatization by the police not only as a way to claim membership within the dominant group, "participatory de-stigmatization strategies" (Mizrachi and Herzog, 2012), but also as a way to maintain trust in the state and its institutions essential for integration.

One attempt to downplay stigmatization was to describe the events as isolated, and the result not of institutional racism, but rather of specific officers and incidents. Police, according to this logic, can be trusted and respected because "acts of racism" are not representative of police conduct but an aberration. Separating the incidences of violence and the undeniable existence of racism among officers from police as a representative institution of the state, allows them to express general trust in police:

There are racist officers, there are officers that like Ethiopians, officers that hate Russians ... officers that hate Arabs, officers that like them. It is human beings. Eventually, they use the power they have, the uniform, it can happen everywhere (focus group, Lod).

Police officers should not hit people. Some officers just come angry to work, someone utters a word, and he will hit without thinking. Smart officers will not do that. So, there are all kinds of officers and, by and large, they don't use violence with no reason ... (focus group, Haifa).

In a similar vein, the mistreatment of Ethiopians was explained by some of the interviewees as the result of the stressful nature of policing and the fact that officers are overburdened with work, alluding to security threats, shared by everyone, that necessarily overshadow concerns of fairness. The important role police perform and the security they provide, and empathy to the difficult tasks police officers face, explains the need for all citizens to cooperate when asked to do so. This is also reflected in the survey data, showing that Ethiopians are similar to other Jewish Israelis in their general evaluation of police work (Table 4.10), evaluation of police judgment (Table 4.11) and the security police provides (Table 4.12). Again, the attempt to identify with police and the work they do signifies moral alignment based on shared citizenship and common concerns:

They treat people differently, but they maintain order ... I feel safe to be out at night, so do my brothers and my sisters, even late at night. Security is fine (focus group, Haifa).

"Many of the officers are worn out, simply worn out, you have no idea how much. And it affects their work ... with all the pressure placed upon them by the system ... citizens eventually pay the price (focus group, Haifa).

When police see a real threat they come to help. I don't think they are not doing their job. Maybe they don't always have enough people (focus group, Hadera).

What can I do, I will give him my ID card [when asked] ... you don't know why he is doing this, maybe there is some information he received ... there is no way to know (focus group, Haifa).

For some, the blame for the tense relations was equally shared between police officers and Ethiopians, especially young people, the latter's behavior often causing friction and suspicion. Citizenship, in this account, is also about responsibility and respect to the state and its institutions. Accordingly, if young people would behave properly, fair and respectable treatment could be expected:

If a person speaks politely, does not take this to be about racism and answers the questions he is asked, friction can be avoided ... the potential for high risk encounters are not always there ... it is about a dialogue (focus group, Kiryat Gat).

We contribute to our negative image. If a police officers arrive we are not always nice, sometimes we talk back ... it is a culture we were exposed to here in Israel and we want to be part of this stupid culture (focus group, Kiryat Gat).

It is important we respect them because at the end of the day they serve us and represent us. So if we treat them with disrespect, and there is a lot of disrespect, maybe sometimes justified ... but if we treat them like this it turns back on us (focus group, Haifa).

Finally, there were those who saw the tensions between Ethiopians and police as a temporary situation, a result of the late arrival of Ethiopians to Israeli society and a "natural" suspicion stemming from a cultural gap or distance, soon to be closed. Successful integration and acculturation, they reasoned, will eventually diminish mistreatment by police and other institutions and would hopefully turn them into full citizens, both formally and informally:

I think the Whites treat us this way because they don't know us. We are the latest immigration and we came from a place that is not that great. They see you are black and treat you accordingly. If they would have known where we come from and what we are about, they would treat us differently (focus group, Lod).

Table 4.10 *Evaluation of Police*

[Considering all the tasks police are expected to fulfil], what is your evaluation of the quality of services police provide to citizens? (%)	Very bad 1	2	3	4	Very good 5	Mean (S.D.)
Ethiopians	13	16	39	16	16	3.07 (1.2)
Control Group	11	21	47	16	5	2.84 (0.99)

Table 4.11 *Judgment*

Police officers use good judgment and make fair decisions (%)	Strongly disagree 1	2	3	4	Strongly agree 5
Ethiopians	18	15	34	21	12
Control Group	10	16	37	29	8

Table 4.12 *Security*

Police provide security for me (%)	Strongly disagree 1	2	3	4	Strongly agree 5	Mean (S.D.)
Ethiopians	22	18	21	24	15	2.90 (1.4)
Control Group	15	22	32	21	10	2.88 (1.2)

The different de-stigmatization strategies are used to narrow the gap between, on the one hand, formal equality and strong desires among Ethiopians for inclusion and, on the other hand, practices and policies of racialization that keep them apart from Israeli/Jewish society. Ethiopians embrace the integrative aspects of the dominant Zionist ideology while struggling to negate, or downplay, its (intra-Jewish) discriminatory elements. These strategies allow many Ethiopian Jews in Israel to downplay the importance and depth of the discrimination they suffer from the police. By doing so, they are able to claim a legitimate and equal status within the mainstream society as well as to maintain trust in the police (Abu et al., 2017). However, discussed below, these focus groups were conducted prior to the outbursts of anger in the summer of 2015.

Sensitivity and Representation

The demonstrations in the summer of 2015 forced police, government and society at large to confront the grim reality of Ethiopians in Israel. The disparity between the formal equality and embracing of Ethiopian immigration and the mounting evidence of racism, discrimination and police violence, could not be ignored. Police, under directions of the government and with representatives of the Ethiopian community, began to search for reforms that would enhance trust and improve their tarnished image. Unlike Arab citizens whose securitization could in the public eye justify harsh treatment, Ethiopians were part of the Jewish collective and within the realm of republican citizenship. The major reforms, however, recruitment of Ethiopians to the police and cultural training for police officers to enable them to better serve the community, suggested by a committee (Israel Police, 2015) formed after the events, were received with suspicion. Recruitment (representation) and cultural training are common practices for police forces in diverse societies across the world and were also raised in the focus groups, with different reactions.

Ethiopians do not share with Arab citizens the ambivalence towards serving in the police, their moral alignment with the state and its institutions being far less problematic. Ethiopians serve in the military and this contribution, they believe, should shield them from discrimination and stigmatization. Being part of the Jewish national collective and able to contribute to the public good provides a potential resource to claim citizenship and makes moral alignment possible and service in the police largely viewed positively. In practice, Ethiopians are well represented in the police force, 663 officers and 2.3 percent of the force, and the police announced, that as part of the reforms, they intend to recruit more Ethiopians and make sure they will have opportunities for promotion. In the focus groups, while there was no strong opposition to more representation, including in higher ranks, some were skeptical it would make a difference. Similar to Arab citizens they were concerned that Ethiopian recruits will adopt police organizational culture, or that they will be unable to make change. These critical voices echo those heard among Arabs:

Ethiopian officer, if he is on patrol and he sees a group of Ethiopians he does not want to be nice to them. Maybe he wants, but he can't (focus group, Lod).
   Bringing Ethiopian officers to the communities will only make things worst. They need to make sure Ethiopians will advance to higher ranks, break the class ceiling, and be in positions where they can make change and explain the profiles are wrong (focus group, Kiryat Gat).

Culture, or the "mental gaps," according to the committee's report was to be addressed by cultural training to officers, giving them the tools to work with the community. But, for some of the participants the problem was not the Ethiopian culture, but rather police's stigmas towards them and the organizational culture that employs racial profiling:

They approach a person by his skin color, they don't treat people equally. I was stopped in the middle of the street for a body search. But. I don't know, they need to protect the public, search people. But every time I see a police officer . . . it is annoying (focus group, Rehovoth).

In the discussions of the committee formed by the Ministry of Justice (2016), where one of the authors was a participant, the use of the term "culture" evoked negative reactions. The Ethiopian participants, many born in Israel, described themselves and demanded that others would see them as Israelis and denounced any significant cultural differences. The problem, they stressed, was racism in Israeli society and police that needs to be addressed, not an imaginary cultural gap. In the survey, Ethiopians tended to agree more than the control groups that proper training is required for officers to understand the problems of their community (Table 4.14). Conversely, in the focus groups, the idea of cultural training of police officers raised concerns that stigmas will be reenforced rather than eradicated, treating Ethiopians as different rather than equals:

There is no need for special training, are we different? They need no training for treating us as equals (focus group, Rehovot).
   They need to rid themselves of all the stigmas they carry (focus group, Kiryat Gat).

I don't want to be treated specially. If I deserve punishment, I should be punished. If I didn't do anything, stay away from me. Don't stop people just because their skin color (focus group, Kiryat Gat).

Reluctance and skepticism towards cultural training and a general acceptance of recruitment and representation are indicative of Ethiopians' perception of citizenship, demands for full inclusion based on Jewish ethnicity, rejection of institutional racism and demonstration of republican contribution. Ethiopians' struggle to be recognized as part of the Jewish collective, and to fend off racialization policies that set them apart, regardless of their intentions, had to reject stigmatizations by different means. The survey data show, again, that Ethiopians' general views of police are similar to that of other Jewish Israelis. Support for recruitment is high, as is the perception that representation is important, both symbolically and practically. Ethiopians believe that recruitment of Ethiopian officers will be of value, but there is no strong support for being policed by Ethiopian officers (Table 4.13), demonstrating, again, a perception of inclusive citizenship. Ethiopians, like other Israeli citizens, while critical of police, see no problem serving in police, and in fact, many of them do.

Oversight

In spite of the reports and documented evidence of police abuse, the demand for oversight of police by Ethiopians does not differ much than that of other Jewish Israelis (Table 4.15). While Ethiopians agree more with the statement that police must be fair and courteous, even at the expense of deterrence, at the same time they support impunity for police officers and that fighting crime and providing order should be a priority, even if it involves hurting innocent people. Here again, Ethiopians demonstrate a desire to be fully included and adopt the general views of society towards police. Like other (Jewish) citizens, concerns of security override other questions, including that of police abuse directed at them. As mentioned several times here, different voices were heard in the focus groups, from younger people, possibly more conscious of racism and discrimination and probably more exposed to it than others. If this was a minority position when the

Table 4.13 *Representation and Recruitment*

Question/statement (%)	Strongly disagree 1	2	3	4	Strongly agree 5	Mean (S.D.)
It is important that police be representative of all groups in Israeli society?						
Ethiopians	9	1	4	9	76	4.43 (1.2)
Control Group	7	5	8	16	64	4.26 (1.2)
How would recruitment of police officers from your community affect the relations between the community and police?						
Ethiopians	7	3	19	19	2	4.07 (1.2)

Would you prefer police in your neighborhood to be:	Ethiopian	Mixed	Not from my group	Not important, professional		
Ethiopian only	0	24	2	80	NR	NR

would you consider becoming a police officer? [For a salary meeting your expectations]	No		Maybe		Yes	
Ethiopians	38	7	8	18	29	2.92 (1.7)
Control Group	38	6	15	18	23	2.81 (1.6)
If a friend or a family member decides to join the police, would you support him/her?						
Ethiopians	10	4	12	16	53	4.09 (1.3)
Control Group	8	8	18	22	44	3.86 (1.3)

Table 4.14 *Training*

Police officers lack proper training to understand real problems in my neighborhood (%)	Strongly disagree 1	2	3	4	Strongly agree 5	Mean (S.D.)
Ethiopians	18	8	22	22	30	3.39 (1.4)
Control Group	22	16	24	18	20	2.97 (1.4)

research took place, the events of 2015 brought those perceptions to the fore.

New Modes of Citizenship

In an ethnographic study of police in a Parisian precinct of working-class ethnic minorities, Didier Fassin describes the dynamics of police violence:

In general, physical violence, when it occurs, takes the form of beating during questioning, interrogation or custody. While bodies and certainly minds retain the traces of violence, the administrative and judicial record is much more forgetful. People who fall victim to it often hesitate to file a complaint. When they do so, the police are generally slow to record their grievances. But even when both conditions are met, investigation is rare, and sanctions exceptional" (Fassin, 2013: 115).

The demonstrations in the summer of 2015 were an outburst of pent-up anger, especially by young Ethiopian people, their minds and bodies retaining the traces of violence Fassin describes. The demonstrations also brought to the fore accusations of institutional racism, translated into acts of citizenship and demands for change. Leading the demonstrations were young people, most of them born in Israel or who arrived at a young age, educated and articulated. No longer willing to explain away incidents of racism as nonrepresentative or temporal, they spoke about institutional racism that pervaded the police, state institutions and society at large. These voices were heard in the focus groups, quoted above, from people who talked about a power equation in which they,

Table 4.15 *Police Oversight*

Question/statement (%)	Group	Strongly disagree 1	2	3	Strongly agree 4	5	Mean (S.D.)
Police must treat citizens with fairness and dignity, even at the expense of deterrence	Ethiopians	6	4	10	19	61	4.25 (1.2)
	Control Group	5	7	15	20	53	4.08 (1.2)
[Police work is difficult and important] Officers should not be charged for their actions	Ethiopians	35	9	14	15	27	2.90 (1.7)
	Control Group	48	17	14	9	12	2.21 (1.4)
Police should prioritize public order and fighting crime even if innocent people are hurt sometimes	Ethiopians	28	9	26	17	21	2.93 (1.5)
	Control Group	26	18	26	16	15	2.76 (1.4)
Strong oversight of police is necessary	Ethiopians	6	4	13	25	52	4.14 (1.1)
	Control Group	3	5	17	27	48	4.12 (1.1)

disempowered, suffered from police abuse that will end only when the equation would change, repeated themselves in the demonstrations:

Change can be created once we will be conscious. If they know that we will stand up for our rights ... change the equation and make clear to the other side that if you wronged us, you will pay (focus group, Kiryat Gat).

Until we will have a society and a leadership committed to reform, nothing will change. The demonstrations could be expected and it will not end here, there is too much anger, poverty and destitution. Every person here could tell you about discrimination, racism or violence, whether he is an academic or a jobless person (Yanovsky, 2015).

It was not incidental that the trigger for the demonstrations was the beating of a soldier in uniform, shattering for many the illusion that acceptance, based on military service, is around the corner:

The military uniform were supposedly the best shield from every police officer, from every racist. But then, something happened, the shocking video of a uniformed soldier beaten by a police officer. It was not only a turning point, but also a realization. The uniform that Ethiopians took pride in were no longer relevant. Even there, where black young people feel Israeli, they suddenly understood, that even dying for your country is no longer enough (Beshach, 2015).

The demonstrators many times held, or wrapped themselves with, Israeli flags and, when interviewed, emphasized their military service and the breached republican equation, their contribution not shielding them from exclusion and racism, also in the military itself. Demonstrators described themselves as a new generation set to change the rules of the game:

Our parents were silenced. We are a different generation we will not be silenced. There is no point in a quiet demonstration, only violence will help. Without violence our situation will stay the same as it was for thirty years (Seidler and Kubowich, 2015).

People think that Ethiopians are those nice people you can simply step over. We came to tell them it is over. My dream was to be a combat soldier, but talking with friends who completed their service, I am no longer certain this is the right thing to do (Yanovsky, 2015).

The anger turned into violence, police and demonstrators blaming each other for aggression, and arrests of demonstrators. The young people who took to the streets did not hesitate to use the word "racism" and rejected attempts to placate them with statements of empathy and promises for committees. They shared their experiences of racial profiling, police violence and discrimination. Explicit demands were made to stop police abuse and bring to trial officers accused of violence. Stories hitherto hidden or marginalized were now headlines and the media exposed various discriminatory practices, as well as data on the high poverty rates and unemployment among Ethiopians. What previously could be excused as isolated and non-representative incidents, now appeared as wider and systemic, and not only within police.

A committee formed by the government, in response to the demonstrations, has used explicitly the term, named "the Committee for Eradication of Racism against Ethiopian Jews." Ethiopians who took part in the committee submitted a document (in the name of the "the joint forum for fighting racism") that explained the sources of distrust in police. The document was explicit in its description of constant police violence, racial profiling, provocations of young Ethiopians that end in unnecessary arrests and charges pressed, and concluded:

This can no longer go on and there is a real and immediate need for drastic changes, changes that would protect normative and law-abiding citizens that the state, by way of its police officers, abuses them only because they are black (Ministry of Justice, 2016: 23).

The influence of the document, and the participants in the committee presenting it, can be seen in the opening words of the committee's report:

For years, Israelis of Ethiopian descent experience discrimination from authorities and Israeli society, exclusion from the public sphere, discrimination in education and employment, stigmas and negative stereotypes – explicit and implicit – and even exposed to verbal and physical violence (Ministry of Justice, 2016: 15).

The report engaged with different aspects of racism and discrimination in different arenas and institutions and submitted fifty-three recommendations for change, fifteen of them directly related to police and policing. The implementation and impact of the report are yet to be examined but the committee and the report, first, provided an official stamp that institutional racism exists, in police and beyond. And, second, possibly reflects a change that occurred during the writing of this work, a rise of a new generation of Israelis of Ethiopian descent with explicit concrete demands for equal and inclusive ethno-republican citizenship.

Conclusions

Ethnicity is part of a stratified citizenship regime, presenting a dilemma for both the state and the ethnic minority. For the state, while ethnic minorities may be different, they are formally part of the collective and discrimination is difficult to justify. For the ethnic minority, when discrimination exists despite formal equality and desire to be part of the collective is strong, the question of how to achieve real equality presents different dilemmas. Everyday encounters with police are part of these dilemmas when police, first, represent state authority, second, provide security to the collective, but, third, also demonstrate discrimination explicit and violent, or more subtle and deniable. Thus, harassment, profiling and violence, when experienced individually, can be explained as coincidental, local and temporal. These mechanisms allow ethnic minorities to maintain allegiance to the state and hope that eventually and gradually equality will be achieved. Allegiances and hopes, however, may be disrupted when discrimination and vulnerability are explicit and appear entrenched.

Being formally part of the Jewish collective allows Ethiopians to demand their rights as citizens – a demand that rests, among other things, on the republican equation of contribution and rights. In the survey, Ethiopians displayed perceptions and attitudes largely similar to other Israelis, demonstrating a surprising trust in police, in light of the reports of police abuse and violence. In the focus groups, however, different voices were heard, many from young people with fresh memories of violence and humiliation violence and humiliation they or others close to them experienced. Institutional racism, in police and society, and the visibility and vulnerability of Ethiopians, often poor and marginalized, exposes them to profiling, abuse and violence. Efforts to compartmentalize discrimination and violence may be part of a (temporarily) successful de-stigmatization strategy, but their effects linger and accumulate.

In January 2019, a police officer shot and killed Yehuda Biadga, a 24-year-old man who suffered mental illness. His family called the police in fear that Biadga, who was holding a knife, would hurt someone. For thousands of Ethiopians, who took again to the streets chanting "Justice for Yehuda," his tragic death was further evidence of police racism, and that nothing has changed.

This incident frustrates the Ethiopian community especially in light of recent efforts made by local authorities to change the attitudes towards the community and fight discrimination and racism. But as it turns out, racism, discrimination, and trigger-happy hands are still at large, and the Ethiopian community has to pay the price—in blood ... Policemen should treat people with dark skin and frizzy hair as equal citizens. If up until now they were treated as immediate suspects, what happened on Friday was a step up: now you're allowed to shoot them dead, without warning. Someone has to stand up and say something. To claim that the matter is being examined by the Police Internal Investigations Department is just throwing dust in our eyes (Abebe, 2019).

The continued targeting of Ethiopians as suspects for no other reason than their skin color, police violence being the tip of an iceberg, conveys a message about citizenship, sets them apart from other citizens and has wider and negative social repercussions. The demonstrations in the summer of 2015, after the documented beating of Damas Pikada and the death of Yosef Salamsa, brought to the fore hitherto denied stories of violence and discrimination. Similar stories surfaced again in the demonstrations of 2019, following the killing of Yehuda Biadga. The demonstrators were frustrated with deep-rooted discrimination, but resolved to fight for equal citizenship. The many Israeli flags, alongside the placards denouncing police racism, signal the desired path for citizenship, but cannot hide disappointment, uncertainty and skepticism.

5 | The Religious Factor: Ultra-Orthodox Jews (Haredim)

Ultra-Orthodox Jews (Haredim) took to the streets in May 1949, after the owner of a movie theater in Jerusalem refused to yield to demands to close on Sabbath. The stormy demonstration on May 25, 1949, was broken up violently by the police, thereby arousing an additional storm of protest by the Haredi public and a government nominated committee of inquiry was set up to investigate the events (Friedman, 1994). The struggle in Jerusalem was unique, as the Haredim were insistent to defend the Sabbath and secular groups, including some from outside the city, organized to thwart Haredi intentions. These battles in Jerusalem between the religious and secular continued, with different reasons and intensities, and with police called in to bring order. In one of the fiercest demonstrations in 1956, Pinchas Segalov, a Haredi protester, was killed; his image became a symbol of the struggle to keep the Sabbath among the Haredi circles, and especially in the Haredi community (Cohen, 1997), and of the tensions between Haredim and the police.

Ultra-Orthodox Jews, or Haredim (meaning "the fearful"), have an ambivalent relation to the Israeli state they perceive as more "secular" than "Jewish," combining hostility, indifference and pragmatism. Since early statehood, Haredim took to the streets to protest alleged infringements of the state on their autonomy and to protect their neighborhoods from secular intrusions. Demonstrations to prevent cars driving near the neighborhoods or theaters opening on Sabbath, archaeological excavations, or military drafting of ultra-Orthodox men, are part of Israel's political landscape with periodic heightened tensions and (mostly limited) violence. For Haredi citizens, often living in separate neighborhoods within a close-knit community, the most important encounter with police is in demonstrations, that at times turn violent.

The fact that Haredim choose isolation from secular society, question the legitimacy of the state and its laws, when those do not conform with religious rules, and with police being the enforcer of laws, their relation to police is expected to range between suspicion and disdain. But, while

143

suspicion and disdain are far from absent, Haredim develop a more complex and nuanced relation with the state and its institutions, and new perceptions of citizenship. Like other fundamentalist groups, the boundaries between Haredim and the rest of society, internal communal dynamics and relation with the state, have all affected their perceptions of state and society, and with it of police and policing, with changes we discuss later.

Religion and the Enclave Society

Religion continues to play an important part in contemporary politics across the world, despite and alongside secularization (Ben-Porat, 2013). The modern state, a secular entity, has taken over many of the authorities and duties previously held by the church, turning religion into a private matter and religious institutions subordinate to state power. The formally secular nature of democracies meant that their modern bureaucracies manage "national systems of education, social control and social welfare that paid little attention to religious affiliation and claimed little by way of divine approval" (Bruce, 2003: 1). But, in many cases, religious organizations and institutions still hold political power and authority and enjoy and wide support. Consequently, the clash between secular forces and religious fundamentalism is regarded central to contemporary politics (Haynes, 2006), raising the specter of a "culture war" (Hunter, 1991: 42–44). The growing gap between secularizing and liberalizing societies and religious individuals and communities underscores different conflicts over (often indistinguishable) private and public matters. These conflicts range from debates over abortions and gay marriage, to questions of dress code and displays of "immodesty" in the public sphere.

Fundamentalist movements, across the world, seek to protect and deepen religious identity and authority, compete with other religions and secular institutions. In these processes, they equate "strong religion" with "purity" and purity with uniformity of belief and practice (Almond et al., 2003: 17). These movements struggle to reinforce internal taboo systems in order to tighten prohibitions that pertain to modesty and morality. Fundamentalists selectively retrieve and amalgamate doctrines, symbols and belief from sacred texts they hold to be of divine origin. While these groups oppose modernity, especially its liberal freedoms, they are the product of the modern era (Stadler, 2012: 20). Scholars who study fundamentalism adopt Douglas' concept of group/grid theory to describe an "enclave," setting boundaries to protect the community. Fundamentalists, who perceive public life to be contaminated by immorality, can use political power to curb liberalism, employ violent means justified by religious interpretation, withdraw from society in order to protect their values and ways of life, or combine different strategies.

Lacking formal authority or at times resources to prevent desertion the most important control the community holds over its members is moral persuasion. The value of each member is highlighted, distinctions between members are minimized and a "wall of virtue" separates the morally superior enclave from the outside world – "there is no mistaking the leitmotif: the outside is polluted, contagious, dangerous" (ibid.: 36).

Enclaves react to modernization and the threats the modern state posits in the making of citizens and citizenship by creating clearly demarcated cultural and moral boundaries. These boundaries, however, are not easy to maintain for several reasons. First, and elaborated below, changes within enclave groups weaken the boundaries previously erected. Second, state laws like those regarding women equality and mandatory education for children can limit religious communities' practices. Third, enclave groups may be unsatisfied by hiding behind walls but also wish to impose their behavioral norms on the rest of society. The contact with state and society, whether chosen or imposed, has the potential for direct conflict that involves disobedience. Decisions not to obey laws or to challenge public order, perceived immoral, will posit the group against the state and directly against police, in charge of law enforcement and public order. And, fourth, the ability of enclave groups to police themselves, based on group solidarity, is often exaggerated. The need for external authority and enforcement, together with incentives for integration, can replace hostility with more pragmatic attitudes towards society, state and its institutions. Perceptions of and expectations from police, and the dilemmas within enclave groups, therefore, may reflect wider questions of citizenship and belonging.

Haredim in Israel

The Hebrew term *Haredim*, meaning "those who fear or tremble," or "one who fears god, truly and completely" (Friedman, 1995: 132, cited in Stadler, 2009: 4), implies devotion and piety (Stadler, 2009: 4). Haredim include several groups that share several important attributes: strict adherence to rules of Halacha (Jewish law), commitment to learning and education, a distinguished uniform look (men dressed in black garments and women fully covered), living with confined geography, the maintenance of social boundaries and an anti-Zionist worldview (Ben-Yehuda, 2010: 17). This Orthodox religious movement emerged in the eighteenth century in response to modernization and its impact on Jewish people, advocating the full and unconditional observance of Jewish religious law. Contemporary Haredim see themselves successors of the East European Jewish tradition of meticulous observation of Halacha, and regard the state of Israel, for not abiding religious laws, foreign, alien and largely illegitimate.

At the end of the nineteenth century, when Zionism and the idea of Jewish statehood was gaining popularity and sympathy among Jews, Haredim remained strongly opposed to Zionism, they saw as a sacrilegious. After statehood, Haredim remained in opposition, labeling Zionism a form of idolatry, but found ways to accommodate and center their efforts on rebuilding the world of Torah (religious studies), destroyed in the holocaust, in the land of Israel (Brown, 2000). Politically, this involved ensuring the autonomy of their educational system, exemption from military service for religious studies and financial support that would allow them to maintain their religious institutions. The more extreme elements among Haredim adopted a clear anti-Zionist stance and refused any cooperation with the state.

Haredim disdained the Zionist idea of the "new Jewish man," being industrious, self-sufficient and able to defend itself, and were not part of the securitized and militarized culture developed in Israel. The diasporic Jew, that the Zionist movement was set to transform, remained the ideal for Haredim, the study of Torah regarded as the ultimate vocation. Against Zionism that strived to uproot the diasporic patterns of Jewish life, advocating a masculine and self-sufficient identity, reconnecting to history, the body and the earthly world, Haredim consider themselves guardians of authentic Judaism (Hakak, 2016: 4). This involves, on the one hand, a distance from Israeli society and rejection of the Republican Equation, but, on the other hand, demand for a mandate over spiritual matters. Consequently, Haredim did not take part in nation and state building missions, excluding themselves from the Jewish collective. Most notably, they were exempted from military service, a mandatory duty and a measurement of republican citizenship. In spite of their opposition to Zionism, Haredim were able to establish themselves and thrive in the new society and state. The Zionist movement, and later the state, seeking compromises with

Jewish religious factions, not only allowed Haredim autonomy but also a stake in the management of public affairs and jurisdiction over issues such as marriage and divorce (Ben-Porat, 2013).

Thus, while Haredim were critical of the Jewish state, not conforming to religious laws, they were able not only to protect their society (Brown, 2000) but also to gain political influence. Haredim, it is important to stress, are part the Jewish collective, able to negotiate their citizenship with the state and society. Their presence and participation, "symbolizing the ethno-national principle of Jewish historical continuity," allows them to shift between pragmatic accommodation and principled rejectionism (Shafir and Peled, 2002: 140). Officially and publicly renouncing Zionism, Haredim developed a complex relationship with the state – rejecting and resisting, but at the same time, depending on the protection and material support of the state, "anti-Zionist in their religious outlook but loyalist to the Jewish state" (Barzilai, 2003: 221). The enclave created, based on piety and differentiation, separating the "purity" of the community from the "polluted" outside, enabled Haredi leadership to control the communal boundaries and regulate members' relations with the state, politics and civil society (Almond et al., 2003: 17; Stadler, 2009: 2).

The ambivalent and often tense relation of Haredim with Israeli state and society at times erupted to demonstrations and violence. The obedience of Haredim remains contingent on the assumption that state law does not contradict Halachic law, for them a major normative source for obedience (Barzilai, 2003: 214). Violence has been used "externally," against state organs and officials to prevent interference in communal affairs. But also "internally" as a disciplinary communal mechanism, consolidating communal solidarity and aiming to prevent the intrusion of liberal and secular values (Barzilai, 2003: 277). The autonomy of a non-liberal community, like elsewhere (Kymlicka, 1995), raised controversies regarding state intervention, on behalf of community members harmed by the community or the need to enforce liberal standards of equality. Social order in some Haredi neighborhoods was enforced not only by the state police, regarded by many as illegitimate, but also by the "modesty guards." This unarmed militia was authorized by the community religious leadership to enforce upon the community, including by violence, Haredi strict rules of modesty and prevent immodest dresses or forbidden engagements between men and women (Ben-Yehuda, 2010: 93).

Violence erupted when Haredi communities were determined to defend issues perceived to be of vital importance. In Jerusalem, Haredi groups waged violent battles to prevent driving near their neighborhoods on Sabbath, against the opening of a public swimming pool and a community center, declaring the rule of the state does not apply in such matters (Sprinzak, 1999: 91). Battles were also waged against cinemas operating on the Sabbath, sex shops, archaeological excavations where human skeletal remains suspected as Jewish were found, and against "immodest" advertisements. In 1986, in an orchestrated campaign, 142 bus stops were raided, 48 burned to the ground (Sprinzak, 1999: 97). The majority of casualties in these riots were Haredim, not police officers or secular Israelis. Haredi violence, in spite of the surrounding rhetoric, was limited and caused no deaths and only a small number of serious injuries, in long years of actions and protests (Sprinzak, 1999: 103). Nevertheless, the public disorder the demonstrations caused, secular disdain to what was perceived as an attempt to coerce them to accept Haredi demands and the fact that Haredim held political power when they were refusing to take part in military service have deepened the schism between the Haredim and the rest of society.

Enclave societies' boundaries are threatened from the outside and contested from within, changing their members' relation to state and society, as well as their perceptions of citizenship. The fear from the Zionist state and the disdain from Zionism was replaced gradually with pragmatic accommodation and political involvement. Haredi politics, and the compromises made, attempted to balance the promotion and protection of interests, while keeping the required distance and boundaries from state and society. Since the 1990s boundaries gradually blurred, and new dilemmas have risen. Growing poverty among Haredim forced or tempted them into the labor market and, consequently, to interact with secular society. These ongoing changes influenced the community "expanding its boundaries, and strengthening alternative models of masculinity, such as the breadwinner and the entrepreneur" (Hakak, 2016: 202). The participation in the labor market meant also a growing participation in consumer society, changing lifestyles and growing use of modern technology (Stadler, 2009: 50). Employment, consumption and leisure, began to undermine enclave boundaries and challenge Haredi leadership.

More importantly, the relation of Haredim to the state and its institutions became more ambivalent, old disdain mixed with new national attachments, expressed "in the massive support for the Israeli forces' action in the occupied territories and the recent vast Haredi enrollment in various defense and aid organizations ..." (Stadler, 2009: 115). For some young

Haredim, it was expressed in a desire to join the military (ibid.), previously considered part of the contaminated outside to be avoided. While the rejection of military service remained strong, a new heroic masculinity developed among Haredim, bringing them closer to Israeli society and to its republican concept of citizenship. While military service remained controversial, volunteering to different organizations associated with security was a more acceptable alternative. For example, ZAKA, a team that identifies the bodies of victims after multiple casualty disasters like terrorist attacks, and if necessary assembles their remains for proper Jewish burial. Taking part in the national struggle and working alongside state institutions like the military and the police has earned new respect for Haredim from Israelis that previously resented their avoidance from military service.

Haredim began to embrace different elements of Israeli society and "ratcheted down the tensions with state and civil society" (Stadler, 2012: 40). The new Haredi discourse combined the religious ideals such as "contribution" and "sacrifice" within the Israeli republican citizenship discourse (Stadler et al., 2011: 139), changing perceptions of citizenship and belonging. Accordingly, surveys demonstrate that the majority of Haredim, of different groups, declare they are proud to be Israeli: 64 percent of Haredim (compared to 86 percent of non-Haredim) declare they feel part of the Israeli state. Yet, Haredim place Jewish identity before Israeli identity and believe that the democratic component is too strong in comparison to the Jewish component in Israel. The strength of the Jewish identity among Haredim might also explain why they are more hawkish on foreign policy matters and less empathic to the discrimination of Arab citizens and more supportive of their exclusion than non-Haredim (Hermann et al., 2016). Haredim, as Shafir and Peled (2002) argue, adopted an ethno-national discourse of citizenship, rejecting both the all-encompassing liberal discourse and the contribution-demanding republican discourse. More recent developments, described above, may suggest they have found alternative paths to republicanism.

Haredi perceptions of state and society has changed and diverged, but remain different from other Israeli Jews. First, they show significantly less trust in institutions like the military, presidency and especially the Supreme Court (Hermann et al., 2016). Second, in spite of belonging to the Jewish collective, they maintain their separation from mainstream Israeli society. And, third, not only have some more extreme elements maintained their distance from the state and remained separated within their communities, divisive issues, like attempts to enforce the military draft upon Haredim, still ignite Haredi disobedience, social disorder and, at times, violence.

Haredim and the State

Our survey findings (Tables 5.1 and 5.2) are in line with the descriptions above. The majority of Haredim feel part of the state (58 percent), but the number is significantly lower than the control group (88 percent), so while the boundaries between Haredim and Israeli society are blurring, gaps remain. The number of Haredim that state they are proud to be Israeli is relatively small, just a little more than half of the control group (43 and 80 percent respectively). The need to be involved in politics and lately in the labor market increases Haredi interaction with others and familiarity with state and societal challenges, but they remain committed first and foremost to their communities and suspicious of state institutions. Consequently, their trust in the state and its institutions is lower than that of the control group (22 compared to 45 percent).

Haredim against Police

Clashes between Haredim and the police were often led by the more extreme elements who do not circumscribe to the changes described.

Table 5.1 *Identification*

Question/statement (%)	Strongly disagree 1	2	3	4	Strongly agree 5	Mean (S.D.)
I feel I belong to this country						
Ultra-Orthodox	10	11	21	18	40	3.67 (1.4)
Control Group	3	1	8	18	70	4.52 (0.9)
I am proud to be an Israeli citizen						
Ultra-Orthodox	20	10	19	9	43	3.48 (1.6)
Control Group	1	2	7	10	80	4.64 (0.8)

Table 5.2 *Trust in State Institutions*

Can state institutions be trusted? (%)	No 0	1	2	3	4	5	6	7	8	9	Yes 10	Mean (S.D.)
Ultra-Orthodox	18	5	7	10	6	25	9	9	7	3	3	4.17 (2.8)
Control Group	8	3	7	8	8	22	11	16	11	3	4	5.06 (2.6)

For the more radical elements, disobeying was all but natural, considering they perceive the secular state illegitimate and its policies sacrilegious. Consequently, when perceiving the state to be encroaching on their autonomy or violating religious mores, resistance, including violence, seemed justified. This uncompromising stance held by a minority impacted also other Haredim, negotiating their citizenship with state and society, that could, at times, identify with the demands of the more radical elements, but not with their tactics. Struggles on some issues, described below, drew larger circles of Haredim, protesting state or municipal policies. Furthermore, while many Haredim disagreed with the aggressive behavior of the more radical elements, they also disdained police violence they perceived unnecessary and discriminatory.

The day of rest, Sabbath, is a constant source of contention between Haredim and secular Jews. In Jerusalem, where many Haredi resided, the battles to prevent cars from driving and opening of cinemas and restaurants were especially fierce, but they also spread elsewhere. In 1984, in Petah Tikvah, the opening of movie theaters on Friday evenings was accompanied by a mass demonstration of about 10,000 religious demonstrators. Only in 1987 the demonstrations, declared illegal, began to die down. While struggles over the Sabbath took place in various places, their intensity was limited, and the focus shifted back to Jerusalem and its Haredi neighborhoods (Ben-Porat, 2013). In Bar-Ilan Street, a major traffic artery in Jerusalem passing through a Haredi neighborhood, struggles lasted for almost twenty years with Haredim demanding that it close to traffic on Sabbath. During the mid-1990s demonstrations turned violent, with Haredim throwing rocks at bypassing cars and clashing with police officers, who responded with force. In 2009, it was the opening of a public parking lot, adjacent to the Haredi neighborhood, on Sabbath that led to demonstrations with officers wounded and many Haredim arrested. The demonstrations continued for almost two years until attentions shifted elsewhere.

Clashes, in the more extreme Haredi areas, erupted also when police entered these neighborhoods to enforce the law. When police attempted to remove the body of a murder victim from a Haredi neighborhood, for example, it encountered a violent protest of residents who wanted to prevent an autopsy to the body, police cars were damaged and eight officers wounded. In another incident, hundreds of Haredim prevented police from taking the body of a nine-year-old, until a court ruled that an autopsy was not necessary (Grossman, 2010). In Beit Shemesh, a town near Jerusalem with a large Haredi population, removal of illegal signposts that called on women to dress modestly by the police resulted in a violent attack on police officers.

For the extreme elements among the Haredim, the attacks against police officers were meant to assert their autonomy, even if it meant defying the state and its institutions. Police attempts to enter the neighborhoods to arrest tax evaders or people suspected of fraud often encountered Haredi resistance (Rosenberg, 2012). The arrest of a Haredi woman, charged with starving her three-year-old child, sparked an extreme violent reaction of Haredim, denouncing police accusations and demanding for the release of the mother. Haredim assaulted city workers, threatened welfare services allegedly responsible for the arrest, vandalized public property and attacked police officers with stones. 110 Haredim were charged with public disorder, 26 police officers and 6 civilians were wounded (Weiss, 2009). The disturbances only subsided after the court released the woman to house arrest. This violent outburst, however, was criticized by more moderate elements among Haredim, appalled by the violence and concerned by the influence of the radical elements on the young people.

Haredim also took to the streets for issues outside their neighborhoods, whether they were about archaeological excavations they thought unearthed Jewish remains, immodest billboards and pride parades. In what became almost a ritual Haredim promised to put their lives on the line to prevent the pride parade and police, in return, announced an emergency situation, bringing in more police officers. Violent demonstrations took place in Haredi neighborhoods and other places before the parade, Haredim wanting to show the police they would not be able to contain the violence and forcing the cancellation of the event (Weiss, 2006). A week of demonstrations against the pride parade, with vandalism and violence, left the police exhausted. Haredi participants explained that this was exactly the strategy, denouncing police cooperation with the LGBT community. The demonstrations against the pride parade drew relatively large numbers, and were dominated by more radical elements while many Haredim preferred to ignore the event, rather than acknowledge it. The attacks, especially on the Jerusalem pride parades, however, were far from benign. Violence exploded when, in 2015, a young woman, Shira Banki, was stabbed to death during the parade, her assailant recently released from prison after serving ten years for a murder attempt in the 2005 pride parade.

In recent years the proposed changes in the military draft laws, designed to enforce military service on Haredim, hitherto able to defer and in practice forgo service, became a major cause of unrest. In 2014, large demonstrations threatened to place Jerusalem "under siege" in response to the Ministry of Finance's treat to cut funding to Haredi institutions that would not comply with new draft laws. The arrest of a young Haredi who, following rabbis' orders, refused to report to the army for deferral request, caused an outburst of Haredi rage, demonstrations in several cities and violent clashes with police. One of the leaders of the demonstrations defiantly stated: "We are not scared, guns don't scare us. We demonstrate to you that you do not rule us. You are meaningless" (Ettinger and Seidler, 2014).

The debate over military service and the new draft laws became one of the core issues dividing Haredi society. New programs of the military to attract and accommodate Haredim and political compromises are matched by the defiant refusal of Haredim to any attempt to enforce upon them military conscription. In March 2014 more than 300,000 Haredim demonstrated against a new draft law (TOI Staff, 2014). A month later, radical Haredi groups blocked streets and clashed with police officers, after the arrest of a Haredi draft dodger. These demonstrations often ended with police arrests and with protestors, usually of more extreme groups, describing their staunch refusal to join the army as "Mesirut Nefesh" (literally: to give one's life). Violent clashes happened also when Haredim in uniform who did join the military, hereby crossing the line, were attacked in Haredi neighborhoods, attackers afterwards clashing with police and arrested (Nachshoni, 2017).

Haredim described their struggles against the state in terms of sacrifice and devotion, frustration with the secularization of the public sphere and concerns for their own way of life. More importantly, they described police behavior as violent and brutal. Several reports in the media have confirmed police violence against Haredim. Videos have clearly shown officers beating Haredi demonstrators, in what appeared as retribution. These violent clashes usually involved radical groups of Haredim and were viewed with disdain by others, as seen in some of the focus groups below. But, police violence, even for those not directly exposed to it, impacts perceptions of police. Overall, these perceptions demonstrate the ambiguity and the debates over citizenship discussed above. As could be expected, trust of Haredim in police is lower than that of our control group (Table 5.3). In the same vein, 49 percent of Haredim do not feel morally aligned with police, compared to only 29 percent of the control group (Table 5.4). But, a majority of Haredim (about 80 percent), similar to the control group, declare that they obey the law and would obey police officers, demonstrating that disobedience and violence is condoned only by a minority.

Perceptions of Police

In a large survey conducted in 2016 (Hermann et al., 2016), Haredim's trust in police (34 percent) was found lower than that of other Jewish Israelis (43 percent), resembling our own results (Table 5.3). Focus groups for Haredim in our research were held separately for men and women, each group was of participants of different parts of the Haredi world but the perceptions and views did not differ much between them. Overall, the views of police were reflective of the citizenship debates above. Unlike Arab citizens and Ethiopians discussed in the previous chapters, Haredim appear less concerned as individuals of being targeted and arrested or vulnerable to crime, and more concerned as a group

Table 5.3 *Trust in Police*

	Strongly disagree				Strongly agree	Mean (S.D.)
I trust police (%)	1	2	3	4	5	
Ultra-Orthodox	20	21	33	15	13	2.80 (1.3)
Control Group	11	14	34	25	16	3.21 (1.2)

Table 5.4 *Moral Alignment*

Police protect values important to me (%)	Strongly disagree 1	2	3	4	Strongly agree 5	Mean (S.D.)
Ultra-Orthodox	29	20	27	14	10	2.56 (1.3)
Control Group	13	16	36	20	15	3.09 (1.2)

regarding police behavior in demonstrations and its perceived encroachment on Haredi communities, unaware of its needs and sensitivities. For some, the need for police was rather limited, due to the nature of the Haredi community and its perceived high morality and internal order: "Overall, the Haredi public is more moral. Off course, not in everything, you always have a few rotten apples" (Shay, men's focus group, Modiin Ilit).

Like other Israelis, Haredim in the focus groups described different incidents in which police were unresponsive – usually burglaries or theft – suggesting that using police services is not entirely rejected. Some stated they would not bother calling the police, believing they would not be able to help. Different voices were also heard in one of the groups, from those who believed police deliberately discriminate against Haredim: "I personally feel that if I call the police they will not treat me as a decent person" (Hanna, women's focus group, Jerusalem), and that police priorities are clear: "When there are demonstrations, there is a lot of police . . . but when you need them, they are not there" (Rachel, women's focus group, Jerusalem). Overall, discrimination was less of a concern in everyday life, and the fear of police misconduct or unfairness was about the community and the Haredi public, as one of the participants explained: "Police are fair for the individual citizen, it is different when it comes to certain groups" (Mordechai, men's focus group, Jerusalem).

Survey results are very much in line with what was heard in the focus groups. Haredim do not differ from the control group in their perceptions of the quality of police services they receive, the fairness of police and their feeling of security (Table 5.5). While in the focus groups they describe police brutality in demonstrations, this does not reflect on the differences between them and the control group. Similarly, while the

Table 5.5 *Police Service*

Question/statement (%)	Group	Very low quality 1	2	3	4	Very high quality 5	Mean (S.D.)
[Considering all the tasks police are expected to fulfil], what is your evaluation of the quality of services police provide to citizens?	Ultra-Orthodox	13	18	44	18	8	2.89 (1.1)
	Control Group	11	21	47	16	5	2.84 (1.0)
Police treat people fairly		Very unfairly	2	3	4	Very fairly	
	Ultra-Orthodox	14	21	6	22	7	2.87 (1.1)
	Control Group	10	18	43	23	6	2.98 (1.0)
How would you rate the quality of services police provide for you?		Very bad	2	3	4	Very good	
	Ultra-Orthodox	19	18	29	21	12	2.89 (1.3)
	Control Group	12	22	36	23	8	2.95 (1.1)
Police provide security for me		No	2	3	4	Yes	
	Ultra-Orthodox	23	21	25	20	11	2.74 (1.3)
	Control Group	15	22	32	21	10	2.88 (1.2)

feeling that police make an effort to improve relations with the community is lower among Haredim (29 compared to 36 percent) and more Haredim believe they are treated worse by police than others (27 compared to 11 percent) they do not differ in the overall score they give for police work (Table 5.6). Essentially as we argue, on a personal level Haredim trust police and feel secure, the disagreements pertaining mostly to the communal and collective levels.

Over-Policing? Police Violence

Many of the participants in the focus groups made an effort to stress they do not take part in demonstrations, and even disdain the radical

Table 5.6 *In Comparison to Others*

If you would file a complaint of a crime, how would you be treated by the police, compared to others? (%)	Worse				Better	Mean (S.D.)
	1	2	3	4	5	
Ultra-Orthodox	12	15	62	7	4	2.75 (0.9)
Control Group	5	6	64	16	9	3.17 (0.9)

Police make efforts to improve relations with my community (%)	Strongly disagree				Strongly agree	Mean (S.D.)
	1	2	3	4	5	
Ultra-Orthodox	29	20	23	15	14	2.65 (1.4)
Control Group	19	15	30	20	16	2.98 (1.3)

Haredim who provoke unnecessary violence that paint all Haredim negatively in the eyes of the public. Nevertheless, observing or hearing the reports of violent police behavior appears to have an important, and negative, impact on the perceptions of police. Thus, memories of the demonstration in Bar-Ilan Street in Jerusalem, back in 1997, were still important almost twenty years later. For many secular Israelis, Haredi struggles to close the road on Sabbath are an example of the latter's violence. For Haredim, especially the women groups, it was a story of police violence, condoned by the secular state:

I can't remember, what the situation was, the whole street talked about police viciousness, the way they came ... with evilness ... using violence, destroying property. So, after that, when you see an officer in uniform it is hard to smile at him, to accept him (Dina, women's focus group, Beitar Ilit).

I still remember the demonstrations in Bar-Ilan street, the cruelty they showed ... really (Sarah, women's focus group, Beitar Ilit).

We saw it with our own eyes, police officers were eating their lunch and suddenly there was a call, they left everything and ran and began hitting ... it was terrible to watch ... and as said, we do not support the demonstrators and the way they do things (Rachel, women's focus group, Jerusalem).

With new technologies and social media, police violence against Haredim (as well as Haredi violence) is more visible to the public. In September 2017, for example, in a demonstration against a new proposed draft law, police officers were documented kicking Haredi demonstrators, chocking them, dragging them on the road and stepping on them. Police also used powerful water cannons that pulled demonstrators off their feet (Porat and Nachshoni, 2017). The images of police using force against Haredim reach the popular press, but more of them can be found in Haredi media and social media, where police violence is a common theme. For participants in the focus groups, who receive information from these sources, police violence was not responsive and incidental, as police explain, but well ingrained in their ideology and practices:

We do not support demonstrations . . . but with Haredim . . . they come with different equipment, with a different attitude (Sarit, women's focus group, Jerusalem).

I was in a Yeshiva for three years, never took part in demonstrations, but saw the police several times acting unfairly, and just because these people were breaking the law . . . once, I saw an officer stepping on purpose on a hat dropped by a demonstrator . . . this symbolizes how they treat Haredim (Aharon-Yaacov, men's focus group, Jerusalem).

Haredim's explanation for alleged police brutality varied; in one case, a personal experience of police violence, the behavior of police was attributed to the quality of police, "I was beaten severely by two officers, they strangled me and hit me . . . some of them are of real low quality" (Aharon, men's focus group Jerusalem). Others, however, related police violence to Haredi status in Israeli society, being viewed as second-rate citizens, due to negative media coverage that teaches police officers, like other Israelis, to hate Haredim (Dina, women's focus group, Beitar Ilit). The media was mentioned several times as influencing the way police operate, highlighting events in which Haredim were involved. These negative perceptions police officers adopt, in turn, are believed to allow police to behave differently in Haredi neighborhoods:

It is not just that they are brutal, but among us we feel that they unload everything on us . . . that they could do anything they want . . . we have no backing, they are not afraid of us, whatever we say . . . we are abandoned (Lea, women's focus group, Beitar Ilit).

Everything about Haredim goes to extremes, until they see my military ID and then they soften-up, I am someone who contributed, not some fanatic and then I am treated differently . . . You will rarely see police here. But when they come, it is for "war," coming in the morning and leave in the evening with a pile of fines (Shay, men's focus group, Modiin Ilit).

Haredim also claimed they, more than others, were targeted and fined for minor offences. Interestingly, this complaint was raised among one focus group of Haredim, all working men, who at the same time, like many Israelis, wanted also more enforcement of public order in their neighborhoods (men's focus group, Modiin Ilit). But the main complaints were about police violence:

We were not exposed to it, because we don't participate in demonstrations. But, judging from what I read in the press, you get a feeling that there is a public interest in Haredim and the police has become political towards Haredim ... even if the police is right in its accusations, her behavior is just terrible, like the way they dragged the "starving mother" in handcuffs ... if she was a different women, not raising public interest, I am sure police would have treated her (Meir, Lithuanian men's focus group, Jerusalem).

In his words Meir refers not only to the feeling that Haredim are singled out, police reflecting deeper currents within Israelis society ("becoming political"), but also alludes to sensitivities among Haredim over questions of state intervention in what is considered private or communal affairs.

The survey findings on fairness (Table 5.7) demonstrate, again, that the difference between Haredim and the control group are small. Haredim score almost similar to the control group on the questions of police fair judgment, willing to explain actions and use of violence. The rather low scores demonstrate not only the similarity between Haredim and the rest of society, but even more so the problematic image of police among all groups. Somewhat similar to other groups, though with different dynamics, Haredim's critical stance towards police is balanced by the changes they undergo, bringing them closer to state and society, and sharing society's security concerns. However, as discussed below, there are important differences in perceptions of police and policing that distinguish Haredim from the rest of society.

Under-Policing?

From what was discussed until now, it is obvious that Haredim are not overly concerned with a lack of policing, a result of both their resentment towards and suspicion of police, and the general feeling they live in safe communities with a high degree of social capital and social solidarity. Haredim often describe their communities as based on strong ties with high level of trust, mutual help and ability to rely upon others

Table 5.7 *Fairness*

Question/statement (%)	Group	Strongly disagree 1	2	3	4	Strongly agree 5	Mean (S.D.)
Police officers use good judgment and make fair decisions	Ultra-Orthodox	12	18	37	23	10	3.02 (1.1)
	Control Group	10	16	37	29	8	3.09 (1.1)
Police officers are willing to explain their decisions and actions	Ultra-Orthodox	32	28	27	9	4	2.24 (1.1)
	Control Group	19	27	36	13	5	2.57 (1.1)
Police must treat citizens with fairness and dignity, even at the expense of deterrence	Ultra-Orthodox	8	8	16	20	48	3.92 (1.3)
	Control Group	5	7	15	20	53	4.08 (1.2)
Officers who use unjustified force should be punished	Ultra-Orthodox	2	1	2	9	86	4.76 (0.7)
	Control Group	2	2	5	10	82	4.67 (0.8)

(Malchi and Ben-Porat, 2018). Consequently, these communities, as several of the respondents argued, could mostly police themselves. Indeed, in the survey, 62 percent of Haredim (compared to 53 in the control group) believe their community can solve most problems by itself.

However, in several focus groups participants complained of the soft hand police show in Mea Shearim, the Jerusalem neighborhood where anti-Zionist radical Haredim reside:

Actually, in Mea Shearim the feeling is that police is rather soft and appears helpless when facing violent people, taking instead their frustrations on innocent bystanders (Betzalel, Lithuanian men's focus group, Jerusalem).

Police never catch the organizers of the demonstrations, they run away so they catch only participants (Asher, men's focus group, Jerusalem).

It is because police are uninvolved and unfamiliar with the Haredi public, they only know what they see in the Media. In Mea Shearim, there are some twenty people responsible for all the problems ... this is not the real Haredi public (Aharon, men's focus group, Jerusalem).

The fact that police are unable or unwilling to deal with these radical elements within the Haredi groups, claimed several participants, harms the rest of the community and its image, a concern for those who are in daily contact with non-Haredim, in the labor market or elsewhere, and bear the consequences of the radicals' behavior:

Police arrests too few, not too many Haredim. There are deranged Haredim that should be locked behind bars who are not stopped because it is Mea Shearim and they are afraid of them and because of politicians (Mordechai, men's focus groups, Jerusalem).

You understand that when there is a demonstration in Mea Shearim I suffer from this in my neighborhood? Why do I need people spitting at me because of them? Again, a Haredi demonstration I am not even aware of? People generalize all the time about the "Haredi public." I never heard they talk about the "secular public" if a young secular boy is doing something wrong (Aharon-Yaacov, men's focus groups, Jerusalem).

Sexual violence, especially against children, is a sensitive topic that participants in several of the focus groups referred to, often hinting rather than explicitly discussing it. The frequency of sexual abuse of children among Haredim is unknown, due to Haredi society's closure, suspicion of the outer world and the power of a close-knit community for silencing. Study of underreporting of children's sexual abuse among ultra-Orthodox Jews in the US was found in isolated communities and explained by prohibitions on reporting to secular authorities, fear and intimidation, stigma and shame, and the reliance of rabbinical courts (Katzenstein and Fontes, 2017). Similar explanations surface in the study of the topic in Israel and by some of the comments in the focus groups. Researchers estimate that the frequency should be at least as high as that in the general society. Haredi children of large families and in a culture that discourages discussions of sexuality might even be more vulnerable to sexual predators. Families might be reluctant to disclose information about sexual abuse in fear of the family name and the child's future and rabbis might discourage involving authorities and urging to keep matters within the community (Ben-Meir and Levavi, 2010). In recent years, concerns and exposure have led to more complaints to authorities of sexual abuse, but also growing concerns, as the following exchange in one of the groups revealed:

A: There is a kind of a paradox here ... when you police will come to your Rabbis to settle the problems "inside," you lose trust of police, because you don't trust all Rabbis.

B: This is one of the most problematic issue among the Haredi public where sensitive issues like sexual abuse of children is silenced and meanwhile among us are terrible people and crimes. It is horrible.

C: This is why the relation between police and Haredi leaders or Rabbis, is not good, it is really bad (Lithuanian men's focus group, Jerusalem).

This exchange, and other comments below, reveals not just the sensitivity of the topic, but also the growing concerns of parents and fears that children are not protected.

The relation of the police and the Rabbis is very sensitive . . . on the one hand there are things the Rabbis cannot take care of and they need police help. But, on the other hand, because of their public, they cannot formally cooperate with police (Aharon-Yaacov, men's focus group, Jerusalem).

Government and police reports indicate growing cooperation between police, social workers, NGOs and Haredi leaders in treatment of victims of sexual abuse (Rabinovitch, 2015). The conversation above, conversely, may allude not only to limited trust of Haredim in police, but also of their leaders and, more importantly, concerns that the lack of cooperation between the two renders children unprotected. In these sensitive matters, as well as the need to contain Haredi radical violence, police presence might be appreciated by mainstream Haredim, despite suspicion and distrust. In other matters, Haredim do not differ from the control group in their perception of under-policing and needs for more police. Yet, in what may be reflecting some of their suspicions, and possibly greater faith in community's power, a larger number of Haredim (49 compared to 38 percent) disagree with the statement that police are not assertive enough in their neighborhoods (Tables 5.8 and 5.9).

Discretion

It is different here . . . If I call the police on a Haredi person, I will turn him in, and how can I say it? . . . I will put a person in risk. Really, I can't call the police (Ora, women's focus group, Beitar Ilit).

Cooperating with police is for many a controversial issue, alluding to dilemmas of citizenship and belonging. For Haredim, living in enclosed communities, maintaining the boundaries between them and the secular world, preferring religious over secular authority, distrusting police and fearing community sanctions, reporting crimes of community members posits a moral dilemma. At the same time, many of them

Table 5.8 *Under-Policing*

Police presence in your neighborhood is too high/too low (%)	Too low 1		2	3	4	Too high 5
Ultra-Orthodox	30		21	31	10	8
Control Group	28		22	30	3	7
In my neighborhood people can solve most problems by themselves (%)	Strongly disagree 1		2	3	4	Strongly agree 5
Ultra-Orthodox	10		9	19	19	43
Control Group	13		9	25	26	27

Table 5.9 *Law Enforcement*

Police do not enforce the law in my neighborhood (%)	Strongly disagree 1		2	3	4	Strongly agree 5
Ultra-Orthodox	32		17	26	13	13
Control Group	20		18	30	17	15

are aware of problems and needs, in face of the community's limitations to deal with violence and crime, that make police presence necessary. An important concern, however, was the lack of discretion they attribute to secular society in general and police in particular, making cooperation all the more difficult.

For the Haredim there is a vital need for discretion and it is just the opposite with police, they hurry to publicize every unusual event and we are hurt enormously by it . . . if police could be more discrete, maybe it would be easier to approach it and complain on sensitive issues (Avraham, Lithuanian men's focus group, Jerusalem).

We are very sensitive to the issue of secrecy because the Haredi community is more aware of the social damage involved and that is why in 95 percent of the cases you will not complain because of the fear of public exposure (Mordechai, Lithuanian men's focus group, Jerusalem).

The sensitivity required for working in the Haredi community, or rather lack thereof, was explained in the focus groups as a reason why the reluctance to cooperate with police impacts issues of domestic abuse and even children's sexual abuse. As mentioned before, even in the groups participants found it difficult to talk about these issues. "There are some things Haredim would rather stay confidential," explained one participants, "unlike others [seculars] who open it up" (David, men's focus group, Jerusalem). Complaining, they believe, will put the person at risk and police are unlikely to help.

Let's say we know a person was seen hitting his son severely. There is a simple way to come up to his house and arrest him ... In the Haredi public there is another question that needs to be answered, to what community or neighborhood he belongs, there are different social circles. And then you call one of the community leaders (Mordechai, men's focus group, Jerusalem).

No one complains [on sexual predators] because we will not receive the response we need from police. If we had the opportunity to reach out and receive the help, these people [predators] will be more afraid. Today, they can do anything they want (Hanna, women's focus group, Jerusalem).

In the statements made about the need for discretion Haredim underscore the difference between themselves and secular society, at times self-critical of their own communities. These statements also, indirectly, allude to Haredim's citizenship debate, no longer able or desiring to fully isolate themselves from state and society, but at the same time wanting to maintain boundaries. The question whether to involve police in delicate matters is at the heart of this ongoing debate.

We don't have television here and people instead gossip, gossip that creates different problems ... so, domestic violence, there are all kinds of sensitivities, not every time you need to bring the suspect to the station, it could be hoax ... (Shay, men's focus group, Modiin Ilit).

If police would understand the cultural nuances in the Haredi sector and would really want to help, rather than media attention, they could end the story differently. this is so sensitive and critical (Meir, Lithuanian men's focus group, Jerusalem).

Consequently, while Haredim are reluctant to cooperate with police like many Israelis (Table 5.10), reflecting the general low trust in police, they are more reluctant than the control group to cooperate with police and identify a person they know committed a crime, torn between the law and communal loyalty.

Table 5.10 *Cooperation*

Would you identify to police a person you saw commit a crime? (%)	Absolutely no 1		2	3	4	Absolutely yes 5
Ultra-Orthodox	21		11	20	15	33
Control Group	16		8	17	8	41

Cultural Sensitivity

Unlike Ethiopian Jews who viewed "cultural sensitivity" with disdain, rejecting any special treatment, and unlike Arab citizens who viewed it with suspicion, that it diverts attention from more important concerns, Haredim seemed to fully embrace the idea. Whether they favor the persistence of an enclave society or maintain a more open relation to Israeli society, the idea that the state and its institutions would respect their way of life was expected. Certain codes and mores, they believe, must be understood by police officers in order for them to gain respect and trust of the community.

They must understand certain things. For a woman to allow you in her house, it is a religious problem that you are alone with her in the house, you can't ask her all kinds of questions (Ora, women's focus group, Beitar Ilit).

We want the police to be better and familiar with our way of life. Before I would like to have police here, I want them to understand us, our needs and to see us as normal people. After that, we will be more willing and able to have them (Shira, women's focus group, Jerusalem).

If in officers' training they would study about Haredim ... a secular police officer should know the consequences for a family that officers entered their house in the middle of the night ... the family will have to face constant shame. In the secular public people let go, here it never ends (Shay, men's focus group, Modiin Ilit).

Cultural sensitivity, as one of the participants explained, could be summarized in one word: "Modesty. That is all you need to know" (Shira, women's focus group, Jerusalem). This related not only to the way officers approach Haredi women and the required discretion described above, but also to the objection to women police officers patrolling the Haredi neighborhoods, especially when paired with male officers or wearing pants.

Table 5.11 *Police and the Community*

Question/statement (%)	Group	Strongly disagree 1	2	3	Strongly agree 4	5
Police make efforts to improve	Ultra-Orthodox	29	20	23	15	14
relations with my community	Control Group	19	15	30	20	16
Police officers lack proper	Ultra-Orthodox	19	12	24	19	26
training to understand real	Control Group	15	13	37	17	18
problems in my neighborhood						
Community policing provides	Ultra-Orthodox	53	13	18	7	9
an answer for my	Control Group	10	10	28	25	28
community's needs						

They need to understand the Haredi public. In all kind of events, it is disrespectful to send a woman officer to a Yeshiva. It doesn't work this way (Avraham, men's focus groups, Jerusalem).

Survey results (Table 5.11) confirm some of the themes raised in the focus groups. A larger number of Haredim compared to the control group (49 compared to 34 percent) disagree with the statement that police make an effort to improve relations with the community, and more (45 percent compared to 35 percent) agree that police lack the proper training to do so. Community policing, however, in its current form, does not receive much support from the Haredim, far less than the control group (16 compared to 53 percent). Overall, while Haredim place a greater emphasis on cultural sensitivity, due to the nature of their relations with the state, they believe that police are not ready or able to make the necessary changes.

Representation: Haredi Police Officers

Question: If your son would want to join the police, how would that be accepted?

"Over my dead body" (Dina, women's focus group, Beitar Ilit).

"God save us" (Dvora, women's focus group, Beitar Ilit).

"I would prefer he will study" (Rachel, women's focus group, Jerusalem).

"The police appears to be . . . bullies, the way the speak, not people of high quality" (Yael, women's focus group, Jerusalem).

The dilemmas surrounding enlistment to the police resemble the question over military service: on the one hand, joining an institution identified with and symbolizing the state, and the higher importance given to religious studies; but, on the other hand, the changing attitudes towards the state described above, practical concerns over employment and the potential to help the community. Police, however, as many of the participants indicated, and similar to perceptions of other Jewish Israelis, do not enjoy the status of the military. In addition, police are being perceived by many as particularly hostile to Haredim. The question therefore in the focus groups was not only whether Haredim would want to join police, whose image remains low, but also whether police, due to their dislike of Haredim, really want them within their ranks, or would be willing to accommodate their needs. Finally, the low image of police officers is another negative factor influencing perceptions towards recruitment.

I think most people who sit here are more intelligent than your average police officer so it is irrelevant for them, they would not find their place in police even if it was socially and religiously excepted (Meir, Lithuanian men's focus group, Jerusalem).

Police is a clique of people that could not find their place in the labor market, they have no skills (Aharon, Lithuanian men's focus group, Jerusalem).

We need to have Haredi officers, but the police does not like Haredi officers, because they will not work on the Sabbath. That is why they place them in office jobs (Yaacov, men's focus group, Jerusalem).

Like other groups, some members raised objections to joining the police under these circumstances:

I can tell you that it is difficult to the public to see them wearing police uniforms (Yaacov, men's focus groups, Jerusalem).

Opposition to enlistment for police stems from the fact we see in police a hostile element, and they view us the same way. Even the military is better than police. You say enlistment to police and everyone is reminded of the beatings in Mea Shearim or some traumatic experience (Aharon, men's focus group, Jerusalem).

When there will be trust between Haredim and police, I will accept that my neighbor will be an officer, because I know he is not just out there to get me (Narkis, Men's focus group, Modiin Ilit).

The close-knit social community structure typical of Haredi neighborhoods has also raised doubts as to whether Haredi officers could be effective. Once again, critical voices of the community alluded to current

problems of keeping things inside the community and overlooking significant issues. Haredi police officers, it was argued, being part of the enclave
society, might take part in covering up problems, rather than solving them.

If there will be too many Haredim in the police, it could create problems
in case the officer will have to arrive to a Haredi area. Haredim are like
family, everyone knows everyone. The police officer will have difficulty
to arrest someone because his grandmother preys with his mother or
something like that. I want Haredim to be in the police, to earn a living,
but not in Haredi neighborhoods (Mordechai, men's focus groups,
Jerusalem).

I am a bit concerned about cooperation with police and with possibility
their will be many Haredi policemen, because they might begin to "make
deals" within the community. It is important that police will be familiar with
Haredim and their sensitivities, not that the police will become Haredi
(Bnayahu, Lithuanian men's focus group, Jerusalem).

Other voices, however, have strongly supported the recruitment of
Haredi officers, stressing not a republican citizenship discourse of
the state or societal common good, but rather a community-
centered one. Haredi officers, they maintained, would be able to
exert the required sensitivity and abide by the moral codes important to the community.

A Haredi police officer will know to keep the rules of modesty. A secular
officer does not know that a women without a headcover is obscene.
A Haredi officer will know to turn his head away and give her respect.
A secular officer will arrest her no matter what. A Haredi officer will be
more sensitive to modesty, not raise his voice on children or try that the
neighbors will not see him ... Do you know how many times these disgraces
destroyed families? ... do you know how humiliating it is for a women to be
without a headcover in front of a strange man? (Shay, men's focus group,
Modiin Ilit).

If I see a Haredi officer in the police car, I know he will care more to listen
to me and I will have more trust in him. He understands me and my problems
(Meir, Lithuanian men's focus group, Jerusalem).

I will be happy to have police in my neighborhood, scan the area five
times a day. It provides security (Avraham, men's focus groups,
Jerusalem).

The dilemmas raised in the focus groups were found also in the survey
(Table 5.12). Haredim in general agree that representation in police is

Table 5.12 Representation

	Strongly disagree 1	2	3	4	Strongly agree 5	Mean (S.D.)
It is important that police be representative of all groups in Israeli society (%)						
Ultra-Orthodox	19	6	14	17	46	3.66 (1.6)
Control Group	7	5	8	16	64	4.26 (1.2)
How would recruitment of police officers from your community affect the relations between the community and police? (%)	Negative effect	2	3	4	Positive effect	
Ultra-Orthodox	11	8	24	21	36	3.63 (1.3)
Control Group	3	4	23	32	38	3.98 (1.0)
Would you prefer police in your neighborhood to be: (%)	Orthodox only	Mixed	Not Orthodox	Not important, professional		
Ultra-Orthodox	9	24	5	62	NR	NR

Table 5.12 (*cont.*)

[For a salary meeting your expectations] would you consider becoming a police officer? (%)	No	2	Maybe	4	Yes	
Ultra-Orthodox	71	4	9	8	9	1.77 (1.3)
Control Group	38	6	15	18	23	2.81 (1.6)

If a friend or a family member decides to join the police, would you support him/her? (%)	Strongly object	2	3	4	Strongly support	
Ultra-Orthodox	28	12	16	14	31	3.10 (1.6)
Control Group	8	8	18	22	44	3.86 (1.3)

important, though the support is lower than among the control group (63 compared to 80 percent). Regarding the background of police officers in their neighborhoods, Haredim show no particular preferences, somewhat similar to other Israelis. A clear majority of Haredim declare they would not consider enlisting (71 percent compared to 38 percent in the control group). However, 45 percent would support a friend or family member that would enlist (compared to 66 percent in the control group), while 40 percent would object (compared to 16 percent in the control group). These numbers demonstrate that for the vast majority of Haredim, being a police officer is not an option, either because of the negative image of police or because the preference for religious studies. Yet, the fact that the attitude towards others of the community enlisting is divided seems to reflect both the wider processes of reluctant integration described above and the particular dilemmas regarding police and policing.

Police Oversight

Unlike Arab citizens and Israelis of Ethiopian descent, Haredim are neither securitized nor subjected to racial profiling. Haredim (Table 5.13) do not perceive themselves exposed to police violence as individuals but may believe they are exposed to police violence when demonstrating. Distanced from the state and less inclined to adopt the security discourse, Haredim are more reluctant to believe that the importance of police work should exempt them from prosecution, though almost similar to the control group. Similarly, Haredim are more reluctant to provide police with more authority but are only slightly more supportive of oversight.

The limited interest of Haredim in the oversight of police is reflective of their needs and concerns, as well as more general perceptions and attitudes. First, their relative immunity from police violence compared to Ethiopians or Arab citizens implies that they are mostly concerned with specific instances of police violence. And, second, their desire to maintain distance from state and society further limits their interest to take part in oversight, implying a more active form of citizenship.

Conclusions

Citizenship is a sensitive issue for Haredim who maneuver between their insistence to remain separated maintain autonomy from state and

Table 5.13 *Oversight*

Question/statement (%)	Group	Strongly disagree 1	2	3	4	Strongly agree 5	Mean (S.D.)
[Police work is difficult and important] officers should not be charged for their actions	Ultra-Orthodox	53	13	18	7	9	2.06 (1.3)
	Control Group	48	17	14	9	12	2.21 (1.4)
Police should prioritize public order and fighting crime even if innocent people are hurt sometimes	Ultra-Orthodox	31	17	30	13	9	2.52 (1.3)
	Control Group	26	18	26	16	15	2.76 (1.4)
Police should have more authority and autonomy to be able to protect the public	Ultra-Orthodox	23	17	24	8	18	2.89 (1.4)
	Control Group	19	12	22	21	26	3.23 (1.4)
Strong oversight of police is necessary	Ultra-Orthodox	3	4	17	22	54	4.24 (1.0)
	Control Group	3	5	17	27	48	4.12 (1.1)

society and the privileges they enjoy being part of the Jewish collective. In recent years, due to internal changes and external incentives, the boundaries between Haredim and the rest of society are slowly blurring. Their integration in the labor market and higher education, and their exposure to consumer culture, as well as particular paths for contribution, brings Haredim into contact with state and society and the development of "inclusive fundamentalism" (Stadler et al., 2011). Like other enclave societies, and in face of changes, Haredim are renegotiating their citizenship status and their relation to state and society. Their perceptions of police and policing are embedded in questions of identity and interests, and reflect the changes Haredi society undergoes and the dilemmas involved.

Previously, contact with police was minimal for Haredim. To begin with, symbolizing state sovereignty, police were to be avoided. Second, not taking part in the security apparatus and discourse, Haredim were largely indifferent to police's role in security provision and their overlap with the military, a source for support among other groups. Third, as an enclave community with strong social capital, policing was performed by the community itself and believed to suffice. And, fourth, encounters with police were often in direct clashes when Haredim were demonstrating and blocking roads. Consequently, the relations with police remained tense and distanced.

While Haredim began to embrace Israeli state and society, this was a gradual process fraught with tensions. Voluntary service in security-related organizations, and the impact of terrorist violence, increased Haredi interest and at times empathy to state security, though police remained suspect. Not only the memory of past violent clashes with police, but also more recent ones, strengthened Haredi perceptions that police are hostile. This perceived hostility of police is less evident at the individual level, as Haredim are not considered a security or a criminal threat, but more on the collective level, where police allegedly use excessive force against them. In addition, more radical elements of Haredi society remain adamant that police not intervene in what they consider internal affairs of the community, strongly reacting against such interferences. At the same time, seen both in focus groups and survey, there are those who believe police have to be brought in to protect those vulnerable to violence and combat the radical elements in Haredi society that instigate violence.

This "reluctant" citizenship, more involved in civic action but refusing full inclusiveness, is reflected also in the level of trust of and expectations from police. As trust is relatively low, and belief in communities' power high, Haredim have limited desire for oversight, almost none for representation, but strong support for cultural sensitivity. These expectations are the result not only of low trust, but also of the importance of maintaining the boundaries between Haredim and the state. Consequently, perceptions of police among Haredim display, on the one hand, some openness and acknowledgment for the need for cooperation; but, on the other hand, reluctance to fully participate and be represented and demand for recognition, as expected from an enclave society.

6 | Integration and Citizenship: Russian Immigrants

While Arab citizens, Israelis of Ethiopian descent and Haredim have all had troubling and notable encounters with police, very few stories of Israelis of Russian descent (henceforth, Russians) have made similar headlines. In spite of their large size and cultural distinction, Russians' experiences with and perceptions of police differ little from that of veteran Israelis. The stark contrast of the experiences of Russians and Ethiopians, immigrating to Israel at the same period, attests both to the stratified nature of Israel's citizenship regime and to the differential experiences of immigrants and their ability to successfully integrate.

Like ethnicity, race and class, immigration often predicts troubled relations with the state and its institutions. Immigrants' unfamiliarity with local culture and practices, on the one hand, and society's prejudice towards immigrants, on the other hand, often underscore a troubled relation with police. Immigrations, however, come in different shapes and forms. Some find themselves on the margins of society, excluded, alienated and suffering discrimination. Others, nonetheless, either successfully adopt local culture and fully integrate into society, or partially integrate, negotiating their identity and status with the surrounding state and society. For the latter group, being at least partially assimilated means they can develop cooperation with and trust in the state and its institutions, including police.

Interaction with police, as mentioned before, teaches citizens about their political standing and social status – negative or positive interactions being indicative of immigrants' place in society (Lerman and Weaver, 2014: 12). For Ethiopians, vulnerable and singled out by their skin color, over-policing is an amplified demonstration of discrimination and racism. Russians, conversely, in spite of difficulties and stereotypes, are largely a strong immigration group, benefiting from high human capital and also more accepted and respected by society. Consequently,

Russians, albeit difficulties, were able to dictate their terms of integration, maintain their cultural distinction, hold a critical stance towards state and society, but, at the same time, perceive themselves as part of both. Their relation to police, strongly resembling that of veteran Israelis of our control group, demonstrates the different paths of integration for minority groups.

The Age of Migration

Studies of migration have shifted from the assimilation model that predicted a single outcome to various models that predict a range of outcomes for immigrants, a result of different motivations, resources and circumstances involved in each migration (Brettell and Hollifield, 2000: 15). Countries, on the one hand, differ in their reception of immigrants, while immigrant groups (and individuals), on the other hand, adapt differently, depending on their levels of social and human capital (Portes and Rumbaut, 1996). Historical experiences of nation and state formation include different models of citizenship, incorporation of minorities and, consequently, immigration policies. Immigration policies determined not only paths and sizes of migration but also societal attitudes towards immigrants, practices of exclusion and inclusion, and, in turn, the consciousness of immigrants themselves. Immigrant groups, even in the same state, may follow different paths of integration, from successful assimilation to the formation of ethnic enclaves, and isolation and separation from the rest of society.

Assimilation, as a policy guiding the absorption of immigrants and a yardstick for successful integration, has gone through several changes. By the early 1990s scholars and policy makers seemed to abandon the assimilation model, considered unfair, restrictive and disrespectful of immigrants' cultural needs, in favor of multicultural approaches that allowed and supported difference. Yet, ten years later multiculturalism itself was under attack, blamed for failing to integrate minorities and creating ethnic enclaves. Some scholars described a return to a more moderate form of assimilation and argued that assimilation is not a unitary process but rather a differential one (Castles and Miller, 2009: 275). Assimilation, as Brubaker (2001) explains, is a process, or a direction of change rather than a final state or a particular degree of similarity. Consequently, assimilation is domain specific, relative to a particular reference population and entails a multidimensional question of "assimilation in what respect, over what period of time, and to what reference population?" (ibid.: 544).

The renewed assimilation debate, beyond its impact on political attitudes and public policies, has also allowed a more nuanced understanding of immigration and immigrants, different paths of integration and the causes underscoring them. Immigrants can follow different strategies for integration (or acculturation) based, first, on the value they (collectively and individually) place on maintaining their identity and, second, the values they place on relationship with wider society. The strategies they can adopt, however, are not always open to choice and can be constrained by state and wider society. Even in states where pluralism is largely accepted there are well-known variations in the relative acceptance of specific cultural groups. Groups that are less accepted – religious, racial or ethnic – experience more hostility, rejection and discrimination and, in turn, are marginalized and are predicted to remain more distant from state and society (Berry, 1997).

Successful integration depends on many factors from immigrants' desire to assimilate, the size of the immigration and its political power, the human and material capital of immigrants, their social networks, their cultural resemblance or distance from the society they enter and the way they are perceived by the host society. A general consistent finding is that the greater the cultural distance between immigrants and the host society, the less positive the adaptation (Berry, 1997). In some instances, deep-seated cultures of racism in host societies coupled with growing inequality resulting from globalization leads to the racialization of ethnic differences:

Minorities may have poor employment situations, low incomes and high rates of impoverishment. This in turn leads to concentration in low-income neighborhoods and growing residential segregation. The existence of separate and marginal communities is then taken as evidence of failure to integrate, and this in turn is perceived as a threat to the host society (Castles and Miller, 2009: 275).

Immigrants can be perceived by society and state as a threat to the social fabric or a burden and, accordingly, different opportunity structures await different groups, some marginalized while others experience rapid social and economic mobility. Cultural bonds (Steinbach, 2001) and the presumed existence of historic, cultural and/or religious heritage shared with host society are expected to enable fast and painless social integration, though these expectations are not necessarily met for first-generation immigrants (Remennick, 2003a). Finally, immigrants with high human capital, on the one hand, and a positive image (hard-working, honest, etc.), on the other hand, are expected to easily integrate. Successful acculturation/integration can be measured by employment in the mainstream economy, diversification of communication circles, gradual reorientation of cultural and media consumption and the attitude of the hegemonic majority towards the specific immigrant groups (Remennick, 2003a).

The strength of immigrant groups can be measured not only by their integration into the host society, but also by their ability to dictate these very terms of integration and preserve their culture. Thus, the fact that immigrants retain their old culture does not necessarily mean a failed integration, but possibly the opposite. First, a greater emphasis on ethnic identity does not come at the expense of national attachment (Wright and Bloemraad, 2012). And, second, integration suggests that a minority group preserves its cultural core while developing additional adaptive skills (Remennick, 2003a, 2003b). Thus, for some immigrant groups cultural and racial distinctions mean marginalization and discrimination. For others, available resources and/or favorable attitudes of host society allow more successful integration and control over the process.

The differences between immigrant groups' ability to integrate have a direct bearing on their citizenship, measured, among other things, by their relations with police. Indeed, issues of immigration and policing became salient with eruptions in French, Australian and English cities in recent years (Wu, 2010). Language barriers, cultural differences, home country experiences, discrimination, marginalization and negative stereotypes are several explanations for troubled relations between police and minority immigrants. Negative perceptions of police, however, are not common to all immigrant groups, some found to have similar or even more favourable views than the rest of society (Wu, 2010). Similarly, not all immigrant groups are negatively stigmatized. Immigrants whose identity is not "visible" and those not perceived as a "threat" are less likely to be over-policed, and, if able to successfully integrate, also not under-policed. "Strong" immigration groups, therefore, are expected to better utilize their citizenship, demonstrated, among other things, by their relation to police and policing.

Russians in Israel

Displaced by threats for personal safety and economic instability in the FSU (former Soviet Union), but not granted refugee status in most cases, Soviet Jews could only immigrate to Israel under the Law of Return. The immigration from the FSU was different from previous large immigration groups to Israel and from the recent Ethiopian immigration. Unlike the large wave of immigrants in the 1950s FSU immigrants in the 1990s arrived to an economically and highly developed country, more affluent, less centralistic and less insistent on cultural assimilation. Israeli Jewish society, and especially the veteran Ashkenazi elite, welcomed the FSU immigrants, seeing them as an asset for strengthening Israel's Jewish demography, security and economy. In addition, some politicians and journalists conveyed the expectation that immigrants will strengthen European/Ashkenazi culture seemingly threatened by a rising Arab/Mizrachi culture, and will secure Israel's western image (Smooha, 2008).

Russian immigrants' entry into the labor market in Israel entailed for many of them a downward social mobility, taking jobs whose requirements were below their education, but they were slowly and steadily able to move upward and improve their economic standing. Their high human capital, positive image and the continuous investment in education, compensated for the absence of material capital (Smooha, 2008). Previously, it was the state that allocated housing to Jewish immigrants, enabling it to decide where they will settle. However, a new policy provided Russian immigrants (unlike Ethiopian immigrants) with an "absorption basket" that allowed them to make their own choices where to live and work.

The size of the immigration, its human capital, and the opportunities afforded by the state enabled the growth of an ethnic community, conscious of its separate interests, outlooks and power (Smooha, 2008). Russian immigrants also saw themselves culturally superior to ordinary Israelis and what they perceived as an Oriental culture prevalent in Israel (Smooha, 2008), strengthening their desire to maintain separation rather than assimilate. Politically, Russian parties, local and national, were quickly formed and gained substantial power. Culturally, newspapers and magazines, radio and television channels in Russian, clubs, theaters and educational networks created a de-facto cultural autonomy (Remennick, 2003b). While immigrants integrated in the public formal realm, labor market or military, they maintained more separation in the private/informal realm (Remennick, 2003a, 2003b).

The few critical voices and concerns, of Mizrahi and Arab citizens, of the negative potential of competition over jobs and resources, was silenced by invoking national resilience, unity and the immigrants' potential, and later real, contribution (Smooha, 2008). Unlike Ethiopian immigrants, FSU immigrants were welcomed in peripheral development towns, mayors hoping that the settlement of educated immigrants in their towns would upgrade them socio-economically (Smooha, 2008). But, in spite of their strength, immigrants also faced difficulties and challenges. The Law of Return provides rights to citizenship for those with one Jewish grandparent or married to a Jew. Consequently, many of the immigrants, estimated one-third, were not considered Jews by Orthodox standards. These non-Jews were not only less welcomed by the general public, they also encountered practical hardships in the right to marriage and burial, under the monopoly of the Jewish Orthodoxy (Ben-Porat, 2013).

Integration involves the preservation of a cultural core alongside the development of adaptive facets of identity, skills and networks (Remennick, 2003b). Like elsewhere (Wright and Bloemraad, 2012), the maintenance of ethnic identity among Russians in Israel did not come at the expense of national identity. Indeed, personal relationships, networks and cultural orientation remained "Russian," but nevertheless integration did take place. This integration, from a point of strength (Al-Haj, 2002), based also on disdain to the perceived Oriental culture prevalent in Israel (Smooha, 2008), allowed immigrants to control the pace and level of integration. Russian immigrants were able to mobilize while maintaining their cultural identity, but also to identify with their new country. The immigrants, although coming from the communist bloc, were strongly oriented to the west and shared with some of the veteran Israelis the disdain for the region's culture.

A decade after their arrival, immigrants were largely satisfied with their absorption, and reported they got along well with veteran Israelis and felt at home in Israel (Al-Haj, 2002). In a different survey, only 8 percent mentioned "feeling second-rate citizens" or that they faced discrimination (Remennick, 2003a). Russian immigrants' desire to institutionalize their separate identity within Israel kept them apart from society. But, at the same time their denigration of the "Oriental other" (Shumsky, 2004) placed them well within right-wing politics and the security discourse. Russian immigrants were secular compared to most Israelis, but this distinction had limited political impact as their secularism was "pragmatic-secular-rightist and ethnic," loosely related to liberalism and liberal politics (Al Haj, 2002; see also Ben-Porat, 2013). As insiders-outsiders in Israeli society Russian immigrants adopted the dominant nationalism, criticizing what they perceived as toleration of Palestinians and stressing their loyalty to the nation and state (Tzfadia and Yacobi, 2007).

Being Israeli

The matter of fact, pragmatic and seemingly emotionally lacking attitude of Russians towards police sets them apart from our other minority groups, and closer to "mainstream" Israelis of the control group. The complaints against police are not devoid of ethnic discourse, but much of the dissatisfaction relates to what is perceived as police inefficiency and lack of capabilities to provide adequate services. Adopting a neoliberal stance, common in contemporary Israeli society, the perceived problem of police is the problem of the public sector in need of reform.

Generally, competition improved many things here in recent years, the level of service is better and we as consumers want more . . . too bad police and other institutions don't make the same changes (focus group, Jerusalem).
    What is needed is a radical reform of the public service . . . this problem is everywhere and police is part of it . . . workers who don't perform well and don't do their jobs, should be sacked . . . standards must be high and those who don't match them must be sent home . . . and people of high quality must be recruited, and paid well (Barry, focus group, Jerusalem).

In the focus groups, Russians, elaborated below, demarcated their differences and cultural distinctions, but at the same time have also expressed confidence in their place within Israeli society and a strong sense of patriotism. As Table 6.1 demonstrates, Russian immigrants hardly differ from the control group in their allegiance to the state, as they take a similar (high) pride as others and feel they belong.
    Consequently, as Table 6.2 shows, Russian immigrants do not differ from the control group in their perceptions of police and attribute the problems of police to insufficient resources and authority. As one of the participants explained: "they lack the means, they lack the ability, they are limited by their resources and by the quality of the manpower they have" (David, focus group, Jerusalem).

Table 6.1 *Identity*

Question/statement (%)	Strongly disagree 1	2	3	4	Strongly agree 5	Mean (S.D.)
I feel I belong to this country						
Russian	2	2	11	27	58	4.37 (0,9)
Control Group	3	1	8	18	70	4.52 (0.9)
I am proud to be an Israeli citizen						
Russian	1	1	6	14	77	4.65 (0.76)
Control Group	1	2	7	10	80	4.64 (0.8)

Table 6.2 *Perceptions of Police*

[Considering all the tasks police are expected to fulfil], what is your evaluation of the quality of services police provide to citizens? (%)	Low quality 1	2	3	4	High quality 5	Mean (S.D.)
Russian	10	16	43	27	4	2.98 (1.0)
Control Group	11	21	47	16	5	2.84 (1.0)

Police treat people fairly (%)	Very unfair	2	3	4	Very fair	Mean (S.D.)
Russian	9	15	44	26	6	3.07 (1.0)
Control Group	10	18	43	23	6	2.98 (1.02)

Table 6.2 (*cont.*)

How would you rate the quality of services police provide for you? (%)	Low quality	2	3	4	High quality	Mean (S.D.)
Russian	17	15	32	25	12	3.01 (1.2)
Control Group	12	22	36	23	8	2.94 (1.1)

I trust police (%)	Strongly disagree	2	3	4	Strongly agree	Mean (S.D.)
Russian	10	13	32	26	19	3.33 (1.2)
Control Group	11	14	34	25	16	3.21 (1.2)

Feeling Secure

Russian immigrants, like many Israelis, are ambivalent in their assessment of police and the security they provide. The blurred boundaries between police and military, Russian immigrants' identification with the state, adoption of society's securitization discourse and the fact they are not targeted as suspects by police explain the similarity between immigrants and the control group. Participants in the focus group did not feel insecure, comparing the Israeli police with the Russian police they were used to, and reflecting their general sense of security in Israel. Their complaints, echoing those of many Jewish Israelis, refer to what they perceive as the inability of police to deal with more ordinary disturbances and crime.

I think they would protect me if I needed. I think police is doing its job. I feel that way because I see them patrolling my neighbourhood. I trust them here more than I trusted them in Russia (Soffa, focus group, Ashkelon).

I would like to say that I am not afraid to walk the streets at night in Israel. I don't know if it is because of the police but I feel personally secure. When I compare this to the Soviet Union I can say that I was afraid there and here, I am not. But, on the other hand, if something would happen at my home, a dispute with a neighbour, I would not call the police. Not because they would not come, but because they would do nothing and only make things worst (focus group, Jerusalem II).

Table 6.3 *Security*

Question/statement (%)	Strongly disagree 1	2	3	Strongly agree 4	5	Mean (S.D.)
Police provide security for me						
Russian	14	12	27	30	18	3.26 (1.3)
Control Group	15	22	32	21	10	2.88 (1.2)
I fear police officers						
Russian	57	15	15	10	4	1.90 (1.2)
Control Group	56	18	12	9	6	1.90 (1.2)
Police do not enforce the law in my neighborhood						
Russian	18	14	30	19	19	3.07) (1.4)
Control Group	20	18	30	17	15	2.89 (1.3)

The difficulties of police in providing public order and preventing disturbance were attributed, among other things, to lack of sufficient authority, a perception that might be related to Russian culture:

It is not the police, it is the laws. When it is a minor issue, like a neighbor that makes noise, the police can solve it easily. Or when it is about a normative person, they can deter him. But when it comes to other situations, the police does not have the tools to deal with the problem (Anna, focus group, Jerusalem).

Russian immigrants (Table 6.3) feel more than the control group that police provide them with security, much like the control group do not fear police officers, and believe more than the control group that the police are not assertive enough.

In some of the focus groups the negative views of police were related to their difficulty in preventing what can be described as minor disorders, such as loud music. Here, the complaints hinted to the perceived difference between orderly and cultured immigrants and the local, less orderly and loud Israelis.

I tried several times to call police when my neighbors downstairs were having an oriental feast, with loud music, when I have an exam to study for. And I am asking them to come and it feels like nobody cares (Elisa, focus group Jerusalem).

This alleged failure to provide order, elaborated below, is part of wider concerns of Russian immigrants that underscores the distance they maintain from Israeli society. For Elisa, an "oriental feast" to referring to local Mizrachi culture stands in stark opposition to studying for an exam, namely being laborious and sophisticated, she and others take pride in.

Fairness and Equality

Now there is no differential treatment. But when we just got here, in the early 2000, there was. After we complained to our [Israeli] neighbours about the behaviour of their children, they called the police and claimed we harassed them. The police officer pushed me . . . (Maria, focus group, Ramla).

Russian immigrants' complaints of police unfairness are limited compared to other groups discussed before. Where concerns of fairness were raised, they were attributed to cultural differences, relevant especially to older Russians who do not speak Hebrew. Accordingly, unfairness is perceived as temporary, or situational, and expected to decline with time.

When my mother wants to call the police, I tell her to let me do it. She has an accent and she can not articulate exactly what she wants . . . she might sound confused . . . so I would rather call because I sound Israeli and I can raise my voice and not be afraid of what they would say (focus group, Jerusalem).

Previously, if Russian adolescents would sit outside and drink, police could stop by them and take away their alcohol. Now, they treat them like Israelis. New immigrants would fear police, hide when it came. Now, they can come out, ask what happened . . . they are no longer afraid (focus group, Ramla).

Yes, there is discrimination against Russians, but it is not special or intended. There is discrimination against Arabs or Haredim, the treatment of all minorities is to some extent discriminating . . . every immigration suffered some unequal treatment and so did the Russians. Although it is much less noticeable these days, it still exists (Roman, focus group Jerusalem II).

This perception of police and policing sits well within the wider aspects of citizenship discussed before, of a relatively strong minority group, assured of its citizenship status and its potential to mobilize.

Whatever discrimination exists was attributed by some of the participants to what can be described as "vulgar" Israeli culture, again setting apart Russian immigration and marking their desire to dictate their terms of integration rather than simply "blending in."

Most immigrants are highly educated people and they should be treated differently than the local population. It upsets me when they yell "come here" what am I, your dog? Israelis might tolerate this, I don't. Our mentality and culture is higher, that is why the treatment must be more respectable (focus group, Ramla).

Where police discrimination was reported, it could be attributed to a defensive reaction against the perceived threat of Russian immigrants, especially for non-educated Israelis, again, demarcating the supposed advantage of the immigrants.

I think discrimination is most noticeable among uneducated people. Think about it, educated people come and threaten the employment of Israelis, their income. I don't want to be harsh but officers that barely have education feel threatened by this collective that can take their place so, in defence, they discriminate against them. Of course, not all [Israelis] are like that (Anja, focus group, Jerusalem II).

Consequently, though acknowledging that other groups are also discriminated, the discrimination Russians perceive is different, based on their strength that evokes threat and the perceived low quality of police officers, susceptible to this threat.

Because there are many Israelis with low education, the arrival of the Russians is a threat to them. Ethiopians are also discriminated, but for different reasons ... if we had more educated officers we would have less discrimination ... too bad most officers in Israel are uneducated. Fortunately, things change. It was worst twenty years ago and gradually they stop treating us like second rate citizens (Svetlana, focus group, Jerusalem II).

Our survey, again, demonstrates the similarity between Russian immigrants and Israelis that do not belong to one of the minority groups studies (Table 6.4). Russians experienced direct discrimination less than the control group (11 compared to 20 percent of respondents) and have similar expectations of police. Like the control group, Russians don't expect to be treated by police worse than others, believe police would respond to their calls and most believe they receive

Table 6.4 *Comparative Stance*

Question/statement (%)	1	2	3	4	5	
If you would file a complaint of a crime, how would you be treated by the police, compared to others?	Worse		Same		Better	Mean (S.D.)
Russian	7	8	74	8	2	2.90 (0.7)
Control Group	5	6	64	16	9	3.17 (0.9)
How quickly would police respond to a call from your neighborhood?	Slow	2	3	4	Fast	Mean (S.D.)
Russian	8	10	26	30	26	3.59 (1.2)
Control Group	10	13	35	28	15	3.25 (1.15)
Police service in your neighborhood compared to others is better/worse	Worse		Same		Better	Mean (S.D.)
Russian	10	9	42	24	15	3.24 (1.1)
Control Group	8	10	45	22	15	3.26 (1.1)

(slightly) better services than others, very similar to the control group. Russian immigrants, in other words, perceive themselves largely protected within Israel's stratified citizenship regime.

Russian immigrants' complaints over the lack of adequate police services are not only limited in scope but mostly lacking an ethnic component of relative deprivation. However, in the focus groups voices were raised, concerning the ability of veteran Israelis to make their demands heard and receive more police attention. Again, the cultural factor was the explanation for what some participants perceived as differential treatment. "Mentality" of veteran Israelis, on the one hand, and stigmas against Russians, on the other hand, allegedly cause police to ignore Russians' concerns and be more attentive to those of veteran Israelis:

The locals have a different mentality, they allow themselves more, they actually demand that the police do their job. It is not clear if police fear them or do the job they are paid for. Police responds quicker to their calls, treats their needs. They are not helpless like us ... we don't know the rules, our rights ... everything takes a long time to resolve and is not always resolved. For Israelis, it is not the same, they are treated differently. It is their police (Ludmila, focus group, Ashkelon).

There are stigmas against Russians, they look down on them. The accent irritates officers. That is how I felt when I called police. They were condescending, as if they are doing me a favour ... it is legitimate to ask for quiet at night and I am sure Israelis would not receive the same answer ... it can't be ignored that Russians are not treated the same, there is some discrimination (Tatiana, focus group, Ashkelon).

Others were less certain of the reasons, acknowledging that other groups, like Ethiopian immigrants, suffer more, language barriers are the main problem and that alleged police inefficiency may be a structural problem pertaining to other citizens as well.

We are newcomers, we don't speak the language well, we don't know the rules ... and they use it against us ... they are unresponsive ... ignore us. They are not punished for not helping the public. If they were punished they would perform better ... we want to see results (Tanya, focus group, Jerusalem II).

Russians don't stand up for their rights, sometime they don't know the language and police know that ... so they can't treat our complaints (Michael, focus group, Jerusalem II).

For the police to have more competent people, salaries must be higher, but also to demand more of them (Michael, focus group, Jerusalem II).

Participants, again, attribute many of the problems to the general quality of police officers, they perceive as lacking the necessary skills to succeed in their jobs. Again, Israeli culture is blamed for the quality of police services by one of the participants, but the word "we" he chose to use may be indicative of de-facto integration:

In Russia they went through the police academy, here, nothing. They receive minimal training, they lack a lot of knowledge (focus group, Ramla).

It should not be: you failed everything else, be a police officer, but the opposite. First, be an officer and then try to be all the rest. It is a long process, but in this country nothing can be long. Everything must be immediate and now, that is why we are like this ... (focus group, Jerusalem).

The survey data (Table 6.5) also demonstrate that Russian immigrants differ little from the control group in their assessment of

Table 6.5 *Over-Policing and Under-Policing*

Question/statement (%)	1		2	3	4	5	Mean (S.D.)
Presence of police in your neighborhood is	Low				High		
Russian	23		17	36	16	8	2.71
							(1.2)
Control Group	28		22	30	13	7	2.50
							(1.2)
Police officers arrest citizens for no reason	Disagree				Agree		
Russian	39		24	22	13	3	2.16
							(1.2)
Control Group	38		26	19	9	8	2.23
							(1.3)

Table 6.6 *Overview of Police*

Question/statement (%)	Strongly disagree 1		2	3	Strongly agree 4	5	Mean (S.D.)
I would obey a police officer even if I disagree							
Russian	6		5	14	22	54	4.14
							(1.2)
Control Group	9		8	21	24	39	3.76
							(1.3)
Police protect values important to me							
Russian	13		12	33	21	21	3.26
							(1.3)
Control Group	13		16	36	20	15	3.09
							(1.2)

police presence in their neighborhood (under-policing) or that police arrest people without cause (over-policing). Also, as described above (Table 6.4), Russian immigrants in general do not perceive themselves to be treated different than others, for better or for worse. Under these circumstances, as Table 6.6 shows, Russian immigrants declare they will obey officers more than our control group, in what could demonstrate obedience (possibly related to Russian experience and culture) but also legitimacy. The following question, of identifying with the values police protect, suggests that police are perceived legitimate and, again, that Russian immigrants' attitudes towards police resemble those of non-minority Israelis and of the strong sense of patriotism developed alongside the critical perceptions of Israeli society.

Representation

Representation, as discussed throughout this book, is especially indicative of minority groups' citizenship status. Groups not represented in police can come to believe that perceived, unfair treatment by officers would diminish with better representation and, accordingly, that representation in police is about acceptance and belonging. In the same vein, the willingness or desire of minorities to join the police, a symbol of the state, might be instrumental but can also attest to their integration and identification with the state and its institutions. Yet, minorities who are more secure of their status as citizens can be less concerned with representation and evaluate the question of enlistment in more pragmatic terms. Russian immigrants, unlike the other groups, neither see representation in police as particularly important, nor as problematic. Again, their attitudes closely resemble those of non-minority Israelis.

In the focus group, participants were more concerned with the performance of officers than their ethnicity. "We would prefer officers of high quality. That is all," as one of them stated (focus group, Jerusalem). In the survey, while Russians strongly supported the idea that police should be representative, they had no preference for the background of police officers in their neighborhoods, both answers almost identical to those of the control group. In the focus groups, some concerns were raised, albeit cynically, of Russians in police.

I think it is complicated, Russians and authority is the worst possible combination. Look at communism (Elisa, focus group, Jerusalem).

If many officers were Russian, we would turn into the Soviet Union. There, most burglaries were done by people sent by police (focus group, Ramla).

If there was a Russian station, it would be corrupted, Russians tend to be mean (focus group, Bat-Yam).

Russians who have made it in Israel think highly of themselves (focus group, Ramla).

These voices did not resonate in the survey, as Russians seemed indifferent to the ethnic make-up of police. Where participants did acknowledge the significance of representation, it was either because of the perceived relevant advantage of Russians in comparison to officers currently in the force, or for the benefit of less fortunate ones in the community.

I think that a person who grew in a Russian family will treat Russians differently, would understand them. It is also about the quality of officers, their education ... it is very low (focus group, Bat-Yam).

    Police work a lot with minorities, with battered women ... drug abuse, with Russians or Ethiopians. So an officer comes to help a Russian woman that finally gathered the courage to complain about her abusive husband. And she does not speak Hebrew, he does not speak Russian, she can't even tell him what is the problem. If there was a Russian officer, she could explain (Yana, focus group, Jerusalem).

At the same focus group, however, another participant was more reluctant, demonstrating again the ambivalence towards integration, and the desire to maintain the boundaries from society.

Enlisting Russians to police is complicated, because if a Russian would enlist, he will be part of them, part of the system, so it will do little good. It is like our children that take more from Israeli culture than from Russian culture. It will work the same way in police, be no good (Angela, focus group, Jerusalem II).

The practical debates about enlisting or the potential that family members or children would enlist demonstrated, on the one hand, the ambivalence towards police and the negative perceptions described above, but, on the other hand, a pragmatic attitude:

I would not want someone from my family to join the police. No way ... police is a problematic body ... a profession where people are daily exposed to human suffering and do nothing about it ... people whose human senses are numb (focus group, Jerusalem).

    If my son would want to join the police I would support him. If he wears a uniform and represents the state – much respect (focus group, Ramla).

    I would not be particularly happy – low salary, unappreciated by most people, officers need endless patience, to control themselves all the time (focus group, Ramla).

Table 6.7 *Representation*

Question/statement (%)	Strongly disagree 1	2	3	4	Strongly agree 5	Mean (S.D.)
It is important that police be representative of all groups in Israeli society						
Russian	10	4	9	14	63	4.16 (1.3)
Control Group	7	5	8	16	64	4.26 (1.2)
Would you prefer police in your neighborhood to be:	From my group	mixed	Not from my group	Not important, professional	NR	NR
Russian	3	11	2	86		
Control Group	3	10	3	84		
[For a salary meeting your expectations] would you consider becoming a police officer?	No		Maybe		Yes	Mean (S.D.)
Russian	27	6	14	21	33	3.91 (1.6)
Control Group	38	6	15	18	23	2.81 (1.6)
If a friend or a family member decides to join the police, would you support him/her?	Strongly object	2	3	4	Strongly support	Mean (S.D.)
Russian	8	6	19	24	44	3.91 (1.2)
Control Group	8	8	18	22	44	3.86 (1.3)

The three different voices echo the concerns about the emotional cost of police service, patriotic support for police service, and cost-benefit calculations that render enlistment unattractive. Russians, however, as the survey shows (Table 6.7), would consider enlistment more than the control group and do not differ in support of a friend or a family member that would consider enlistment. The fact that Russians still lag behind economically but are in the process of integration can explain this pragmatic attitude towards enlistment, police providing a secure job with social benefits.

Conclusions

Russians' attitudes towards and perceptions of police are very different from the three other minority groups, demonstrating the stratified nature of Israel's citizenship regime and the diverse paths of integration for different groups. While Russian immigrants suffered a fair share of negative stigmatization, they were able to transcend many of the difficulties not only to gradually integrate, but also to set the pace and terms of integration. Language and culture set Russians apart from Israeli society, but do not marginalize them like other minority groups. The size of the immigration and its human capital allowed Russians to organize politically and for many to successfully integrate. The fact that many of the immigrants were non-Jewish and the majority of them secular caused rifts and conflicts, but those were mostly contained and minimized against the perceived advantage of the immigration to state and society. Consequently, Russian immigrants maintained their difference and were reluctant to part with the "Russian" component of their identity. At the same time, Russians adopted a patriotic, nationalistic stance, well within the republican equation of citizenship.

Russian immigrants' citizenship was described as "passive" and alienated from political participation and suspect of political authorities (Philippov and Bystrov, 2011). Nevertheless, most immigrants adopted a patriotic Zionist vision and right-wing and hawkish attitude based on, among other things, a negative or hostile attitude towards the Arab minority. In addition, an undemocratic outlook imported from the Soviet Union entails reservation also towards other groups construed as deviant or disloyal (Philippov and Knafelman, 2011). These attitudes add an active component to the otherwise passive Russian citizenship, correspond with (a version) of the national ethos and, despite segregation from Israeli society and ethnocentrism, position Russian immigrants within the collective boundaries of the nation.

The strong resemblance of Russian perceptions of police and policing to that of non-minority Israelis demonstrates the integration patterns described above. Russian immigrants do not suffer stigmas that expose them to over-policing. The encounters with police they describe do not differ much from that of non-minority Israelis, although at times are influenced by language and cultural barriers. Immigrants' complaints of police, not being effective enough or lacking in service, are also hardly distinguishable from those of Israelis, even when they attribute them to Israeli "culture" or "mentality." This pragmatic attitude towards police, devoid of victimhood or overt discrimination, is reflected in the question of representation that is largely a personal, cost-benefit calculation rather than a collective concern of a distressed minority.

7 | Conclusions

Happy families are all alike; every unhappy family is unhappy in its own way

(Tolstoy, *Anna Karenina*, p. 1).

Police violence against minorities, or clashes between minorities and police, seem to tell the same story – everywhere. It could be young black men beaten by police officers in American cities, second-generation North African migrants fleeing police officers in a Parisian poor suburb, Israelis of Ethiopian descent humiliated by police officers, or a Bedouin man shot to death during house demolitions. Indeed, they are all identifiable minorities, stigmatized by surrounding society and more vulnerable than others. Historically, policing emerged to contain social changes that could no longer be managed by existing private, communal or informal mechanisms (Bayley, 1998). The "order" police enforce, everywhere, is a particular order that delineates and reinforces boundaries and hierarchies of a particular citizenship regime. The study of the enforcement of this order in policies and everyday operations of police forces, and in the perceptions and expectations of different groups, often unmasks the illusion of universal citizenship.

The "heavy symbolic load" (Bradford, 2014: 22) police officers carry with them has an immediate and practical importance for citizens. Interactions with police, the coercive apparatus of the state (Williams, 2015), whether as suspected offenders or victims seeking help, allow citizens to evaluate their status as citizens. For some, respect, and the expectation to be respected, demonstrate confident citizenship. For others, disrespect, securitization and stigmatization reaffirm the limitations of their citizenship. Encounters with police officers and their expected outcomes, therefore, can influence perceptions of political standing, membership and efficacy (Lerman and Weaver, 2014: 12), reaffirming belonging or alienation.

Minorities often share vulnerability and marginalization, but at the same time, like unhappy families, they have different histories, everyday

194

experiences, grievances and expectations. National minorities may differ from ethnic minorities in their desire to be included, immigrant minorities might be judged differently and afforded different opportunities according to the way they are viewed by society and visible minorities might be more vulnerable to abuse than those more similar to the majority. Minorities differ, first, in the resources or human capital they possess, and their class status. Second, they differ in the perceptions state officials and members of society hold towards them and, consequently, opportunities they are afforded for meaningful integration. And third, they differ in their desire to integrate or maintain their distinction and separation. These differences combine to create particular social positions, institutionalized paths of integration and a complex stratified citizenship regime.

Whether it is a stop and search procedure or response to a call, police officers and citizens do not engage each other as neutral bureaucrats and abstract individuals. Rather, it is an encounter loaded, on both sides, with personal and collective histories, negative or positive perceptions, and sets of expectations. These encounters often challenge the formal definitions of citizenship and expose its hierarchical order. Citizens belonging to groups deemed dangerous or a threat to public order, burdened by social stereotypes carried also by police officers, are more likely to be treated with suspicion and force. Complaints and concerns of citizens of lower status, social or economic, might not be taken seriously as those of more powerful groups, rendering them vulnerable to violence. The monopoly over legitimate violence, characteristic of the modern state and placed in the hands of police, therefore, is hardly neutral. Citizens identified with the state and integrated in society, or those desiring to integrate, are more likely to perceive police as legitimate and trustworthy, even when they fail them. Conversely, alienated and marginalized citizens of minority groups are more likely to identify police with the state they fear or distrust and treat their policies and actions with suspicion, regardless of their declared or intended purpose.

Being a Citizen

Citizenship is a contested concept in diverse societies, where majorities and minorities struggle over the definition of its boundaries and content. Arab citizens, Israelis of Ethiopian and Russian descent and ultra-

Orthodox (Haredim), through their perceptions of police (Table 7.1), demonstrate the stratification and hierarchies of Israel's citizenship regime, and articulate their concerns, demands and expectations. The symbolic significance of police, on the one hand, and their practical importance, on the other hand, underscore dilemmas and paradoxes for individuals and groups. Arab citizens are reluctant to identify with police, but in dire need of effective policing and attribute its lack (and their insecurity) to intended discrimination and defunct citizenship. Ethiopians, racially profiled and subjected to abuse, still declare trust in police, echoing their desire to be part of society and overcome marginal citizenship. Haredim, negotiating their position within state

Table 7.1 *Belonging and Citizenship*

Question/statement (%)	Strongly disagree 1	2	3	4	Strongly agree 5	Mean (S.D.)
I feel I belong to this country						
Arab	15	13	27	21	24	3.26 (1.4)
Haredim	10	11	21	18	40	3.67 (1.4)
Ethiopian	4	10	14	17	56	4.12 (1.2)
Russian	2	2	11	27	58	4.37 (0,9)
Control Group	3	1	8	18	70	4.52 (0.9)
I am proud to be an Israeli citizen						
Arab	14	8	23	20	35	3.53 (1.4)
Haredim	20	10	19	9	43	3.48 (1.6)
Ethiopian	3	2	9	8	78	4.57 (1.0)
Russian	1	1	6	14	77	4.65 (0.76)
Control Group	1	2	7	10	80	4.64 (0.8)

and society, and reconsidering previous chosen segregation, demonstrate their reluctant citizenship and ambivalence also in relation to police. And, finally, Russians' pragmatic if critical attitude towards police, very similar to that of non-minority citizens, attests to their relatively successful integration and secured sense of citizenship.

Israelis of Russian and Ethiopian descent, despite differences in their integration and status, are similar in pride and belonging to attitudes of the control group, demonstrating, respectively, their successful integration and the strong desire to do so. For Ethiopians, the fight against discrimination is about the demand for equal citizenship based on belonging to the nation and relies, especially among the younger generation, upon republican perceptions of contribution. Arab citizens and Haredim demonstrate lower feelings of belonging and pride, and distance from state and society. Arabs, formally full citizens, are in practice discriminated and marginalized, their potential for meaningful citizenship limited by not belonging to the national collective. For Haredim, an integral part of the Jewish nation, the exclusion from the state is largely by choice. The way the different groups relate to the state naturally affects their perceptions of police and their expectations from them. Similarly, encounters with police officers, whether as suspects or victims, teach citizens about their status and confirm their image of the state and its institutions.

Our Police?

In many societies across the world, minority populations consistently display lower levels of satisfaction with, trust in and legitimacy of the police. This, as described in the previous chapters, is the result of both the symbolic significance of police and their everyday practices that are perceived as discriminatory. From a symbolic perspective, it could be expected that it would be difficult if not impossible for minority groups to identify with a state perceived as exclusionary and non-neutral (Marx, 2002). Alienation from the state, consequently, should also have a negative effect on perceptions of its institutions, including police. In the survey, however, the differences between the groups were small or insignificant over most questions regarding trust and identification, seemingly blurring differences between the groups. Only ultra-Orthodox differ in their reluctance to identify with police (Table 7.2) and in their lower trust in police

Table 7.2 *Values*

Police protect values important to me (%)	Strongly disagree 1	2	3	4	Strongly agree 5	Mean (S.D.)
Arab	12	12	36	21	19	3.21 (1.2)
Haredim	29	20	27	14	10	2.56 (1.3)
Ethiopian	18	16	27	17	22	3.08 (1.4)
Russian	13	12	33	21	21	3.26 (1.3)
Control Group	13	16	36	20	15	3.09 (1.2)

Table 7.3 *Trust*

I trust police (%)	Strongly agree 1	2	3	4	Strongly disagree 5	Mean (S.D.)
Arab	18	12	30	20	22	3.17 (1.4)
Haredim	20	21	33	15	13	2.80 (1.3)
Ethiopian	19	12	24	15	29	3.23 (1.5)
Russian	10	13	32	26	19	3.33 (1.2)
Control Group	11	14	34	25	16	3.21 (1.2)

(Table 7.3). Focus groups, however, and other qualitative resources, show a more nuanced picture regarding identification and trust.

Trust in general, and in the police in particular, is a "fuzzy" concept (Worrall, 1999) subjected to different ideas about what constitutes good policing, based upon varied concerns, interests and experiences.

While ultra-Orthodox's distrust and Russians' trust of police is not difficult to explain by their respectively critical stance towards the state and largely successful integration, the trust of Ethiopians and Arabs requires explanation. Ethiopians' trust, we argue (see also: Abu et al., 2017), can be explained by their strong desire to integrate, expression of trust reflecting shared values and belonging. However, in the focus groups, especially among young people, different voices were heard, highly critical of police and of discrimination. Also, the documented beating of Ethiopians by police officers and the demonstrations that took place since 2015 (described in Chapter 4) brought forth new voices, mostly from young people, confident and assertive, with new demands for equal and inclusive citizenship. These new voices, of people born in Israel, or who immigrated when very young, rejected attempts to explain away their discrimination as the result of "cultural differences." Raised in Israel, educated in its school system and serving in the military, their demands to put an end to discrimination placed responsibility on the state and its institutions.

Arab citizens' alignment and trust, close to that of all other groups but the Haredim, attests to other dilemmas we explore, torn between disdain of police (representing the state and with a history of violence) and the dire need for policing to curb rising crime and violence. A more recent survey (Hermann et al., 2016) finds much greater gaps between Jewish and Arab citizens in their trust of police (42 compared to 27 percent). Also, a study comparing perceptions of Jews and Arabs in a mixed town (Jaffa) finds significant differences, the proximity of the groups allowing comparisons and evoking perceptions of relative deprivation (Mentovich et al., 2018). Finally, also among Arab citizens, in the focus groups more voices and concerns were raised, as well as more negative feelings towards police. For Arab citizens, the combined perception of police violence (especially fatal shootings) and police neglect demonstrate their vulnerability and unequal citizenship.

To Serve and Protect I: Over-Policing

The use of excessive force against citizens and their targeting as suspects for no other reason than being part of a minority group conveys a powerful message about the differential structure of citizenship. The targeting of "visible minorities," and their securitization, sets them apart from other citizens and has wider and negative social repercussions. Visibility, stigmatization, securitization and vulnerability subject minorities to being profiled by police officers and more likely to experience verbal and physical abuse. "Racial profiling," explicitly or implicitly adopted by police, uses generalizations based on race, ethnicity, religion or national origin as the basis for suspicion in directing law enforcement actions (Closs and McKenna, 2006; Wortley and Tanner, 2003). In this process of racialization, skin color becomes a category that triggers police actions, from stop and search, to arrests and, at times, more use of force than otherwise (Walker et al., 2000).

Ethiopians are the most susceptible among the groups for racial profiling, being visible, suffering from stigmatization and vulnerability. Arab citizens, possibly less visible than Ethiopians, also suffer stigmatization and are strongly securitized and, consequently, vulnerable. Finally, ultra-Orthodox are highly visible, self-segregating and unpopular, but less stigmatized and vulnerable than the other two groups. In the survey (Table 7.4) Ethiopians expressed stronger concern over police violence than other groups, indicating that visibility and vulnerability are central. In the focus groups, Arab citizens and ultra-Orthodox have also expressed concerns about police violence directed against them, signaling prejudice and inequality.

Police violence underscores the troubled history of the relations between Arab citizens and police – the use of deadly force against them a reminder of their securitization. Securitization, for Arab citizens,

Table 7.4 *Over-Policing*

Police stop or arrest people in your neighborhood for no reason (%)	Strongly disagree 1	2	3	4	Strongly agree 5	Mean (S.D.)
Arab	31	22	27	12	9	2.45 (1.3)
Haredim	40	26	19	10	7	2.19 (1.2)
Ethiopian	22	13	24	21	20	3.04 (1.4)
Russian	39	24	22	13	3	2.16 (1.2)
Control Group	38	26	19	9	8	2.23 (1.3)

implies that national security is first and foremost the security of the Jewish people, that security concerns often trump citizenship rights and, consequently, that Arab citizens are over-policed. The lingering memory of the 2000 events when thirteen demonstrators were killed by police fire, more recent shootings of Arab citizens during raids, and police violence against Arab political activists, all lead Arab citizens to conclude that police are violent and biased. At the same, explained below, Arab citizens are more vulnerable to "internal" violence, the result of rising crime and require more rather than less policing to provide them with security. While this need does not diminish the importance of over-policing, it evokes, both symbolically and practically, acute dilemmas and uncertainties for Arab citizens' engagement with police that we discuss below.

Over-policing of Haredim is limited and contained. While they are visible, standing out in their black garb and head covers, they are neither perceived a security threat nor are they associated with crime. Violent clashes with police take place during demonstrations that escalate, but in most cases only the more radical elements of Haredi society are actively involved in these demonstrations. Thus, while Haredim view police violence with disdain, and even anger, most are not exposed to it unless they take part in those demonstrations or happen to be unfortunate bystanders. Unlike Arab citizens and Israelis of Ethiopian descent they are not exposed to racial profiling and are largely able to maintain distance from police.

Visible, stigmatized and vulnerable, Ethiopians are the group most exposed to racial profiling and police violence. In the focus groups, young men described their fear and disdain from police officers, explained by their own negative experiences or those of their friends and relatives. Stories of profiling and abuse became abundant, first, after the documented beating of Damas Pikada and, second, the killing of Yehuda Biadga, with the pent-up anger of young Ethiopians who took to the streets and made their voices heard. For Ethiopians, who perceive themselves, unlike Arabs and Haredim, as an integral part of both Israeli society and the Jewish nation, the significance of over-policing cannot be overstated. Also, the fact that Ethiopians are formally part of the nation and perform their duties as republican citizens makes their discrimination difficult to justify. Consequently, the demonstrations and public sympathy have led to the formation of a government commission that officially acknowledged that systemic racism against Ethiopians exists.

To Serve and Protect II: Under-Policing

Feelings of inadequate police services and insecurity can exist among both majority and minority groups. These perceptions can be the result of real rise in crime and unsafe neighborhoods or unfounded concerns from sensationalist media coverage of events that raise concerns and fears. What sets apart minorities from majorities is that under-policing is attributed to discrimination and at times intended neglect. "Relative deprivation" (Gurr, 1970), when minorities compare themselves to others, affects their evaluation of citizenship, alignment with the state and judgment of policies. This group position of unfair and exclusionary treatment is directed not only against dominant groups, perceived to be better off, but also against social institutions (Weitzer and Tuch, 2006) and the state, perceived as responsible for discriminatory allocation of resources. As the survey findings demonstrate (Table 7.5) Arab citizens believe more than all other groups that they receive less attention from police when needed, and that less police resources are employed for their benefit, making them more vulnerable to crime and violence than other groups.

Arab citizens feel less secure in their neighborhoods than Jewish citizens. The growing crime rate, especially violent crime and murders, is a major concern for Arab citizens. While police took pride that crime-related violence was successfully curbed among the Jewish citizens, among Arab citizens the picture was very different. Crime rates soared, the murder rate being three times higher than among Jewish citizens. Rampant crime, needless to say, can neither be explained nor solved simply by the presence of police officers or more authority. Rather it requires addressing the structural inequality and the lack of opportunities that breed alienation and crime. Arab citizens, as described in Chapter 3, suffer residential, educational and occupational segregation; higher unemployment and poverty.

Consequently, police inability to curb crime is part of a vicious cycle where poverty and crime feed each other. In the focus groups, participants alluded to the connection between lack of opportunities, poverty and crime, but also to police responsibility for the dire situation of Arab towns and neighborhoods. The large number of illegal weapons used at large, gangs taking over the streets and unsolved murders were attributed not to police inability but rather their lack of will to invest necessary efforts.

Table 7.5 *Under-Policing*

Question/statement (%)	Worse 1	2	3	4	Better 5	Mean (S.D.)
If you would file a complaint of a crime, how would you be treated by the police, compared to others?						
Arab	13	10	67	5	5	2.79 (0.9)
Haredim	12	15	62	7	4	2.75 (0.9)
Ethiopian	27	8	47	13	5	2.61 (1.2)
Russian	7	8	74	8	2	2.90 (0.7)
Control Group	5	6	64	16	9	3.17 (0.9)
Police service in your neighborhood compared to others is worse/better						
Arab	24	19	33	12	12	2.69 (1.3)
Haredim	13	20	41	17	10	2.92 (1.1)
Ethiopian	19	10	33	18	21	3.12 (1.4)
Russian	10	9	42	24	15	3.24 (1.1)
Control Group	8	10	45	22	15	3.26 (1.1)

Simultaneously under- and over-policed, alienated from the state and indifferent to symbolic importance of police, yet with no viable alternative for security provision, Arab citizens develop a complex relationship with police. This relationship, mixing disdain and dependency, is embedded in wider questions of citizenship and belonging. The Israeli government, in reference to new plans for Arab towns and villages, declared once and again it will enhance personal safety, quality of life and economic growth (see Chapter 3). Under government directives, new police stations will be opened in Arab towns, existing stations will be expanded and Arab citizens will be recruited to police. Arab citizens, especially political activists, have raised concerns that police expansion is aimed at political control rather than equal service, and that eradicating discrimination and poverty, and other structural causes of inequality, need to be addressed. The simultaneous, and similarly contradictory, government policies of declared resource allocation to narrow economic inequality and legislation that entrenches political inequality raises more suspicion and potentially more difficulties.

Fairness

Fairness, and perceptions of fairness, are essential components of meaningful citizenship. If equality of treatment is the main parameter to assess the exercise of citizenship, it is measured by citizens in their everyday interaction with state institutions, and often in comparison to their fellow citizens. Judgments of fairness include evaluations of how decisions are made by authorities and how people over whom authority is exercised are treated. Specifically, citizens' trust in the police is primarily dependent on whether they perceive police actions to be fair, namely respectful and just (Sunshine and Tyler, 2003b; Tyler 2001, 2006). Fairness means that police officers treat citizens with respect, maintain the rule of the law, and allow them to have a voice in decisions concerning them. Fairness, however, especially when minorities are concerned, is based not only on evaluated specific interactions with individual officers, but also on general policies that police carry out and their perceived implications for different groups. This means not only egalitarian status between citizens, but also attention to different sensitivities and needs of particular groups.

Like trust, fairness is a fuzzy concept that can mean different things for different people, so that general questions about "police fairness" may tell only part of the story. Indeed, our survey (Table 7.6) shows little, if any, difference is found between the groups in assessment of police fairness, as all groups rate police fairness as not very high. This evaluation, also, is based not on personal encounters with police officers, as most respondents, in all groups, declared that they have not personally experienced unfair treatment by police. Our focus groups, however, and other survey questions discussed above, not only show that unfairness is a concern, but also that different groups

Table 7.6 *Fairness*

Question/statement (%)	Strongly disagree 1	2	3	4	Strongly agree 5	Mean (S.D.)
Police treat people fairly						
Arab	19	16	40	16	9	2.81
						(1.2)
Haredim	14	21	36	22	7	2.87
						(1.1)
Ethiopian	22	20	35	15	9	2.70
						(1.2)
Russian	9	15	44	26	6	3.07
						(1.0)
Control Group	10	18	43	23	6	2.98
						(1.0)
Have you personally experienced discriminatory policing?	No	Yes				
Arab	81	19				
Haredim	79	16				NR
Ethiopian	78	22				
Russian	89	11				
Control Group	80	20				

have different concerns regarding fairness and different measurements they use for evaluating police fairness.

Russian immigrants' relative integration and confident citizenship, and Haredim's distance from state and society, limit their concerns of police fairness. For Russians, problems of police are structural and universal rather than particular and discriminatory. Haredim, reluctant to involve police, alluded to police violence, but were largely unthreatened personally as most violence took place in demonstrations. Conversely, for Ethiopians and Arab citizens police unfairness was a concern, albeit for different reasons. For Arab citizens, police unfairness is in both over-policing and under-policing, demonstrating defunct citizenship, where their lives appear to matter less than those of others. Arab citizens shot or beaten by police officers, on the one hand, and police failure to provide security, perceived to be of intended neglect, on the other hand, explain resentment and alienation associated with unfairness. For Ethiopians, unfairness is about over-policing and police violence, perceived as part of wider discriminatory practices of the state and its institutions. The gap between state-led celebration of their coming to Israel, their formal belonging, desire to belong and contribution to the common good, and between racial discourse and practices that keep them apart, has both symbolic and practical costs.

Overall, groups' assessments of police fairness demonstrate that minorities not only differ from the majority in their perception of police, they also differ among themselves, demonstrating the complex structure of citizenship. While procedural justice is likely to positively affect perceptions of fairness, where Arab citizens and Ethiopians are concerned it might not be enough to satisfy significant concerns and demands. Politeness, respect and dignity will have to be supplemented with measures that eradicate police biased treatment, allocate resources in a fair manner, commit to protect all citizens and make police accountable.

Representation

The presence of minorities in police could be an indication of success-ful integration and alignment with the state, but also the result of individual decisions based on practical, instrumental considerations. Excluded and marginalized minority groups who harbor negative perceptions of police are likely to object to the enlistment of their members. Wearing the uniform of police may symbolize unwarranted identification with the state and, more importantly, mean taking part in securing political and social order they find objectionable. Minorities, however, may also see benefits in members who join the police, if they believe they could positively influence police and serve their communities. Also, for minority groups who seek future integra-tion, and believe it is possible, members serving in police demonstrate the group's loyalty and contribution. For members of minority groups, enlistment considerations include individual benefits (like a steady job), but also collective sentiments and concerns over their standing in their communities.

For minority groups in Israel these considerations (Table 7.7) may be especially complex. The blurred boundaries between military and police, many police officers coming from the army and police involved

Table 7.7 *Representation*

Question/statement (%)	Strongly disagree 1		2	3	4	Strongly agree 5	Mean (S.D.)
It is important that police be representative of all groups in Israeli society?							
Arab	10		6	12	15	57	4.04 (1.4)
Haredim	19		6	14	17	46	3.66 (1.6)
Ethiopian	9		1	4	9	76	4.43 (1.2)
Russian	10		4	9	14	63	4.16 (1.3)
Control Group	7		5	8	16	64	4.26 (1.2)
	No 1		2	3	4	Yes 5	Mean (S.D.)
[For a salary meeting your expectations] would you consider becoming a police officer?	1		2	3	4	5	Mean (S.D.)
Arab	58		7	11	10	14	2.16 (1.5)
Haredim	71		4	9	8	8	1.77 (1.3)
Ethiopian	3		7	8	18	29	2.92 (1.7)
Russian	27		6	14	21	33	3.91 (1.6)
Control Group	38		6	15	18	23	2.81 (1.6)
If a friend or a family member decides to join the police, would you support him/her?	1		2	3	4	5	Mean (S.D.)
Arab	35		8	15	17	26	2.90 (1.6)
Haredim	28		12	16	14	31	3.10 (1.6)
Ethiopian	10		4	12	16	53	4.09 (1.3)
Russian	8		6	19	24	44	3.91 (1.2)
Control Group	8		8	18	22	44	3.86 (1.3)

in military-type operations, makes the police attractive to some groups but problematic to others. In addition, police suffer from a low image, salaries for young recruits considered low and working hours that are long and intense. Yet, police work may be attractive to individuals, driven by patriotism or adrenalin, and provide a steady and stable job. These considerations, as discussed in the previous chapters, create collective and individual dilemmas and debates that provide a powerful demonstration of the ways the minority groups studied articulate their citizenship and belonging.

For the majority of Jewish Israelis, represented by our control group, questions regarding enlistment seem to carry little if any ideological weight. Only a minority would consider becoming police officers, probably because of the low pay and hard work. Conversely, the majority of them would not object to a friend or a family member who would choose to do so. As expected, minority groups have different perspectives about serving in the police, perspectives related to their status and place in the hierarchy of the citizenship regime and their expectations for the future.

Haredim, more than all other groups, are reluctant to consider becoming police officers, largely uninterested in questions of representation. This is partly due to the occupational aspirations of young religious men, and families' expectations, to become religious scholars and remain within the community confines. The lack of interest in representation also demonstrates the distance they maintain from the state and its institutions. Nevertheless, the fact that support for representation exists, though lower than among other groups, possibly alludes to the changes (described in Chapter 5) in the relations between Haredim and the state, with growing patriotism and greater involvement in security-related organizations. Still, the meaning of citizenship and belonging remains unresolved and, in practical terms, the negative image of police and the dominant model of religious scholarships also explain their tepid view of enlistment and representation.

Turning our attention to Russians, Ethiopians and Arab citizens, for whom steady employment might be considered important, particular patterns and dilemmas emerge. For Russians, who hold a patriotic stance and are relatively secure in their citizenship, enlistment to police does not appear to carry any collective dilemmas but only pragmatic individual calculations. Ethiopians are well represented in police (and even more in the border police, under the jurisdiction of the military), would consider police service more than most groups and would strongly support others who would enlist. The perceived institutional racism of police (and other institutions) that might turn people away from enlistment is matched by a strong sense of patriotism, a desire to belong as well as practical employment considerations. While in the focus groups the actual impact of Ethiopian police officers on the police and community was doubted, these doubts did not challenge the basic desire and demand to belong and the importance of representation to demonstrate belonging and citizenship.

Obviously, for Arab citizens, becoming police officers was most problematic among all groups, but also strongly disputed within. The troubled history and continued police violence, the role of police in execution of policies considered illegitimate like house demolitions in Arab towns and villages, and the symbolic significance of wearing a police uniform, all make enlistment difficult. It is hardly surprising, therefore, that Arab citizens are less likely to consider enlistment and to support others who would enlist. But, in practice, while Arab citizens are underrepresented in police, there is also a growing support for having Arab citizens in the force. In April 2016, Jamal Hakrush, a Muslim Arab, was appointed deputy commissioner to lead a new unit aimed at improving police service in Arab communities. A campaign to encourage Arab citizens to join the police was launched, drawing many applications and enabling the recruitment of more than 300 Muslim officers, including women.

Recruitment, as discussed in Chapter 3, remains a divisive issue among Arab citizens, with the lingering memory of the past and more recent violent clashes. But, despite the troubled history and present concerns, enlistment is not ruled out by many. This cannot be explained only by individual instrumental decisions of secure employment but must take into account collective considerations and concerns, which legitimize recruitment. The rise of violent crime and insecurity in Arab towns and villages is a major cause of concern, police held responsible for their perceived lack of efforts and intended neglect. At the same time, however, demands to take responsibility and action also arise within Arab communities. Under these circumstances, support for recruitment is less about the symbolic importance of representation in police, and more about expected practical and "local" impact of Arab police officers, possibly also in an attempt to de-politicize the debate.

Oversight and Accountability

Police misconduct is a critical issue, especially for minorities who are more vulnerable and disempowered – unable to hold police accountable. Allegations of police violence will often be denied by police, described as a necessary use of force, or explained away as isolated events of "rotten apples." While majorities, more concerned with police effectiveness, might be satisfied with minimal measures to increase accountability, minorities would demand more comprehensive changes. These would include making violent officers accountable for their actions and expansion of public oversight over police work. Accountability and oversight may sound natural for any democracy, but when police officers perceive themselves as a bulwark between order and chaos, and minorities are securitized, these demands would encounter resistance from police with support of other citizens. Charges that oversight is required because police deliberately fail to investigate complaints, and that violent officers are not punished, will be met by claims that such measures will undermine police ability to operate and provide security. For Arab citizens, the fact that no charges were pressed against officers involved in the death of thirteen people in 2000, or more recently in the killing of Yacoub Abu Al-Qia'an, is a reason not to trust police; similarly, in demonstrations Ethiopian young people chanted repeatedly: "A violent officer's place is in jail."

Responses to the survey (Table 7.8) not only demonstrate little, if any, differences between the groups concerning accountability and oversight, but also apparent contradictions within them. Citizens of all groups believe that police use force indiscriminately but, at the same time, also agree that it is not assertive enough. Similarly, they hold that police should be given more freedom of action, but also that strong oversight is required. These contradictions attest to real dilemmas when citizens want police to be both fair and effective and remain uncertain about their priorities. Even minorities who are over-policed and demand to be treated as equal citizens cannot escape these dilemmas as security concerns may be significantly important. Ethiopians, part of the Jewish collective and aligned with the state, prioritize security like others and take part in its production through military service and police roles. Oversight and accountability, while supported, are matched by security concerns and a demonstration of

Table 7.8 *Oversight*

Question/statement (%)	Strongly disagree 1	2	3	4	Strongly agree 5	Mean (S.D.)
Officers who use unjustified force should be punished						
Arab	4	1	2	7	86	4.72 (0.9)
Haredim	2	1	2	9	86	4.76 (0.7)
Ethiopian	6	2	5	5	81	4.53 (1.1)
Russian	2	1	2	6	89	4.81 (0.7)
Control Group	2	2	5	10	82	4.67 (0.8)
Police do not enforce the law in my neighborhood						
Arab	18	13	38	16	15	2.98 (1.3)
Haredim	32	17	26	13	13	2.58 (1.4)
Ethiopian	18	17	34	16	15	2.93 (1.3)
Russian	18	14	30	19	19	3.07 (1.4)
Control Group	20	18	30	17	15	2.89 (1.3)
Police should have more authority and autonomy to be able to protect the public						
Arab	12	11	28	23	27	3.42 (1.3)
Haredim	23	17	24	18	18	2.89 (1.4)
Ethiopian	18	12	20	15	36	3.38 (1.5)
Russian	22	11	22	17	27	3.16 (1.5)
Control Group	19	12	22	21	26	3.23 (1.4)

21121221121221221122112212212121121221221221221212

Table 7.8 (*cont.*)

Question/statement (%)	Strongly disagree 1	2	3	4	Strongly agree 5	Mean (S.D.)
Strong oversight of police is necessary						
Arab	3		2	11	23 60	4.34 (1.0)
Haredim	3		4	17	22 54	4.24 (1.0)
Ethiopian	6		4	13	25 52	4.14 (1.1)
Russian	22		11	22	17 27	3.16 (1.5)
Control Group	3		5	17	27 48	4.12 (1.1)

loyalty. Arab citizens, on their behalf, insist that police be held accountable for violence against them. Demands for accountability, however, are matched by rampant crime and growing insecurity that could explain the desire for strong and assertive police.

While the importance of oversight does not surface in surveys, it cannot be entirely discarded. To begin with, fairness and effectiveness, in spite of popular opinions, do not necessarily stand in opposition to each other. Rather, as procedural justice theory (Chapter 1) suggests, perceptions of fairness, trust and effectiveness can reinforce each other. Second, while minorities' security concerns might overshadow in surveys their concerns of police fairness, they do not diminish them. In the focus groups, complaints of police's unjust use of violence and abuse were significant. These pent-up feelings come out either in angry demonstration or in more subtle reluctance to cooperate with police. And, third, from a normative point of view, accountability and oversight of police are important even if they protect "only" citizens of minority groups, or the more vulnerable members of these groups, and are overlooked by majorities more concerned with security and hesitant to undermine police authority associated with it.

Citizenship and Policing

Interactions with representatives of government implicitly mediate to citizens their relation to the state (Lipsky, 1980: 4) and their status, in comparison to other citizens. Citizenship is not only a legal and political membership in a state, but also a set of practices through which individuals and groups articulate their claims for rights (Isin and Wood, 1999: 4), sometimes against the state and its institutions and often in competition with other groups (Ben-Porat and Turner, 2011: 7). Ethnic, racial and national hierarchies, demonstrated among other things by the way groups and individuals are policed, mean that citizenship is a site of negotiation, contest and contention. Citizens' contact and exchanges with police, symbolizing and performing state power, as suspects or victims, are affected by questions of status and belonging, often delineating differences between majority and minorities and between minorities. These interactions, differently stated, are "institutionalized" through citizenship regimes, where minorities hold different statuses and resources, have different expectations, desires and needs, and, accordingly, relate differently to the state and institutions. Minorities' relation with and to police, as argued throughout the book, tell a greater story of equality, belonging and citizenship.

The four minority groups studied in the book are positioned differently, or institutionalized, in Israel's citizenship regime. Institutions are largely stable and "path dependent," but are also affected by external and internal developments and may change, incrementally or rapidly. The minority groups we study are implicated by their status and belonging that affect their relations with police, making even simple interactions all but neutral. Whether they perceive themselves as over- or under-policed, they draw from over-policing and neglect conclusions about the lower value of their citizenship, and vice versa. Minorities, however, are not necessarily passive or submissive. Rather, struggles they wage against police, choices whether to avoid or cooperate and decisions to enlist all contribute to the dynamic reality of citizenship and to possible future changes.

If police are "the state in a shining armour," with extraordinary power over citizens, their significance in creation and maintenance of social hierarchies cannot be overstated. Police policies and practices have a direct bearing on individuals' ability to exercise their citizenship. The hierarchy of citizenship we described throughout this book is determined by the visibility, negative stereotypes and political vulnerability of the groups. Minority groups who are visibly identifiable and negatively stereotyped are more likely to be stopped and searched and more exposed to police abuse. Negative stereotypes and securitization, in turn, also impact minorities' legitimacy and political efficacy, namely their ability to demand equal treatment. Being repeatedly stopped and searched, and in fear of police or, conversely, neglected by police and left unprotected from violence, limit individuals' ability to move freely in public space and, consequently, their citizenship.

Russian immigrants' pragmatic and often critical stance towards police, (resembling attitudes of non-minority Israelis), represents both their largely successful integration but also some distance from Israeli society that they choose to maintain, described elsewhere as "passive citizenship" (Philippov and Bystrov, 2011). With rapid economic mobilization, high educational achievements, taking active part in both military service and the labor market, even if distinguishable, Russian immigrants' distinction carries limited, if any, negative stereotypes. Russian immigrants may be more distant from authorities and the state than the rest of the Jewish Israelis (ibid.), their citizenship is passive but at the same time secure and largely unthreatened by police.

Haredi relations to police demonstrate common conceptions of fundamentalist citizenship, hostility and resistance, but alongside an instrumental approach. At the same time, the gradual and careful integration and new patriotism, forming what Stadler et al. (2011) describe as "inclusive fundamentalism," can be identified through some of the voices. Haredim are highly distinguishable, standing out in their unique garb, but usually not stereotyped as security or crime threats. Yet, historically, Haredi communities developed a suspicious if not hostile relation to police. The symbolic importance of police is minimal for Haredim, distanced by choice from state and society, and indifferent to republican conceptions of citizenship. Descriptions of police brutality are part of Haredim history, but their significance may have declined as it is limited to demonstrations and affects mostly those who chose to take part in them. More important was the Haredim concern of autonomy that demanded to keep police outside community affairs.

Careful but steady integration in the labor market and academic education, growing patriotism and identification with the state, and recognition of problems within the community that require intervention, all explain a more ambivalent attitude towards police and policing, and of citizenship in general. Trust in police remains relatively low and the belief in communities' power high, as is the importance attributed to maintaining the community boundaries, typical of an enclave society. Yet, growing interest in security issues, volunteering in civil society organizations involved in security related issues (Chapter 5) and recognition of the need for policing may (as part of a more general renegotiation of citizenship) narrow the alienation from police.

Police and policing have a direct and important, albeit different, impact on Arab citizens and Israelis of Ethiopian descent. Contrary to the relatively secure citizenship of Russian immigrants and Haredim, visible and distinct, but not stigmatized, Arabs and Ethiopians are visible, stigmatized and vulnerable. Consequently, encounters with police are loaded with suspicion and at times fear, reflecting wider concerns and frustrations. Securitization, profiling, use of force, humiliation or, conversely, neglect and insecurity have a direct bearing on citizens' capacity to exercise their full citizenship, to move and be present in public spaces and, consequently, on their perceptions of their place in society.

"When a police officer comes into contact with a person from a community more involved in crime, it is natural he will suspect him," explained Israel's Police Commissioner when asked about racial profiling of Ethiopians (Ginat, 2016). Racial profiling and police violence against Ethiopians, mostly young men, has been for a long time denied, ignored or described as temporal. The immigration of Ethiopian Jews to Israel was described as the successful accomplishment of a national mission, and current hardships as a "natural" consequence of a "cultural gap."

Over-policing, namely racial profiling and police violence, has been the major concern of Ethiopians, especially young men. High visibility, negative stereotypes and especially vulnerability are the explanations they provide for police abuse. The limited political resources of the community, due to its relatively small number, and the older generation's lack of familiarity with the bureaucratic systems render young Ethiopians vulnerable to police abuse. Also, the constant attempts to use cultural frames of explanation, termed "cultural gaps," shifts the focus from institutional racism to the community's difficult integration.

The demonstrations in the spring of 2015 brought to the fore not only the pent-up anger of young Ethiopians, frustrated with discrimination and marginalization, but also an articulation of republican citizenship discourse. Highlighting belonging and contribution and rejecting the cultural frames, a new generation of Ethiopians demanded equality and justice. Juxtaposing military service and being Israeli with discrimination and profiling, the demands could not be ignored. The ability to evoke sympathy among mainstream Israelis to their distress and, more importantly, the rise of an assertive and articulate young leadership, have put both government and the police on the defensive. While actual changes are yet to be seen, Ethiopians seem to successfully claim their place and articulate their citizenship.

Police and policing both demonstrate and maintain the qualitative difference between Jewish and Arab citizenship. First, securitization renders Arab citizens threats, subjected to constant scrutiny and, at times, violence. Second, Arab citizens are insecure and vulnerable to violence and crime in their own towns and villages. The police shooting of Yacoub Abu Al-Qia'an (described in Chapter 3) is exemplary of the former. It began with the military-like operation for a house demolition, led to a tragic result (the death of Al-Qia'an and of a police officer, Erez Levi), in turn excused or explained by "security" – police's attempts to link Al-Qia'an with ISIS. The securitization of Arab citizens, implicated by the Israeli–Palestinian and Israeli–Arab conflicts, is gradually extended to political struggles, framing demands for equality as threats and constraining citizenship. Accordingly, politically active Arab citizens view police as oppressive and discriminatory, enforcing an unjust political order.

For the majority of Arab citizens, however, police violence is of secondary importance. Rather, it is the dire situation of rampant crime and violence, illegal weapons and a murder rate more than twice as high as in Jewish towns and neighborhoods. Over-policing, in the form of violence, and under-policing, interpreted as neglect, explain Arab citizens' distrust of police and of the state. The government has shown a contradictory attitude, investing resources to close economic gaps between Jewish and Arab citizens, but at the same time promoting legislation that undermines their equal political status, thereby simultaneously inflating and deflating citizenship. Similarly, while police-suggested reforms of more forces might alleviate the dire security situation in Arab towns and villages, Arab citizens still harbor doubts as to whether a strong and present police force, by itself, is the road to equal citizenship.

The perceptions of police and policing we studied here teach us where different groups in Israel position themselves within the hierarchy of citizenship. The "thin blue line" is not a simple division of order and disorder, with citizens aligned according to their behavior. Order and disorder, as demonstrated here, are often associated with and provided to individuals by group affiliations. Everyday decisions, to stop and search young Ethiopian men, or to assign capable forces to Arab neighborhoods, are critical for individuals to exercise their citizenship and trust the state and its institutions. In a complex web of citizenship, the blue line delineates ethnic, racial and class divides, demarcating those who are served and protected from those securitized and neglected. For the latter, equal citizenship is yet to be achieved.

Bibliography

Abebe, Dany Adeno. 2015, May 3. "The Problem Is Also Yours." *Yedioth Aharonot.*

2019, January 20. "The Israeli Police Badge of Shame." Ynet.

Abraham Fund. 2018. Personal Security Index: Crime, Violence and Policing in Arab Cities 2017, www.abrahamfund.org/webfiles/fck.

Abu, Ofir, Fany Yuval and Guy Ben-Porat. 2017. "Race, Racism and Policing: Responses of Ethiopian Jews in Israel to Stigmatization by the Police." *Ethnicities* 17(5): 688–706.

Abu Suiss, Ahmed. 2016, January 26. "Who Killed Sami El Jaer." *Walla News,* https://news.walla.co.il/item/2929759.

Adams, Brian. 2004. "Public Meetings and the Democratic Process." *Public Administration Review* 64: 43–54.

Albrecht, Hans Jorg. 1997. "Ethnic Minorities, Crime, and Criminal Justice in Germany." *Crime and Justice* 21: 31–99.

Al-Haj, Majid. 2002. "Ethnic Mobilization in an Ethno-National State: The Case of Immigrants from the Former Soviet Union in Israel." *Ethnic and Racial Studies* 25(2): 238–257.

Ali, Nohad. 2014. *Crime and Violence in Arab Society in Israel: Institutional Conspiracy or a "Cultural Crime."* Haifa: Haifa University, Jewish-Arab Center (Hebrew).

Almond, Gabriel A., R. Scott Appleby and Emmanuel Sivan. 2003. *Strong Religion: The Rise of Fundamentalisms around the World.* Chicago: University of Chicago Press.

Andrews, Rhys, George A. Boyne, Kenneth J. Meier, Laurence J. O'Toole and Richard M. Walker. 2005. "Representative Bureaucracy, Organizational Strategy, and Public Service Performance: An Empirical Analysis of English Local Government." *JPART* 15: 489–504.

Arian, Asher, Tamar Hermann, Nir Atmor, Yael Hadar, Yuval Lebel, and Hila Zaban. 2008. *Auditing Israeli Democracy 2008: Between the State and Civil Society.* Jerusalem: Israel Democracy Institute (Hebrew).

Archer, Margaret. 1990. "Foreword." In M. Elbrow and E. King (eds.), *Globalization, Knowledge and Society.* London: Sage, pp. 1–13.

Axtmann, Ronald. 1996. *Liberal Democracy into the Twenty-First Century: Globalization, Integration, and the Nation-State.* Manchester, UK: Manchester University Press.

Balibar, Etienne. 1991. "Is There a 'Neo-Racism'?" In E. Balibar and I. Wallerstein (eds.), *Race, Nation, Class: Ambiguous Identities.* London: Verso, pp. 17–28.

2005. "Difference, Otherness, Exclusion." *Parallax* 11(1): 19–34.

Banting, Keith, and Will Kymlicka. 2003. "Are Multiculturalism Policies Bad for the Welfare State?" *Dissent* (Fall): 59–66.

Barlow, David E., and Melissa H. Barlow. 2000. *Police in a Multicultural Society – An American Story.* Minnesota: Waveland Press.

Bar-On Maman, Shani. 2018. "Protest and Class in Beer-Sheva, 1948–1963." *Iyunim* 29: 82–110.

Barzilai, Gad. 2003. *Communities and Law: Politics and Cultures of Legal Identities.* Ann Arbor, MI: University of Michigan Press.

Bayley, David H. 1985. *Patterns of Policing: A Comparative International Analysis.* New Brunswick, NJ: Rutgers University Press.

1994. *Police for the Future.* New York: Oxford University Press.

1998. "The Development of Modern Policing." In L. Gaines (ed.), *Policing Perspectives: An Anthology.* New York: Oxford University Press, pp. 67–68.

2002. "Law Enforcement and the Rule of Law: Is There a Tradeoff?" *Criminology & Public Policy* 2(1): 133–154.

2005. *Changing the Guard: Developing Democratic Police Abroad.* Oxford: Oxford University Press.

Beetham, David. 1991. "Max Weber and the Legitimacy of the Modern State." *Analyse & Kritik* 13(1): 34–45.

Ben-Dor, Gabriel, Ami Pedhazur, and Badi Hasisi. 2003. "Anti-Liberalism and the Use of Force in Israeli Democracy." *Journal of Military Sociology* 31(1): 119–142.

Ben-Eliezer, U. 1997. "Rethinking the Civil-Military Relations Paradigm: The Inverse Relation between Militarism and Praetorianism through the Example of Israel." *Comparative Political Studies* 30(3): 356–374.

2004. "Becoming a Black Jew: Cultural Racism and Anti-Racism in Contemporary Israel." *Social Identities* 10(2): 245–266.

2008. "Multicultural Society and Everyday Cultural Racism: Second Generation of Ethiopian Jews in Israel's 'Crisis of Modernization'." *Ethnic and Racial Studies* 31(5): 935–961.

Ben-Porat, Guy. 2008a. "We Are Here, They Are There: Between Peace and Exclusion in Israel/Palestine." *Citizenship Studies* 12(3): 307–320.

2008b. "Policing Multicultural States: Lessons from the Canadian Model." *Policing and Society* 18(4): 411–425.

2013. *Between State and Synagogue: The Secularization of Modern Israel.* New York: Cambridge University Press.

Ben-Porat, Guy, and As'ad Ghanem. 2017. "Introduction: Securitization and the Shrinking of Citizenship." *Citizenship Studies* 12(3): 195–201.

Ben-Porat, Guy, Omri Shamir, and Fany Yuval. 2016. "Value for Money: Political Consumerism in Israel." *Journal of Consumer Culture* 16(2): 592–613.

Ben-Porat, Guy, and Bryan S. Turner. 2011. "Introduction." In Guy Ben-Porat and Bryan S. Turner (eds.), *The Contradiction of Israeli Citizenship.* Oxford: Routledge, pp. 1–22.

Ben-Porat, Guy, and Fany Yuval. 2012. "Minorities in Democracy and Policing Policy: From Alienation to Cooperation." *Policing and Society* 22(2): 235–252.

Ben-Meir, Heli, and Yeela Levavi. 2010. "Unique Aspects of Treating Child Victims of Sexual Assault from the Haredi Sector." *Society and Welfare* 30(3–4): 453–475.

Ben-Rafael, Eliezer, and Yochanan Peres. 2005. *Is Israel One? Religion, Nationalism, and Multiculturalism Confounded.* Leiden: Brill.

Ben-Yehuda, Nachman. 2010. *Theocratic Democracy: The Social Construction of Religious and Secular Extremism.* New York: Oxford University Press.

Ben Zikri, Almog, and Josh Breiner. 2018, May 1. "State Attorney Closes the Um Al Hiran Case." *Haaretz.*

Berry, John W. 1997. "Immigration, Acculturation, and Adaptation." *Applied Psychology* 46(1): 5–34.

Beshach, Daniel. 2015, April 5. "Not Enough to Die for the Country." *Walla News.*

Blecherman, Avi. 2015, February 2. "Ethiopian Youth Protest: Police Marks Us All Criminals." *Sicha Mekomit.*

Boggs, Carl. 2000. *The End of Politics: Corporate Power and the Decline in Public Sphere.* New York and London: Guilford Press.

Bonilla-Silva, Eduardo. 2006. *Racism without Racists: Color-Blind Racism and the Persistence of Racial Inequality in America.* Lanham, MD: Rowman & Littlefield.

Boston, Jonathan, and Paul Callister. 2005. "Diversity and Public Policy." *Policy Quarterly* 1(4): 34–44.

Bottoms, Anthony, and Justice Tankebe. 2012. "Beyond Procedural Justice: A Dialogic Approach to Legitimacy in Criminal Justice." *J. Crim. L. & Criminology* 102(1): 119–167.

Bouckaert, Geert, Steven Van De Walle, Bart Maddens, and Jarl K. Kampen. 2002. *Identity vs. Performance: An Overview of Theories Explaining Trust in Government.* Leuven: Katholieke Universitat.

Bradford, Ben. 2014. "Policing and Social Identity: Procedural Justice, Inclusion and Cooperation between Police and Public." *Policing and Society* 24(1): 22–43.

Brass, Paul. 1985. *Ethnic Groups and the State*. London and Sydney: Croom Helm.

Brettell, Caroline B., and James F. Hollifield. 2000. "Introduction: Migration Theory." In Caroline B. Brettell and James F. Hollifield (eds.), *Migration Theory: Talking across Disciplines*. New York: Routledge, pp. 1–17.

Brown, Ben, and William R. Benedict. 2002. "Perceptions of the Police." *Policing: An International Journal of Police Strategies and Management* 25(3): 543–580.

Brown, Benjamin. 2000. *Orthodox Judaism*. Oxford: Blackwell.

Brown, Lee P. 1989. *Community Policing: A Practical Guide for Police Officials*. No. 12. Washington, DC: US Department of Justice, Office of Justice Programs, National Institute of Justice.

Brubaker, Rogers. 1996. *Nationalism Reframed: Nationhood and the National Question in the New Europe*. Cambridge, UK: Cambridge University Press.

    2001. "The Return of Assimilation? Changing Perspectives on Immigration and Its Sequels in France, Germany, and the United States." *Ethnic and Racial Studies* 24(4): 531–548.

Bruce, Steve. 2003. *Politics and Religion*. Cambridge, UK: Blackwell.

Brunson, Rod K., and Jody Miller. 2006. "Gender, Race and Urban Policing: The Experience of African American Youths." *Gender and Society* 20(4): 531–552.

Burstein-Hadad, Noa. 2014. "What Killed Yosef Salamsa?" Hamakom, www.ha-makom.co.il/noa-burshtein-hadad-yosef.

Casey, John. 2000. "International Experiences in Policing Multicultural Societies." *International Journal of Police Science and Management* 3(2): 165–177.

Caspi, Yehoshua. 1990. "From the Mandate Police to the Israel Police." In V. Pilovski (ed.), *From Yishuv to a State 1947–1949*. Haifa: Haifa University Press (Hebrew), pp. 279–290.

Castells, M. 1997. *The Power of Identity*. Vol. 2 of The Information Age: Economy, Society and Culture. Oxford: Basil Blackwell.

Castles, Stephen. 2005. "Nation and Empire: Hierarchies of Citizenship in the New Global Order." *International Politics* 42: 203–224.

Castles, Stephen, and Mark J. Miller. 2009. *The Age of Migration: International Population Movements in the Modern World*. New York and London: The Guilford Press.

Central Bureau of Statistics. 2013. *Population Statistical: Abstract of Israel* 64. Jerusalem: CBS.

Cesari, Jocelyne. 2009. "Securitization of Islam in Europe." In Jocelyne Cesari (ed.), *Muslims in the West after 9/11*. London: Routledge, pp. 19–37.

Chakraborti, N., and Garland, J. 2003. "Under-Researched and Overlooked: An Exploration of the Attitudes of Rural Minority Ethnic Communities towards Crime, Community Safety and the Criminal Justice System." *Journal of Ethnic and Migration Studies* 29(3): 563–572.

Chan, Janet B. 2011. "Racial Profiling and Police Subculture." *Canadian Journal of Criminology and Criminal Justice* 53(1): 75–78.

Channel 10 News. 2017. "Um Al Hiran," www.10.tv/news/150316.

Closs, William J., and Paul F. McKenna. 2006. "Profiling a Problem in Canadian Police Leadership: The Kingston Police Data Collection Project." *Canadian Public Administration* 49(2): 143–160.

Cohen, Asher. 1997. "Religion and State: Secularists, Religious and Haredim." In Z. Zameret and H. Yablonka (eds.), *The First Decade*. Jerusalem: Yad Ben-Zvi, pp. 227–242.

Coicaud, Jean-Marc. 2002. *Legitimacy and Politics: A Contribution to the Study of Political Right and Political Responsibility*. Cambridge, UK: Cambridge University Press.

Coleman, Selden Sally, and Frank Selden. 2001. "Rethinking Diversity in Public Organizations for the 21st Century: Moving toward a Multicultural Model." *Administration and Society* 33: 303–329.

Collier, David, and Steven Levitsky. 1997. "Democracy with Adjectives: Conceptual Innovation in Comparative Research." *World Politics* 49(April): 430–451.

Connor, Walker. 1994. *Ethnonationalism: The Quest for Understanding*. Princeton: Princeton University Press.

Cordner, Gary. 2014. "Community Policing." In Michael D. Reisig and Robert J. Kane (eds.), *The Oxford Handbook of Police and Policing*. New York: Oxford University Press, pp. 148–171.

Crawford, Beverly. 1998. "The Causes of Cultural Conflict: An Institutional Approach." Research Series-Institute of International Studies, University of California Berkeley: 3–43.

Daghash, Maha Taji. 2011. *The Arab Minority and Police Relations: Rising Arab Intra-Communal and Criminal Violence and the Crisis of Citizenship*. Jerusalem: Floersheimer Studies.

Desroches, Frederick J. 1992. "The Occupational Subculture of the Police." In B. K. Cyderman, C. N. O'Toole, and A. Fleras (eds.), *Police, Race and Ethnicity: A Guide for Police Services*. Toronto: Buttersworths.

Dobrowolsky, Alexandra. 2007. "(In)Security and Citizenship: Security, Im/migration and Shrinking Citizenship Regimes." *Theoretical Inquiries in Law* 8(2): 629–662.

Dolev, Daniel. 2018, May 2. "Two Victims, Zero Found Guilty." *Walla News*, https://news.walla.co.il/item/3154546.

Dwivedi, O. P. 2001. "The Challenge of Public Diversity for Good Governance." United Nations Expert Meeting on Managing Diversity in the Civil Service. New York: United Nations Headquarters.

Easton, David. 1965. *A Framework for Political Analysis*. Englewood Cliffs: Prentice Hall.

Efrati, Ido. 2017, June 6. "One Killed as Riots, Clashes with Police Erupt in Israeli Arab City of Kafr Qasem." *Haaretz*, www.haaretz.com/israel-n ews/one-killed-in-clashes-with-police-in-israeli-arab-town-of-kafr-qasem-1.5480701.

Ellison, Graham. 2007. "A Blueprint for Democratic Policing Anywhere in the World? Police Reform, Political Transition, and Conflict Resolution in Northern Ireland." *Police Quarterly* 10(3): 243–269.

Enloe, Cynthia. 1981. "The Growth of the State and Ethnic Mobilization: The American Experience." *Ethnic and Racial Studies* 4(2): 123–136.

Epp, Charles R., Steven Maynard-Moody, and Donald Haider-Markel. 2014. *Pulled Over: How Police Stops Define Race and Citizenship*. Chicago, IL: University of Chicago Press.

Esman, Milton J. 1999. "Public Administration and Conflict Management in Plural Societies: The Case for Representative Bureaucracy." *Public Administration & Development* 19(4): 353–366.

Ettinger, Yair, and Shirley Seidler. 2014, March 19. "Haredi Demonstrations across the Country." *Haaretz*.

Fassin, Didier. 2013. *Enforcing Order: An Ethnography of Urban Policing*. Cambridge: Polity.

Fishbein, Einat. 2018. "Maybe My Arrest Was the Most Effective Thing I Have Ever Done," www.ha-makom.co.il/article/einar-jafer-farah.

Fenton, Steve. 2003. *Ethnicity*. Cambridge, UK: Polity Press.

Fenton, Steve, and Stephan May. 2002 "Ethnicity, Nation and Race: Connections and Disjunctures." In Steven Fenton and Stephan May (eds.), *Ethnonational Identities*. London: Palgrave, pp. 1–20.

Findlay, Mark. 2004. *Introducing Policing: Challenges for Police and Australian Communities*. Oxford: Oxford University Press.

Fixler, Philip E., and Robert W. Poole Jr. 1988. "Can Police Services Be Privatized?" *The Annals of the American Academy of Political and Social Science* 498(1): 108–118.

Forman, James Jr. 2017. *Locking Up Our Own*. New York: Farrar, Straus and Giroux.

Fox, John E., Laura Moroşanu, and Eszter Szilassy. 2012. "The Racialization of the New European Migration to the UK." *Sociology* 46(4): 680–695.

Fraser, Nancy. 2009. "Social Justice in the Age of Identity Politics." In George L. Henderson and Marvin Waterstone (eds.), *Geographic Thought: A Praxis Perspective*. New York: Routledge, pp. 72–91.

Fredrickson, George H. 1990. "Public Administration and Social Equity." *Public Administration Review* 50(2): 228–237.

Friedman, Menachem. 1994. "Neturei Karta and the Sabbath Demonstrations in Jerusalem: 1948–50." In A. Bareli (ed.), *The Divided Jerusalem 1948–1967*. Jerusalem: Yad Ben-Zvi, pp. 224–240.

1995. "Life Tradition and Book Tradition in the Development of Ultraorthodox Judaism." In S. Deshen, C. S. Leibman, and M. Shokeid (eds.), *Israeli Judaism: The Sociology of Religion in Israel*. Brunswick, NJ: Transaction Publishers, pp. 127–148.

Fung, Archon, and Erik Olin Wright. 2001 "Deepening Democracy: Innovations in Empowered Participatory Governance." *Politics & Society* 29(1): 5–41.

Gans, Herbert J. 2017. "Racialization and Racialization Research." *Ethnic and Racial Studies* 40(3): 341–352.

Gazal-Ayal, Oren, and Raanan Sulitzeanu-Kenan. 2010. "Let My People Go: Ethnic In-Group Bias in Judicial Decisions—Evidence from a Randomized Natural Experiment." *Journal of Empirical Legal Studies* 7(3): 403–428.

Ghanem, As'ad, and Ibrahim Khatib. 2017. "The Nationalisation of the Israeli Ethnocratic Regime and the Palestinian Minority's Shrinking Citizenship." *Citizenship Studies* 21(8): 889–902.

Ghanem, As'ad, and Mohanad Mustafa. 2011. "The Palestinians in Israel: The Challenge of the Indigenous Group Politics in the 'Jewish State'." *Journal of Muslim Minority Affairs* 31(2): 177–196.

Ginat, Gali. 2016, August 30. "Commissioner Alsheich on Police Violence against Ethiopians." *Walla News*.

Goldsmith, A. 2005. "Police Reform and the Problem of Trust." *Theoretical Criminology* 9(4): 443–470.

Gorman, Michael F., and John Ruggiero. 2008. "Evaluating US State Police Performance Using Data Envelopment Analysis." *International Journal of Production Economics* 113(2): 1031–1037.

Grossman, Shmuel. 2010. "Riots in Beit Shemesh and Jerusalem." Ynet.

Gurr, Ted R. 1970. *Why Men Rebel*. Princeton, NJ: Princeton University Press.

Hadid, Dia. 2016, September 3. "Israel Seeking Police Recruits: Eager, and Arab." *New York Times*.

Hakak, Yohai. 2016. *Haredi Masculinities between the Yeshiva, the Army, Work and Politics: The Sage, the Warrior and the Entrepreneur*. Leiden: Brill.

Harpaz, Amikam. 2012. *Policing Strategies*. Jerusalem: Nevo Publisher (Hebrew).

Harris, Fredrick C., and Robert C. Lieberman. 2013. "Beyond Discrimination: Racial Inequality in the Age of Obama." In Fredrick C. Harris and Robert C. Lieberman (eds.), *Beyond Discrimination: Racial Inequality in a Postracist Era*. New York: Russel Sage, pp. 1–36.

Har-Zahav, Chaim. 2017. "After the Police Car Hit the 16 Year Old, He Was Arrested," www.ha-makom.co.il/article/haim-rahat-police.

Hasisi, Badi, and David Weisburd. 2014. "Policing Terrorism and Police–Community Relations: Views of the Arab minority in Israel." *Police Practice and Research* 15(2): 158–172.

Hasisi, Badi, and Ron Weitzer. 2007. "Police Relations with Arabs and Jews in Israel." *British Journal of Criminology* 47(5): 728–745.

Hawdon, James. 2008. "Legitimacy, Trust, Social Capital, and Policing Styles: A Theoretical Statement." *Police Quarterly* 11(2): 182–201.

Haynes, Jeff. 2006. "Religion and International Relations in the 21st Century: Conflict or Cooperation?" *Third World Quarterly* 27(3): 535–541.

Held, D., A. McGrew, D. Goldblatt, and J. Perraton. 1999. *Global Transformations*. London: Polity Press.

Herbert, Steve. 2006. "Policing the Contemporary City." In V. E. Kappeler (ed.), *The Police and Society*. Illinois: Waveland Press.

Hermann, Tamar, Chanan Cohen, Fadi Omar, Ella Heller, and Tzipy Lazar-Shoef. 2017. *A Conditional Partnership: Jews and Arabs, Israel 2017*. Jerusalem: Israel Democracy Institute.

Hermann, Tamar, Ella Heller, Chanan Cohen, Dana Bublil, and Fadi Omar. 2016. *The Israeli Democracy Index 2016*. Jerusalem: Israel Democracy Institute.

Hermann, Tamar, Ella Heller, Or Anabi, and Fadi Omar. 2018. *Israel Democracy Index 2018*. Jerusalem: Israel Democracy Institute.

Høigård, Cecile. 2011. "Policing the North." *Crime and Justice* 40(1): 265–348.

Holdaway, Simon, and Megan O'Neill. 2006. "Institutional Racism after Macpherson: An Analysis of Police Views." *Policing and Society* 16(4): 349–369.

Hood, Christopher. 1995. "The 'New Public Management' in the 1980s: Variations on a Theme." *Accounting, Organizations and Society* 20(2–3): 93–109.

Hough, Mike, Jonathan Jackson, and Ben Bradford. 2013. "Police Futures and Legitimacy: Redefining 'Good Policing'." In Jennifer M. Brown (ed.), *The Future of Policing*. Oxford: Routledge, pp. 109–130.

Hough, Mike, Jonathan Jackson, Ben Bradford, Andy Myhill, and Paul Quinton. 2010. "Procedural Justice, Trust, and Institutional Legitimacy." *Policing: A Journal of Policy and Practice* 4(3): 203–210.

Howell, Susan E., Huey L. Perry, and Matthew Vile. 2004. "Black Cities/White Cities: Evaluating the Police." *Political Behavior* 26(1): 45–68.

Hunter, James D. 1991. *Culture Wars: The Struggle to Define America.* New York: Basic Books.

Inglis, Christine. 1996. "Multiculturalism: New Policy Responses to Diversity." *MOST Policy Papers* 4. UNESCO, https://unesdoc.unesco .org/ark:/48223/pf0000105582.

Irvin, Renee A., and John Stansbury. 2004. "Citizen Participation in Decision-Making: Is It Worth the Effort?" *Public Administration Review* 64: 55–65.

Isaac, Jeffrey C. 2015. "The American Politics of Policing and Incarceration." *Perspectives on Politics* 13(3): 609–616.

Isin, Engin F., and Particia K. Wood. 1999. *Citizenship and Identity.* London: Sage.

Israel Police. 2015. "Strengthening Trust between Police and the Ethiopian Community," (internal document).

Jabareen, Yousef T. 2015. "The Arab-Palestinian Community in Israel: A Test Case for Collective Rights under International Law." *Geo. Wash. Int'l L. Rev.* 47: 449.

Jackson, Jonathan, and Ben Bradford. 2010. "Police Legitimacy: A Conceptual Review," https://papers.ssrn.com/sol3/papers.cfm?abstract_id=1684507.

Jackson, Jonathan, Ben Bradford, Mike Hough, Andy Myhill, Paul Quinton, and Tom R. Tyler. 2012. "Why Do People Comply with the Law? Legitimacy and the Influence of Legal Institutions." *British Journal of Criminology* 52(6): 1051–1071.

Jackson, Jonathan, and Jacinta M. Gau. 2016. "Carving Up Concepts? Differentiating between Trust and Legitimacy in Public Attitudes towards Legal Authority." In Ellie Shockley, Tess M. S. Neal, Lisa M. PytlikZillig, and Brian H. Bornstein (eds.), *Interdisciplinary Perspectives on Trust.* Cham: Springer, pp. 49–69.

Jamal, Amal. 2011. *Arab Minority Nationalism in Israel: The Politics of Indigeneity.* Oxford: Routledge.

Jamieson, Dave. 2014, December 7. "Bill De Blasio Explains Why His Son Needs to Be Careful around Cops." *Huffington Post,* www .huffingtonpost.co.uk/2014/12/07/bill-de-blasio-son_n_6283774.html.

Jonathan, Tal. 2009. "Police Involvement in Counter-Terrorism and Public Attitudes towards the Police in Israel—1998-2007." *The British Journal of Criminology* 50(4): 748–771.

Jones, Trevor, and Ronald van Steden. 2013. "Democratic Police Governance in Comparative Perspective: Reflections from England & Wales and the

Netherlands." *Policing: An International Journal of Police Strategies &*
Management 36(3): 561–576.

Jost, John T., and Avital Mentovich. 2010. "The J-Curve Hypothesis." In J.
Levine and M. Hogg (eds.), *The Encyclopedia of Group Processes and*
Intergroup Relations. Thousand Oaks, CA: Sage Publications.

Kääriäinen, J. T. 2007. "Trust in the Police in 16 European Countries: A
Multilevel Analysis." *European Journal of Criminology* 4(4): 409–435.

Kacen, Lea. 2006. "Spousal Abuse among Immigrants from Ethiopia in
Israel." *Journal of Marriage and Family* 68: 1276–1290.

Kahn, Kimberly Barsamian, and Karin D. Martin. 2016. "Policing and Race:
Disparate Treatment, Perceptions, and Policy Responses." *Social Issues*
and Policy Review 10(1): 82–121.

Kaplan, Steven. 1999. "Can the Ethiopian Change His Skin? The Beta Israel
(Ethiopian Jews) and Racial Discourse." *African Affairs* 98: 535–550.

Kaplan, Steven, and Chaim Rosen. 1993. "Ethiopian Immigrants in Israel:
Between Preservation of Culture and Invention of Tradition." *Jewish*
Journal of Sociology 35(1): 35–48.

Kaplan, Steven, and Hagar Salamon. 2004. "Ethiopian Jews in Israel: A Part
of the People or Apart from the People?" In U. Rebhun and C. I.
Waxman (eds.), *Jews in Israel: Contemporary Social and Cultural*
Patterns. Hanover, NH: Brandeis University Press, pp. 118–148.

Kashua, Sayed. 2016, January 14. "Welcome to the Ghetto of Arab Society,
Where Would You Like to Live?" *Haaretz*.

Katzenstein, David, and Lisa Aronson Fontes. 2017. "Twice Silenced: The
Underreporting of Child Sexual Abuse in Orthodox Jewish
Communities." *Journal of Child Sexual Abuse* 26(6): 752–767.

Keiser, Lael R. 2010. "Representative Bureaucracy." In R. Durant (ed.), *The*
Oxford Handbook of American Bureaucracy. Oxford: Oxford
University Press, pp. 714–737.

Kelling, George L., and Mark Harrison Moore. 2006. "The Evolving
Strategy of Policing." In V. E. Kappeler (ed.), *The Police and Society*.
Illinois: Waveland Press.

Kennedy, Randall. 1997. *Race, Crime and the Law*. New York: Vintage
Books.

Khamaisi, Rassem. 2013. "Barriers to Developing Employment Zones in the
Arab Palestinian Localities in Israel and Their Implications." In N.
Khattab and S. Miaari (eds.), *Palestinians in the Israeli Labor Market*.
New York: Palgrave Macmillan, pp. 185–212.

Khazzoom, Aziza. 2003. "The Great Chain of Orientalism: Jewish Identity,
Stigma Management, and Ethnic Exclusion in Israel." *American*
Sociological Review 68: 481–510.

Khoury, Jack. 2016, June 5. "Arabs Involved in 59% of Murders." *Haaretz,*
www.haaretz.com/israel-news/.premium-arab-citizens-involved-in-59-
percent-of-murders-in-israel-1.5391537.

Kimmerling, Baruch. 1999. "Patterns of Militarism in Israel." *European Journal
of Sociology/Archives Européennes de Sociologie* 34(2): 196–223.

Knesset Committee for Internal Affairs. 2016. "Protocol 6.1.2016."

  2017. "Protocol 450," www.nevo.co.il/law_word/Law103/20_
ptv_390907.doc.

Knesset Committee for Women and Gender Equality. 2003. "Protocol
30.9.2003," https://main.knesset.gov.il/Activity/committees/Women/P
ages/CommitteeProtocols.aspx?ItemID=2007601.

  2016. "Protocol 6.10.2016," https://main.knesset.gov.il/Activity/commit
tees/Women/Pages/CommitteeProtocols.aspx?ItemID=2007601.

Kook, Rebecca. 2017. "Representation, Minorities and Electoral Reform:
The Case of the Palestinian Minority in Israel." *Ethnic and Racial
Studies* 40(12): 2039–2057.

Kopelowitz, Ezra. 2001. "Religious Politics and Israel's Ethnic Democracy."
Israel Studies 6(3): 166–190.

Korn, Alina. 2003. "Rates of Incarceration and Main Trends in Israeli
Prisons." *Criminal Justice* 3(1): 29–55.

Kubowich, Yaniv. 2014, September 24. "Internal Affairs Rejects 93 percent
of Citizens' Complaints." *Haaretz.*

  2016a, November 20. "With No Police, Arab Society Enforces the Law by
Itself." *Haaretz.*

  2016b, May 4. "Protest of Israelis of Ethiopian Descent: Dozens Wounded
and Arrested in Tel-Aviv." *Haaretz.*

Kymlicka, Will. 1995. *Multicultural Citizenship: A Liberal Theory of
Minority Rights.* Oxford: Clarendon Press.

  2004. "Justice and Security in the Accommodation of Minority
Nationalism." In Stephen May, Tariq Maqdood, and Judith Squires
(eds.), *Ethnicity, Nationalism, and Minority Rights.* Cambridge:
Cambridge University Press, pp. 144–175.

  2010. "The Rise and Fall of Multiculturalism? New Debates on
Inclusion and Accommodation in Diverse Societies." In S.
Vertovec and S. Wessendorf (eds.), *The Multiculturalism Backlash:
European Discourses, Policies and Practices.* London: Routledge,
pp. 32–49.

Kymlicka, Will, and Wayne Norman. 1994. "Return of the Citizenship: A
Survey of Recent Work on Citizenship Theory." *Ethics* 104: 352–381.

Lamont, Michele. 2009. "Responses to Racism, Health, and Social Inclusion
as a Dimension of Successful Societies." In P. Hall and M. Lamont

(eds.), *Successful Societies: How Institutions and Culture Affect Health*. Cambridge, MA: Harvard University Press, pp. 151–168.

Lamont, Michele, and Nissim Mizrachi. 2012. "Ordinary People Doing Extraordinary Things: Responses to Stigmatization in Comparative Perspective." *Ethnic and Racial Studies* 35(3): 365–381.

Lavie, Ephraim. 2010. "Arabs in Israel: Between Integration and Alienation." In Shlomo Brom and Anat Kurz (eds.), *Strategic Survey for Israel*. Tel Aviv: INSS, pp. 37–58.

Lenard, Patti Tamara. 2012. *Trust, Democracy, and Multicultural Challenges*. University Park, PA: Pennsylvania State University Press.

Lerman, Amy E., and Vesla M. Weaver. 2014. *Arresting Citizenship: The Democratic Consequences of American Crime Control*. Chicago: University of Chicago Press.

Lev, Tali, and Yehouda Shenhav. 2010. "The Social Construction of the Enemy from Within: Israeli Black Panthers as a Target of Moral Panic." *Israeli Sociology* 1: 135–158.

Levy, Yagil. 2008. "Israel's Violated Republican Equation." *Citizenship Studies* 12(3): 249–264.

Lewin, Alisa C., Haya Stier, and Dafna Caspi-Dror. 2006. "The Place of Opportunity: Community and Individual Determinants of Poverty among Jews and Arabs in Israel." *Research in Social Stratification and Mobility* 24(2): 177–191.

Lewin-Epstein, Noah, and Moshe Semyonov. 1993. *The Arab Minority in Israel's Economy*. Boulder, CO: Westview Press.

Lewis, Amanda E. 2003. "Everyday Race-Making: Navigating Racial Boundaries in Schools." *American Behavioral Scientist* 47(3): 283–305.

Lewis, Colleen. 1999. *Complaints against Police: The Politics of Reform*. Riverwood, NSW: Hawkins Press.

2005. "Police, Civilians and Democratic Accountability," http://demo cratic.audit.anu.edu.au/papers/200508_lewis_police.pdf.

Lijphart, A. 1984. *Democracies: Patterns of Majoritarian and Consensus Government in Twenty-One Countries*. New Haven, CT: Yale University Press.

Lipsky, Michael. 1980. *Street-Level Bureaucracy*. New York: Russel Sage.

Loader, Ian. 1997. "Policing and the Social: Questions of Symbolic Power." *British Journal of Sociology* 48(1): 1–18.

Loader, Ian, and Neil Walker. 2001. "Policing as a Public Good: Reconstituting the Connections between Policing and the State" *Theoretical Criminology* 5(1): 9–35.

Lorbiecki, Anna, and Gavin Jack. 2000. "Critical Turns in the Evolution of Diversity Management." *British Journal of Management* 11: S17–S31.

Loveman, Mara. 2014. *National Colors: Racial Classification and the State in Latin America*. New York: Oxford University Press.

Lustick, Ian. 1980. *Arabs in the Jewish State: Israel's Control of a National Minority*. Austin: Texas University Press.

MacPherson, William. 1999. "The Stephen Lawrence Inquiry," https://asse ts.publishing.service.gov.uk/government/uploads/system/uploads/attac hment_data/file/277111/4262.pdf.

Malchi, Asaf, and Guy Ben-Porat. 2018. "Home and Away: Volunteering among Ultra-Orthodox Men in Israel." *International Journal of Sociology and Social Policy* 38(5–6): 411–425.

Mandel, Robert. 2001. "The Privatization of Security." *Armed Forces & Society* 28(1): 129–151.

Manna, Adel (ed.). 2008. *Arab Society in Israel, 2: Population, Society, Economy*. Jerusalem: Van-Leer Institute.

Manning, Peter K. 2006. "The Police: Mandate, Strategies and Appearances." In V. E. Kappeler (ed.), *The Police and Society*. Illinois: Waveland Press.

Mansbridge, J. 1999. "Should Blacks Represent Blacks and Women Represent Women? A Contingent 'Yes'." *The Journal of Politics* 61(3): 628–657.

Marshall, T. H. 1950. "Citizenship and Social Class." Reprinted in T. H. Marshall and T. Bottomore (eds.) (1992), *Citizenship and Social Class*. London: Pluto Press.

May, Stephen. 2004. "Ethnicity, Nationalism, and Minority Rights: Charting the Disciplinary Debates." In Stephen May, Tariq Maqdood, and Judith Squires (eds.), *Ethnicity, Nationalism, and Minority Rights*. Cambridge: Cambridge University Press.

Marx, Anthony W. 2002. "The Nation-State and Its Exclusions" *Political Science Quarterly* 117(1): 103–126.

2005. *Faith in Nation: Exclusionary Origins of Nationalism*. New York: Oxford University Press.

Maxwell, Rahsaan. 2010. "Trust in Government among British Muslims: The Importance of Migration Status." *Political Behavior* 32(1): 89–109.

Mazepus, Honorata, Wouter Veenendaal, Anthea McCarthy-Jones, and Juan Manuel Trak Vásquez. 2016. "A Comparative Study of Legitimation Strategies in Hybrid Regimes." *Policy Studies* 37(4): 350–369.

McGarry, John, and Brendan O'Leary. 2006. "Consociational Theory, Northern Ireland's Conflict, and Its Agreement 2.-What Critics of Consociation Can Learn from Northern Ireland." *Government and Opposition* 41(2): 249–277.

Mears, Tracey L., Tom R. Tyler, and Jacob Gardner. 2015. "Lawful of Fair? How Cops and Laypeople Perceive Good Policing." *The Journal of Criminal Law and Criminology* 105(2): 297–344.

Meier, Kenneth J., and Daniel P. Hawes. 2009. "Ethnic Conflict in France: A Case for Representative Bureaucracy?" *The American Review of Public Administration* 39(3): 269–285.

Meier, Kenneth J., and Jill Nicholson-Crotty. 2006. "Gender, Representative Bureaucracy, and Law Enforcement: The Case of Sexual Assault." *Public Administration Review* 66(6): 850–860.

Meier, Kenneth J., Robert D. Wrinkle, and J. L. Polinard. 1999. "Representative Bureaucracy and Distributional Equity: Addressing the Hard Question." *The Journal of Politics* 61(4): 1025–1039.

Melchers, Ron. 2003. "Do Toronto Police Engage in Racial Profiling?" *Canadian Journal of Criminology and Criminal Justice* 45(3): 347–366.

Mentovich, Avital, Guy Ben-Porat, Natalie Levy, Phillip A. Goff, and Tom Tyler. 2018. "Policing Alienated Minorities in Divided Cities." *Regulation & Governance*, https://doi.org/10.1111/rego.12232.

Michels, Ank. 2011. "Innovations in Democratic Governance: How Does Citizen Participation Contribute to a Better Democracy?" *International Review of Administrative Sciences* 77(2): 275–293.

Michelson, Melissa R. 2003. "The Corrosive Effect of Acculturation: How Mexican Americans Lose Political Trust." *Social Science Quarterly* 84(4): 918–933.

Ministry of Justice. 2016. "Final Report of the Task Force for the Eradication of Racism against Israelis of Ethiopian Descent," www.justice.gov.il/Pubilcations/Articles/Documents/ReportEradicateR acism.pdf.

Mizrachi, Nissim, and Hanna Herzog. 2012. "Participatory Destigmatization Strategies among Palestinian Citizens, Ethiopian Jews and Mizrahi Jews in Israel." *Ethnic and Racial Studies* 35(3): 418–435.

Mizrachi, Nissim, and Adane Zawdu. 2012. "Between Global Racial and Bounded Identity: Choice of Destigmatization Strategies among Ethiopian Jews in Israel." *Ethnic and Racial Studies* 35(3): 436–452.

Mosher, Frederick C. 1982. *Democracy and the Public Service*. Vol. 2. New York: Oxford University Press.

Muller, Benjamin J. 2004. "(Dis)Qualified Bodies: Securitization, Citizenship and 'Identity Management'." *Citizenship Studies* 8(3): 279–294.

Murphy, Kristina, and Adrian Cherney. 2011. "Understanding Cooperation with Police in a Diverse Society." *The British Journal of Criminology* 52(1): 181–201.

Nachshoni, Kobi. 2017, February 6. "16 Haredim Arrested in Mea Shearim for Attacking IDF Soldiers." Ynet.

Nardy, Guy. 2017, September 5. "Arab Citizens Want Security but Not Police Stations." *Globes*.

2018, April 6. "Minister Galant Declared War on the Bedouin Settlements." *Globes.*

Newburn, Tim. 2003. "The Future of Policing." In Tim Newburn (ed.), *Handbook of Policing.* Cullompton: Willan Publishing, pp. 707–721.

Nield, Rachel. 2006. "Democratic Reform in War-Torn Societies" *Conflict, Security and Development* 1(1): 21–43.

Nobles, Melissa. 2000. *Shades of Citizenship: Race and Census in Modern Politics.* Stanford, CA: Stanford University Press.

Nyers, Peter. 2004. "Introduction: What's Left of Citizenship?" *Citizenship Studies* 8(3): 203–215.

Oakley, Robin. 2001. "Police and Recruitment in a Multiethnic Britain." Paper presented at the Policing Partnerships in a Multicultural Australia, Brisbane, 25–26 October.

Offer, Shira. 2004. "The Socio-Economic Integration of the Ethiopian Community in Israel." *International Migration* 42(3): 29–55.

Olesker, Ronnie. 2014. "National Identity and Securitization in Israel." *Ethnicities* 14(3): 371–391.

Omi, Michael, and Howard Winant. 2014. *Racial Formation in the United States.* New York: Routledge.

Orr Commission. 2000. "The Official Summation of the Orr Commission Report," https://web.archive.org/web/20071001144625/ and www.ha aretz.com/hasen/pages/ShArt.jhtml?itemNo=335594 .

Pakulski, Jan. 1997. "Cultural Citizenship." *Citizenship Studies* 1(1): 73–86.

Parmar, Alpa. 2011. "Stop and Search in London: Counter-Terrorist or Counter-Productive?" *Policing and Society* 21(4): 369–382.

Peffley, Mark, Marc L. Hutchison, and Michal Shamir. 2015. "The Impact of Persistent Terrorism on Political Tolerance: Israel, 1980 to 2011." *American Political Science Review* 109(4): 817–832.

Peled, Yoav. 1992. "Ethnic Democracy and the Legal Construction of Citizenship: Arab Citizens of the Jewish State." *American Political Science Review* 86(2): 432–443.

Philippov, Michael, and Evgenia Bystrov. 2011. "All by Myself? The Paradox of Citizenship among the FSU Immigrants in Israel." In Guy Ben-Porat and Bryan S. Turner (eds.), *The Contradiction of Israeli Citizenship.* Oxford: Routledge, pp. 258–277.

Philippov, Michael, and Anna Knafelman. 2011. "Old Values in the New Homeland: Political Attitudes of FSU Immigrants in Israel." *Israel Affairs* 17(1): 38–54.

Pierre, Jon. 2000. *Debating Governance: Authority, Steering and Democracy.* Oxford: Oxford University Press.

Pieterse, Jan N. 2004. "Ethnicities and Multiculturalisms: Politics of Boundaries." In Stephen May, Tariq Maqdood, and Judith Squires (eds.), *Ethnicity, Nationalism, and Minority Rights*. Cambridge: Cambridge University Press, pp. 27–49.

Piquero, Alex R., Raymond Paternoster, Greg Pogarsky, and Thomas Loughran. 2011. "Elaborating the Individual Difference Component in Deterrence Theory." *Annual Review of Law and Social Science* 7: 335–360.

Pitts, David W. 2005. "Diversity, Representation, and Performance: Evidence about Race and Ethnicity in Public Organizations." *Journal of Public Administration Research and Theory* 15(4): 615–631.

Pitts, David W., Alisa K. Hicklin, Daniel P. Hawes, and Erin Melton. 2010. "What Drives the Implementation of Diversity Management Programs? Evidence from Public Organizations." *Journal of Public Administration Research and Theory* 20(4): 867–886.

Pitts, David W., and Elizabeth Jarry. 2007. "Ethnic Diversity and Organizational Performance: Assessing Diversity Effects at the Managerial and Street Levels." *International Public Management Journal* 10(2): 233–254.

Pollitt, Christopher, and Geert Bouckaert. 2011. *Continuity and Change in Public Policy and Management*. Cheltenham: Edward Elgar Publishing.

Porat, Ishai, and Kobi Nachshoni. 2017, September 17. "8 Arrested in Haredi Demonstration in Jerusalem." Ynet.

Portes, Alejandro, and Ruben Rumbaut. 1996. *Immigrant America: A Portrait*. Berkeley, CA: University of California Press.

Pulwer, Sharon, and Yaniv Kubowich. 2016, August 31. "Police Commissioner on Violence against Ethiopians: It Is Natural They Are More Suspected." *Haaretz*.

Putnam, Robert D. 1993. *Making Democracy Work: Civic Traditions in Modern Italy*. Princeton, NJ: Princeton University Press.

Rabad, Achia. 2010, August 8. "I Go to Prison with My Head Held High." Ynet, www.ynet.co.il/articles/0,7340,L-3931659,00.html.

2018, May 21. "Human Rights Activist in Court: Police Officer Broke My Leg." Ynet, www.ynet.co.il/articles/0,7340,L-5266169,00.html.

Rabinovitch, Maria. 2015, July 20. "Issues in Identifying and Treating Sexual Abuse of Minors in Haredi Society." Jerusalem: Knesset Research and Information Center.

Rabinowitz, Dan, and Khawla Abu-Baker. 2005. *Coffins on Our Shoulders: The Experience of the Palestinian Citizens of Israel*. Berkeley, CA: University of California Press.

Rattner, Arye. 2010. *The Legal Culture: Law and the Legal System in the Eyes of the Israeli Public*. Jerusalem: The Shasha Center for Strategic Research, The Hebrew University (Hebrew).

Rattner, Arye, and Gideon Fishman. 2009. "Micro and Macro Analysis of Violence in Israel." Report submitted to the Israeli Ministry of Science.

Rattner, Arye, Hagit Turjeman, and Gideon Fishman. 2008. "Public versus Private Defense: Can Money Buy Justice?" *Journal of Criminal Justice* 36(1): 43–49.

Remennick, Larissa. 2003a. "What Does Integration Mean? Social Insertion of Russian Immigrants in Israel." *Journal of International Migration and Integration/Revue de l'integration et de la migration internationale* 4(1): 23–49.

Remennick, Larissa. 2003b. "The 1.5 Generation of Russian Immigrants in Israel: Between Integration and Sociocultural Retention." *Diaspora: A Journal of Transnational Studies* 12(1): 39–66.

Rice, Mitchell F. 2005. *Diversity and Public Administration: Theory, Issues and Perspectives.* New York: Sharpe.

    2007. "A Post-Modern Cultural Competency Framework for Public Administration and Public Service Delivery." *International Journal of Public Sector Management* 20(7): 622–637.

    2015. *Diversity and Public Administration: Theory, Issues and Perspectives.* New York: ME Sharpe.

Roberg, Roy R., Jack L. Kuykendall, and Kenneth Novak. 2002. *Police Management.* Los Angeles: Roxbury Publishing Company.

Roh, Sunghoon, and Matthew Robinson. 2009. "A Geographic Approach to Racial Profiling: The Microanalysis and Macroanalysis of Racial Disparity in Traffic Stops." *Police Quarterly* 12(2): 137–169.

Ronen, Yaniv. 2010. "Data on Crime in Arab Society in Israel." Jerusalem: Knesset Research and Information Center.

Rosenberg, Oz. 2012, January 15. "Hundreds of Haredim Confronted Police in Jerusalem." *Haaretz.*

Rothschild, Joseph. 1981. *Ethnopolitics: A Conceptual Framework.* New York: Columbia University Press.

Rouhana, Nadim, and As'ad Ghanem. 1998. "The Crisis of Minorities in Ethnic States: The Case of Palestinian Citizens in Israel." *International Journal of Middle East Studies* 30(3): 321–346.

Saba-Habesch, Lina, and Mordechai Kremnitzer. 2010. "Ten Years since October 2000 Events: Writing Is Still on the Wall." Jerusalem: Israel Democracy Institute, www.idi.org.il/articles/8101.

Salamon, Hagar. 2003. "Blackness in Transition: Decoding Racial Constructs through Stories of Ethiopian Jews." *Journal of Folklore Research* 40(1): 3–32.

Sasson-Levy, Orna. 2013. "A Different Kind of Whiteness: Marking and Unmarking of Social Boundaries in the Construction of Hegemonic Ethnicity." *Sociological Forum* 28(1): 27–50.

Scharpf, F. W. 2007. "Reflections on Multilevel Legitimacy." MPIfG working paper, www.econstor.eu/handle/10419/41671.

Schildkraut, Deborah J. 2005. "The Rise and Fall of Political Engagement among Latinos: The Role of Identity and Perceptions of Discrimination." *Political Behavior* 27(3): 285–312.

Schmemann, Serge. 1996, January 29. "Ethiopians in Israel Riot over Dumping of Donated Blood." *New York Times*.

Schmidt, Vivien A. 2013. "Democracy and Legitimacy in the European Union Revisited: Input, Output and 'Throughput'." *Political Studies* 61(1): 2–22.

Schneider, Cathy Lisa. 2008. "Police Power and Race Riots in Paris." *Politics & Society* 36(1): 133–159.

Seeman, Don. 1999. "One People, One Blood: Public Health, Political Violence, and HIV in an Ethiopian-Israeli Setting." *Culture, Medicine and Psychiatry* 23: 159–195.

Seidler, Shirley, and Yaniv Kubowich. 2015, May 4. "Protests of Israelis of Ethiopian Descent." *Haaretz*.

Shaalan, Hassan. 2014, November 10. "Riots in Kafr Kanna." Ynet, www .ynet.co.il/articles/0,7340,L-4590472,00.html.

2017a, November 26. "Suspected Murder in Tira." Ynet, www .ynet.co.il/articles/0,7340,L-5034024,00.html.

2017b, October 2. "Shooting and Demonstrating." Ynet, www .ynet.co.il/articles/0,7340,L-5023917,00.html.

Shabtay, Malka. 1999. *Best Brother: The Identity Journey of Ethiopian Immigrant Soldiers*. Tel Aviv: Tcherikover (Hebrew).

2001. *Between Reggae and Rap: The Integration Challenge of Ethiopian Youth in Israel*. Tel Aviv: Tcherikover (Hebrew).

Shachar, Ayelet. 1998. "Whose Republic? Citizenship and Membership in the Israeli Polity." *Georgetown Immigration Law Journal* 13: 233–272.

Shadmi, Erella. 2012. *The Fortified Land, Police and Policing in Israel*. Tel Aviv: Hakibbutz Hameuchad (Hebrew).

Shafir, Gershon, and Yoav Peled. 2002. *Being Israeli: The Dynamics of Multiple Citizenship*. Vol. 16. Cambridge: Cambridge University Press.

Shani, Ayelet. 2016, June 11. "Domestic Violence Is a Major Threat for Israeli Arab Women: Why Wont the Police Intervene?" *Haaretz*.

Shumsky, Dimitry. 2004. "Post-Zionist Orientalism? Orientalist Discourse and Islamophobia among the Russian-Speaking Intelligentsia in Israel." *Social Identities* 10(1): 83–99.

Sklansky, David A. 2007. "Seeing Blue: Police Reform, Occupational Culture, and Cognitive Burn-In." In Megan O'Neill, Monique Marks, and Anne-Marie Singh (eds.), *Police Occupational Culture*. Bingley: Emerald Group Publishing Limited, pp. 19–45.

Skogan, Wesley, and Kathleen Frydl (eds.). 2004. *Fairness and Effectiveness in Policing: The Evidence*. Washington, DC: National Academies Press.

Skolnick, Jerome H., and David H. Bayley. 1988. "Theme and Variation in Community Policing." *Crime and Justice* 10: 1–37.

Smith, David J. 2007. "The Foundations of Legitimacy." In Tom R. Tyler (ed.), *Legitimacy and Criminal Justice: International Perspectives*. New York: Russel Sage, pp. 30–58.

Smooha, Sammy. 1990. "Minority Status in an Ethnic Democracy: The Status of the Arab Minority in Israel." *Ethnic and Racial Studies* 13 (3): 389–413.

   1997. "Ethnic Democracy: Israel as an Archetype." *Israel Studies* 2(2): 198–241.

   1999. "The Advances and Limits of the Israelization of Israel's Palestinian Citizens." In Kamal Abdel-Malik and David C. Jacobson (eds.), *Israel and Palestinian Identities in History and Literature*. New York: St. Martin's Press, pp. 9–33.

   2008. "The Mass Immigrations to Israel: A Comparison of the Failure of the Mizrahi Immigrants of the 1950s with the Success of the Russian Immigrants of the 1990s." *Journal of Israeli History* 27(1): 1–27.

   2009. "The Israeli Palestinian-Arab Vision of Transforming Israel into a Binational Democracy." *Constellations* 16(3): 509–522.

   2015. *Still Playing by the Rules: Index of Jewish–Arab Relations 2013*. Jerusalem: Israel Democracy Institute.

Soni, Vidu. 2000. "A Twenty-First-Century Reception for Diversity in the Public Sector: A Case Study." *Public Administration Review* 60(5): 395–408.

Spinner, Jeff. 1994. *The Boundaries of Citizenship: Race, Ethnicity and Nationalism in the Liberal State*. Baltimore, MD: Johns Hopkins University Press.

Sprinzak, Ehud. 1999. *Brother against Brother: Violence and Extremism in Israeli Politics from Altalena to the Rabin Assassination*. New York: Simon and Schuster.

Stadler, Nurit. 2009. *Yeshiva Fundamentalism: Piety, Gender and Resistance in the Ultra-Orthodox World*. New York: NYU Press.

   2012. *A Well-Worn Tallis for a New Ceremony: Trends in Israeli Haredi Culture*. Boston, MA: Academic Studies Press.

Stadler, Nurit, Edna Lomsky-Feder, and Eyal Ben-Ari. 2011. "Fundamentalist Citizenships: The Haredi Challenge." In Guy Ben-Porat and Bryan S. Turner (eds.), *The Contradictions of Israeli Citizenship*. London: Routledge, pp. 151–173.

Steinbach, Anja. 2001. "Intergenerational Transmission and Integration of Repatriate Families from the Former Soviet Union in Germany." *Journal of Comparative Family Studies* 32(4): 505–515.

Stenning, Philip C. 2003. "Policing the Cultural Kaleidoscope: Recent Canadian Experience." *Police and Society* 7(3): 13–47.

Stenning, Philip C., and Clifford D. Shearing. 2005. "Reforming Police: Opportunities, Drivers and Challenges." *Australian & New Zealand Journal of Criminology* 38(2): 167–180.

Stoker, Gerry. 2006 "Public Value Management: A New Narrative for Networked Governance?" *The American Review of Public Administration* 36(1): 41–57.

Stone, Christopher E., and Heather H. Ward. 2000. "Democratic Policing: A Framework for Action." *Policing and Society* 10(1): 11–45.

Strassman-Shapira, Tal. 2012. "The Wadi Salib Events and the Reflection of Ethnic Differences in Israel, Maariv Correspondents Reporting." *Kesher* 41: 66–73.

Squire, V. 2015. "The Securitisation of Migration: An Absent Presence?" In Gabriella Lazaridis and Khursheed Wadia (eds.), *The Securitisation of Migration in the EU*. Basingstoke: Palgrave Macmillan, pp. 19–36.

Sunshine, Jason, and Tom R. Tyler. 2003a. "The Role of Procedural Justice and Legitimacy in Shaping Public Support for Policing." *Law and Society Review* 37(3): 513–548.

2003b. "Moral Solidarity, Identification with the Community, and the Importance of Procedural Justice: The Police as Prototypical Representatives of a Group's Moral Values." *Social Psychology Quarterly* 66(2): 153–165.

Tankebe, Justice. 2013. "Viewing Things Differently: The Dimensions of Public Perceptions of Police Legitimacy." *Criminology* 51(1): 103–135.

Tator, Carol, and Frances Henry. 2006. *Racial Profiling in Canada: Challenging the Myth of "A Few Bad Apples."* Toronto: University of Toronto Press.

Thomas, Craig W. 1998. "Maintaining and Restoring Public Trust in Government Agencies and Their Employees." *Administration and Society* 30(2): 166–193.

Thomas, David A. 2004. "Diversity as Strategy." *Harvard Business Review*, https://hbr.org/2004/09/diversity-as-strategy.

Times of Israel. 2017, February 23. "Minister Promises Apology If Probe Finds Um Al-Hiran Not Terror," www.timesofisrael.com/minister-promi ses-apology-if-probe-finds-umm-al-hiran-incident-not-terror/.

2018, May 20. "Police to Be Probed for Alleged Violence in Dispersing pro-Gaza Protest in Haifa."

Tinor-Centi, E. and M. Hussain. 2000. "Policing in a Multicultural Society: The Background and Experience of a Danish Project." Australasian Police Multicultural Advisory Bureau.

TOI Staff. 2014, March 2. "Hundreds of Thousands Protest Haredi Draft in Jerusalem." *Times of Israel.*

Tolstoy, Leo. 2012. *Anna Karenina.* Chelmsford, MA: Courier Corporation.

Treitler, Vilna Bashi. 2013. *The Ethnic Project: Transforming Racial Fiction into Ethnic Factions.* Stanford, CA: Stanford University Press.

Troper, Harold, and Morton Weinfeld. 1999. *Ethnicity, Politics and Public Policy: Case Studies in Canadian Diversity.* Toronto: University of Toronto Press.

Tully, James. 2001 "Introduction." In A. G. Gagnon and J. Tully (eds.), *Multinational Democracies.* Cambridge: Cambridge University Press.

Turner, Bryan S. 1993. "Contemporary Problems in the Theory of Citizenship." In Bryan S. Turner (ed.), *Citizenship and Social Theory.* London: Sage.

    2000. "Islam, Civil Society and Citizenship." In N. A. Butenschon, U. Davis, and M. Hassassian (eds.), *Citizenship and the State in the Middle East.* New York: Syracuse University Press, pp. 28–49.

    2001. "The Erosion of Citizenship." *British Journal of Sociology* 52(2): 189–209.

Tyler, Tom R. 2001. "Public Trust and Confidence in Legal Authorities: What Do Majority and Minority Group Members Want from the Law and Legal Institutions?" *Behavioral Sciences and the Law* 19(2): 215–235.

    2004. "Enhancing Police Legitimacy." *The Annals of the American Academy of Political and Social Science* 593 (1): 84–99.

    2005. "Policing in Black and White: Ethnic Group Differences in Trust and Confidence in the Police." *Police Quarterly* 8(3): 322–342.

    2006. *Why People Obey the Law: Procedural Justice, Legitimacy, and Compliance.* Princeton, NJ: Princeton University Press.

Tzfadia, Erez, and Haim Yacobi. 2007. "Identity, Migration, and the City: Russian Immigrants in Contested Urban Space in Israel." *Urban Geography* 28(5): 436–455.

U.S. Department of Justice. 2016. "Investigation of the Baltimore City Police Department," www.justice.gov/crt/file/883296/download.

Van Craen, Maarten. 2013. "Explaining Majority and Minority Trust in the Police." *Justice Quarterly* 30(6): 1042–1067.

Van Craen, Maarten, and Wesley G. Skogan. 2015. "Differences and Similarities in the Explanation of Ethnic Minority Groups' Trust in the Police." *European Journal of Criminology* 12(3): 300–323.

Van de Walle, Steven, and Geert Bouckaert. 2003. "Public Service Performance and Trust in Government: The Problem of Causality." *International Journal of Public Administration* 26(8–9): 891–913.

Vigoda-Gadot, Eran, Nissim Cohen, and Shlomo Mizrahi. 2016. Public Sector Performance in Israel. Policy Paper 15. Haifa: Haifa University Israel (Hebrew), https://pmpc.hevra.haifa.ac.il/images/NAPPA-01122016.pdf.

Waddington, Peter A. J. 1999. *Policing Citizens: Authority and Rights.* London: Psychology Press.

Walker, Samuel, Cassia Spohn, and Miriam DeLone. 2000. *The Color of Justice: Race, Ethnicity and Crime in America.* Belmont, CA: Wadsworth.

Weber, Max. 1948. *From Max Weber: Essays in Sociology.* London: Routledge and Kagan Paul.

Weimer, David, and Aidan R. Vining. 1998. *Policy Analysis: Concepts and Practice.* New Jersey: Prentice Hall.

Weisburd, David, Badi Hasisi, Tal Jonathan, and Gali Aviv. 2009. "Terrorist Threats and Police Performance: A Study of Israeli Communities." *The British Journal of Criminology* 50(4): 725–747.

Weisburd, David, Jerome McElroy, and Patricia Hardyman. 1988. "Challenges to Supervision in Community Policing: Observations on a Pilot Project." *American Journal of Police* 7(2): 29–50.

Weisburd, David, Orit Shalev, and Menachem Amir. 2002. "Community Policing in Israel: Resistance and Change." *Policing: An International Journal of Police Strategies & Management* 25(1): 80–109.

Weiss, Efrat. 2006, November 3. "Open House: Police Can Secure the Parade." Ynet.

2009, July 17. "Injuries and Arrests in Jerusalem." Ynet.

Weiss, Yfaat. 2007. *Wadi Salib: A Confiscated Memory.* Jerusalem: Van-Leer.

Weitz, Gidi. 2010, December 23. "The Most Ungrateful Job in Israel." *Haaretz.*

Weitzer, Ronald. 2000. "White, Black, or Blue Cops? Race and Citizen Assessments of Police Officers." *Journal of Criminal Justice* 28(4): 313–324.

Weitzer, Ronald, and Badi Hasisi. 2008. "Does Ethnic Composition Make a Difference? Citizens' Assessments of Arab Police Officers in Israel." *Policing & Society* 18(4): 362–376.

Weitzer, Ronald, and Steven A. Tuch. 1999. "Race, Class, and Perceptions of Discrimination by the Police." *Crime and Delinquency* 45(4): 494–507.

2002. "Perceptions of Racial Profiling: Race, Class, and Personal Experience." *Criminology* 40(2): 435–456.

2006. *Race and Policing in America: Conflict and Reform.* Cambridge: Cambridge University Press.

Wiatrowski, Michael D., and Jack A. Goldstone. 2010. "The Ballot and the Badge: Democratic Policing." *Journal of Democracy* 21(2): 79–92.

Williams, Michael C. 2003. "Words, Images, Enemies: Securitization and International Politics." *International Studies Quarterly* 47(4): 511–531.

Williams, Kristian. 2015. *Our Enemies in Blue: Police and Power in America*. Chico, CA: AK Press.

Wimmer, Andreas. 2013. *Ethnic Boundary Making: Institutions, Power, Networks*. New York: Oxford University Press.

Worrall, John L. 1999. "Public Perceptions of Police Efficacy and Image: The 'Fuzziness' of Support for the Police." *American Journal of Criminal Justice* 24(1): 47–66.

Wortley, Scot, and Akwasi Owusu-Bempah. 2009. "Unequal before the Law: Immigrant and Racial Minority Perceptions of the Canadian Criminal Justice System." *Journal of International Migration and Integration/Revue de l'integration et de la migration internationale* 10(4): 447–473.

Wortley, Scot, and Julian Tanner. 2003. "Data, Denials, and Confusion: The Racial Profiling Debate in Toronto." *Canadian Journal of Criminology and Criminal Justice* 45(3): 367–390.

Wright, Matthew, and Irene Bloemraad. 2012. "Is There a Trade-Off between Multiculturalism and Socio-Political Integration? Policy Regimes and Immigrant Incorporation in Comparative Perspective." *Perspectives on Politics* 10(1): 77–95.

Wu, Yuning. 2010. "Immigrants' Perceptions of the Police." *Sociology Compass* 4(11): 924–935.

Wünsch, Daniela, and Katrin Hohl. 2009. "Evidencing a 'Good Practice Model' of Police Communication: The Impact of Local Policing Newsletters on Public Confidence." *Policing: A Journal of Policy and Practice* 3(4): 331–339.

Yalo, Tal. 2015, May 1. "Put an End to Racism." *Yedioth Aharonot*.

Yanay, Uri. 1997. "The Safety of the Neighborhood: Community and Police Interface." *Social Security* 49: 78–96 (Hebrew).

Yanovsky, Roi. 2015, May 1. "Nine Hours of Protest." Ynet.

———. 2016, October 27. "Arab Officers to Young Arabs: Join the Police." Ynet, www.ynet.co.il/articles/0,7340,L-4870756,00.html.

Yanovsky, Roi, and Hassan Shaalan. 2016, April 15. "Blessing and Cursing: Debate over Arab Recruitment to the Police." Ynet, www.ynet.co.il/articles/0,7340,L-4791554,00.html.

Yedioth Aharonot. 2006, September 19. "They Killed Our Children Again."

Zoabi, Haneen. 2018. "Crime in Arab Society: Lessons for Police Work," A report submitted to the State Comptroller (unpublished, personal correspondence with authors).

Index

Abu Al-Qiyan
  Yacoub, 69, 78, 86, 103,
    210, 216
accountability, 5, 38, 48
African American, 1, 33, 36, 45, 101,
    110, 112, 113

Black Lives Matter, 1, 36, 108, 111
Black Panthers, 117
bureaucracy
  representative, 41
bureaucrats
  street level, 28

citizenship, 5, 8, 25, 35
  and inclusion/exclusion, 26
  and police, 9
  and policing, 7, 20, 28, 49
  and trust, 8–9
  and voice, 46
  Arab citizens, 13, 52, 64, 70, 72–75,
    79, 105
  custodial, 33
  demands, 6, 10
  diversity, 21–23
  Ethiopian Citizens, 114
  Ethiopians, 124, 131, 133, 137
  hierarchy, 1, 13, 63, 70, 72, 109, 113
  hierarchy, Israel, 55
  inclusion, 25
  Israel, 13, 14, 62–64
  law, Israel, 54
  minorities, 41
  participation, 46
  republican, 55
  republican equation, 55, 61
republican equation
  Ethiopians, 107, 123
  ultra-Orthodox, 146, 214
  securitization of, 27–28

status, 2
stratification, 3
ultra-Orthodox, 144, 147, 148, 154,
    164, 171
Committee for Eradication of Racism
  against Ethiopian Jews, 139
Community Policing, 12, 15, 40, 47, 57
  Arab Citizens, 100
  Israel, 59
  ultra-Orthodox, 147, 166
crime, 7, 9, 10, 13, 20, 33, 34, 40, 202
  Arab Cities, 17, 52, 69–70, 77, 81,
    82, 94, 98, 105, 209
  crime rates, 38, 47, 91, 202
  Israel, 60, 62
  ultra-Orthodox, 163
cultural Sensitivity, 45, 46, 173
  Ethiopians, 165
  ultra-Orthodox, 163, 166
cultural training, 45, 46, 135
  Arab citizens, 98
  Ethiopians, 134

democratic policing, 35, 40, 46
demonstrations
  Arab citizens, 68, 84, 88
  Ethiopians, 107, 115, 122, 137–139,
    199, 210, 215
  ultra-Orthodox, 14, 143, 151–153,
    157, 201
deterrence, 7
discrimination, 10, 21, 176
  Arab citizens, 17, 52, 73, 78, 82
  Ethiopians, 14, 65, 107, 117, 121,
    139, 140, 199, 215
  ethnicity, 115
  FSU Immigrants, 14, 179, 185
  minorities, 2, 33, 49
  Mizrahim, 116
  police, 5, 6, 113

CPSIA information can be obtained
at www.ICGtesting.com
Printed in the USA
LVHW010600180920
666365LV00013B/239

9 781108 404747